Time-Limited Psychotherapy in Practice

Therapists and counsellors are under increasing pressure from employers, clients and insurance companies to provide effective treatment in a time-limited, demonstrably effective form. Various types of brief therapy have developed in response, including time-limited psychotherapy (TLP). This is the first comprehensive textbook on TLP since James Mann's seminal books of 1973 and 1982.

TLP draws on psychodynamic principles and is designed to give clients an intense course of therapy over twelve sessions, with a small number of follow-up sessions. *Time-Limited Psychotherapy in Practice* presents in a clear manner the necessity of such a treatment modality, the clinical model of TLP, patient selection and the course of treatment. Using vivid and rich clinical descriptions of treatments and up-to-date research findings, the book describes what the treatments entail and discusses their outcome. The final chapter deals with the teaching and learning of TLP, in the context of the changes in the mental health realm and the changing conditions in public needs and in public services.

Time-Limited Psychotherapy in Practice will appeal to psychotherapists and counsellors, both in practice and in training. It will also be of interest to researchers and academics in the mental health field.

Gaby Shefler is a clinical psychologist and a psychoanalyst. He is Chief Psychologist of Herzog Hospital and head of the clinical training programmes at the Department of Psychology at the Hebrew University, Jerusalem. He has written numerous books and articles on time-limited psychotherapy.

Time-Limited Psychotherapy in Practice

Gaby Shefler

First published 2001 by Brunner-Routledge
27 Church Road, Hove, East Sussex, BN3 2FA

Simultaneously published in the USA and Canada
by Taylor & Francis Inc
29 West 35th Street, New York, NY 10001

Brunner-Routledge is an imprint of the Taylor & Francis Group

Typeset in Garamond by Mayhew Typesetting, Rhayader, Powys
Printed and bound in Great Britain by Biddles Ltd, Guildford and
King's Lynn

British Library Cataloguing in Publication Data
A catalogue record for this book is available from the British Library

Library of Congress Cataloging in Publication Data

Shefler, Gaby.
    Time limited psychotherapy in practice / Gaby Shefler.
      p. ; cm.
    Includes bibliographical references and index.
    ISBN 1-58391-139-1 (hbk) – ISBN 1-58391-140-5 (pbk)
    1. Brief psychotherapy.   I. Title.
    [DNLM: 1. Psychotherapy, Brief. WM 420.5.P5 S542t 2001]
  RC480.55+
  616.89'14–dc21

                                2001025462

ISBN 1-58391-139-1 (hbk)
ISBN 1-58391-140-5 (pbk)

In beloved memory of my parents,
Bejy and Yacob Shefler

And to my TLP mentor,
James Mann

Contents

Figures and tables

FIGURES

TABLES

Acknowledgments

Upon completion of this book, I am pleased to find myself feeling grateful to many collaborators, at different times and in various settings.

I first wish to express my deep gratitude to Professor Haim Dasberg, who led me through the initial stages of learning short-term dynamic psychotherapy. Under his direction and leadership, the Herzog-Ezrat Nashim Community Mental Health Center developed the unit for treatment and research in short-term dynamic psychotherapy where most of the work presented in this book was conducted.

I appreciate and thank all the therapists that took part at various stages of this project, and will list them in alphabetical order: Varda Amir, Rachel Kellerman, Ilana Navon, Yael Lavi, Hadassa Neeman, Ilana Roman, Ruth Viniar, and Eliezer Witztum at the Herzog-Ezrat Nashim Community Mental Health Center, and Lea Abudi from Meir Hospital in Hadera.

I wish to thank my friends, Dr Hadas Wiseman and Professor Jaques Barber, for their helpful remarks on various parts of the manuscript and their constant personal and professional friendship.

I am deeply thankful to my friend and colleague, Dr David Greenberg, the director of the Herzog-Ezrat Nashim Community Mental Health Center, for his ability to create and maintain an environment at the clinic that enables the implementation of any new project.

I very much appreciate Deja Dominguez for her helpful co-operation in the translation and adaptation of the material into English.

I thank Ida Mann and the Mann family for their friendship and support.

I wish to thank Kate Hawes and Dominic Hammond at Brunner-Routledge, for their excellent editorial work.

The publication of this book was made possible by the generous contribution of the Albert and Temmy Latner Institute for the Study of Social Psychiatry and Psychotherapy at Herzog Hospital and by the Schaeffer Endowment for Research in Depression at the Hebrew University of Jerusalem.

And last but not least, my wife Michal and my daughters, Tali, Naomi and Yaeli, for their constant love and support. They know best how time-consuming time-limited psychotherapy can be.

Gaby Shefler, Jerusalem
January 2001

Introduction

A thirty-year perspective on time-limited psychotherapy

James Mann

The issue of time in psychological and existential terms with particular reference to the psychotherapeutic encounter has captured
my interest for many years. In the early 1950s, I was the director of
a state-supported outpatient clinic and was soon confronted with
the problem of increasing numbers of patients and the establishment of waiting lists which generally created more anxiety and
uncertainty about whether the clinic would ever really call and
offer help.

It occurred to me that since I had considerable experience with
group psychotherapy why not find a way to use this approach with
patients already in treatment in the clinic? I knew that there were
numbers of patients who remained in treatment for long periods of
time with the result that our treatment personnel had as many
patients as they could treat at any one time with little or no
prospect of having regular openings that could accommodate new
patients. I asked several of our therapists to consider bringing
together a group of four to eight patients who had made progress
but whose dependent desires prolonged treatment. I suggested
further that a proposal be made that the group would meet for
eight sessions to discuss the prospect of all treatment coming to an
end upon the completion of six to eight sessions. In other words,
would pressing patients toward termination of treatment be a
means of reducing their dependency and also reducing our waiting
list?

The immediate reports were encouraging. The awareness that
their treatment would come to an end after a designated number
of sessions stimulated active affective discussion, and the group
co-operated in meeting the challenge. Shortly thereafter I was
appointed clinical director of the state hospital of which the

1

outpatient clinic was a part and drifted away from further consideration of that particular effort.

About twelve years later, as the Director of Psychiatric Education
of the Boston School of Medicine, I was challenged with the same
kind of problem in our outpatient department: too many patients
and an insufficient number of therapists. I embarked on an active
campaign to test the theory that a substantial number of patients
could be selected for whom twelve sessions of dynamic, psychoanalytically oriented psychotherapy following an evaluative interview would be sufficient if an appropriate method was used to
gain rapid access to a significant issue of central importance to the
patient. Further, that with the central issue in hand, twelve sessions
would be sufficient to work through that issue and bring treatment
to termination.

Intrigued by the possibilities, I then began a long series of
seminars in which psychiatric residents chose a patient for me to
treat in this manner. Initially my work was observed behind a
one-way mirror preceded and followed by a discussion of what
had transpired. Eventually this gave way to closed-circuit tele-
vision of the treatment process. In due course, my private practice
was confined to the two extremes of psychological treatments in
terms of duration, psychoanalysis and time-limited psychotherapy.
I learned that the method I had devised was both clinically useful
and could be taught to other clinicians. It also was apparent to me
that any variety of brief dynamic psychotherapy was not easy and
certainly this applied also to time-limited psychotherapy. There
are important prerequisites for the use of this modality. They
include experience first with patients in long-term psychotherapy
which is, after all, the training ground for learning about the many
aspects of mental life, conscious and unconscious, about defenses,
resistance, positive and negative transference, countertransference,
the therapeutic alliance and about living with patients' anxiety
without reacting against the patient. All these can be learned in
long-term psychotherapy but even more is necessary. Each of
us in the mental health field bring with us certain blind spots,
certain areas of our own problems which may serve to prevent
us from recognizing the same problem in the patient, or, more
important, may move us to protect the patient and ourselves by
denial and avoidance. Awareness of those of our problems which
could be anti-therapeutic serves also to prevent anti-therapeutic
interventions.

Continuing seminars, supervision of therapists and my own experience in treating patients in time-limited psychotherapy slowly crystallized for me what appeared to be two major aspects that fuel the clinical process. The first of these is the specific limitation of time to twelve sessions following initial evaluation. The patient is informed of the date of the final session in the first treatment session. The second is the particular method of choosing the central issue, which will facilitate direct entrance into a basic problem. The central issue is very different from the usual focus as it appears in brief psychotherapy.

Added to the requirements already noted as necessary for the effective practice of time-limited psychotherapy, must be the understanding and knowledge of, and experience with, basic psychoanalytic concepts. Time-limited psychotherapy includes knowledge of and experience with the structural hypothesis, the theory of narcissism, and the developmental perspective.

Stated succinctly, Freud's structural hypothesis (id, superego and ego) says that when conflict exists between these agencies of the mind we can expect that it will be expressed as one or other variety of symptoms, or as some kind of character defect. This concept prevails as fundamental to considerations of psychopathology. Freud also maintained that narcissism plays a significant role in the development of psychotic illness. More recently, many analysts have followed Kohut and Kernberg in elaborating the importance of narcissism in non-psychotic illness and in viewing the vicissitudes of narcissism in early life as one of the crucial determinants in some of the more severe neuroses and so-called higher forms of emotional disturbances. The structural hypothesis and the newer developments (self-psychology) are complementary. Object relations theory brings into consideration aspects of psychopathology, whether of Oedipal or pre-Oedipal origin, arising out of environmental failure, which is as potent as constitutional or biological factors. Such environmental failures will be related to the behavior of a parent or both parents or to accidents of fate such as the arrival of a sibling or the illness or death of parental objects. In the Oedipal period, the seductive or overly competitive parent can induce overwhelming conflict that leads to symptom formation. In the pre-Oedipal area, failures of mothering and of fathering may lead to disturbances in the development of stable, healthy self-esteem. In almost all patients in time-limited psychotherapy, transference reflects pre-Oedipal and Oedipal failures.

The developmental perspective stresses the notions of progression and regression as the child moves through the conflicts that are so much part of the process of emotional, biological and physical growth. It also implies that a specific conflict or emotional hurdle may be mastered by psychotherapy or other means, to be followed by 'normal' maturation.

In many patients the removal of one particular difficulty can lead to powerful changes. A developmental perspective provides an important theoretical basis for understanding how time-limited psychotherapy can produce lasting improvement in so short a time without emphasizing the direct experience of instinctual wishes as they related to Oedipal or pre-Oedipal infantile drives.

The apparent universal inclusion of major psychoanalytic theories as affect practice is possible if one considers union and separation as a central life dynamic. Union and separation, separations and losses are recurrent experiences from infancy to death and necessarily include all levels and all vicissitudes of development. Given an order of priorities among unconscious problems in which a central encompassing locus can be found, time-limited psychotherapy operates on the assumption that those which arise from separation and loss are more global in their impact and more readily accessible in a brief treatment model than are Oedipal problems.

To be precise, time-limited psychotherapy with its specific time limit and its particular kind of central issue brings to the forefront of the treatment process the major human psychological plague, namely the wish to be as one with another, to experience and enjoy intimacy with another and yet learn how to tolerate separation and loss without undue damage to one's feeling about the self. In a direct, realistic manner the time limit promptly confronts the patient with a deadline, that the work of treatment is to be concluded on a stated date. It is the ambiguity about duration in long treatment that leads to intensification of infantile, childhood wishes and this becomes apparent in the various manifestations of regression and resistance that ensue. This effect is a considered one in both psychoanalysis (including the influence of lying on a couch) and long-term psychotherapy so that the regression becomes a major lever in working through layers of defense toward some resolution. The greater the specificity about the duration of the treatment, the more rapidly are the regressive wishes confronted with real time, with reality and the work to be done. The result is an effective and dramatic reduction in regression. Such reduction is more than welcome and, in fact, is a necessity for any model of brief treatment. In my book, *Time Limited Psychotherapy* (1973), I have written about other aspects of time in its categorical and existential dimensions; the former relating primarily to reality and the latter to time as experienced and lived in both consciously and unconsciously.

The aspect of time that is particularly pertinent to the theory of time-limited psychotherapy is best described as part of its enmeshment in the second of its major premises, that is the central issue. The complaints that bring the patient for help are regarded as defensive means to keep out of consciousness a particular kind of present and chronically endured pain. It is pain that is experienced repetitively in situations that may be and most often are different in reality from one another but to which the patient responds automatically to their personal symbolic meaning. The central issue is further defined as a statement by the patient to himself or herself as to how he or she feels and has always felt about the self. It is always a negative perception; it is preconscious and may appear fleetingly in consciousness only to be warded off and dispelled by the prompt introduction of the person's usual coping or adaptive means.

The therapist's awareness of how this patient has always felt about the self is facilitated by adopting a particular manner of listening. The facts of the case are important and as the patient relates the succession of painful events in his life it is incumbent upon the therapist to ask of himself how must this person have felt about himself or herself as this painful event was happening, and not only how this person felt about the one inflicting the pain.

Most therapists achieve sufficient interviewing skill so that within one to three evaluation sessions an extensive, wide-ranging psychiatric history is obtained. The data are sufficient to warrant an understanding of what the patient had to endure, how well or poorly he has coped with the long-standing difficulties and also why the patient feels as he does. The facts are all present, we know all the important dates, all the significant characters, most of the life incidents that have more or less devastated the patient and how all these gave rise to the patient's present affective state. However, one highly important piece of information is missing and it is the one that the patient cannot offer to us, because he has been aware of it, at best, in only a fleeting moment. This awareness as I have noted, is closed off by the immediate introduction of automatic, characteristic devices that serve to ward off the awareness of negative feelings about the self.

The awareness that is avoided in all cases is what the patient felt and has always felt and expects in the future to feel about himself or herself repeatedly, in all situations experienced as psychologically painful, whether those situations be truly similar or, in most instances, only experienced as similar symbolically. It is the therapist's obligation to comprehend, to understand, to recognize the patient's feeling about the self, despite his inability to tell us. That comprehension becomes a test of the therapist's capacity for empathy. By empathy I mean the measure of flexibility in the therapist's own emotional life that allows him to move into the patient's emotional experience, to share with and to feel the patient's pain, to experience a kind of intimacy that goes only so far as allowing the therapist to know the agony of another person's lifelong internal experience of self-denigration.

At the same time, to be empathic also dictates the necessity for not entering so completely into the patient's life as to become identified with the patient. Should this happen there follows an immediate loss of any degree of objectivity in the patient's helper. The patient's problems and the therapist's problems become inextricably entangled to the gain of neither. Countertransference is not always negative but this particular variety is invariably totally negative. When I speak of the therapist's emotional flexibility I mean, therefore, the necessity for the therapist to be able to enter and to experience the patient's affect but at the same time to maintain a necessary distance in order to remain effectively therapeutic. One implication, of course, directs attention to the need for all therapists to be aware of their own internal lives whether through personal analysis or personal long-term psychotherapy. It becomes exquisitely pointed when the central issue in TLP is on (and it will always happen) a subject that the therapist actually shares but has come to terms with in his own therapy and can therefore maintain the necessary distance that allows him to continue to be useful to the patient.

A history taken with all the necessary facts that include the question addressed by the therapist to himself as to how the patient might have felt as he or she endured various psychological injuries, make it possible for the therapist to review his notes and to be able to present to the patient that which the therapist sees as the patient's central problem. The central issue derived and formulated in this way includes *time, affect,* and the *negative self-image.* A statement is made at the beginning of treatment that links a profound notion about the self to factors of time (as duration) and intense affect. At the same time it conveys to the patient the therapist's awareness of the patient's long-standing feelings of helplessness and hopelessness insofar as expectations of future contentment and fulfillment are concerned.

The particular method of formulating the central issue invariably reaches into the deepest recesses of the patient's feelings in a way probably not experienced since early childhood. The central issue is not an interpretation. It is a clarification that puts into words something the patient has always known, sometimes clearly but most often as a vague, never-ending, disturbing haze of consciousness. For the patient it echoes unconscious recollections of moments of intense gratification and of love when in episodes of frustration and helplessness mother entered and restored a sense of satiation and fulfillment. In consciousness the patient experiences the central issue with gratitude and trust.

The patient's response to this kind of central issue is that he or she has *always* felt this painful way about the self. In some instances it may be possible to date specifically traumatic occurrences. In TLP this is not particularly important since it is the 'always' that the patient feels has dictated the substance of his life.

Powerful traumata influence profoundly either unconscious guilt or narcissistic equilibria or both. They affect relationships back to the primary internal objects, the parents. Because they have their origin in childhood when the earliest introjections occur, objective time is obliterated so far as *affective experience* is concerned so that the negative image of the self is experienced as having always been there. To aggravate matters, the negative image remains uninfluenced and unaltered despite conscious awareness that the reality of one's present existence clearly negates the validity of the negative image. Apart from the rare exception, the negative self-image is a continuing *fiction about the self* in the patient's life as an adult. What may have been true in the life of the child is continued into adult life as objective time and affect are obliterated and the fiction about the self nourished by the automatic distortions of present reality as dictated by the *always.*

A poignant example is seen frequently in the person who seeks help either for depression or its counterpart, a work block, or even because of generalized anxiety, who recognizes that he or she has been and is successful in work or career and is recognized as such by those important to him. The symptoms that bring the person for help may conceal a lifelong image of the self as a fraud or a faker who will sooner or later be exposed. In such instances, continuing recognition of success does nothing to diminish the sense of life as daily terror.

The central issue in this case could be formulated and then presented to the patient as follows: 'You are a person who is able, competent and recognized as such by those important to you. Nevertheless what troubles you now, and has always troubled you, is your feeling that you are a fraud or a faker soon to be exposed.' Note that the first part of the central issue speaks to the person's assets and competence in coping with the bad image of the self; the second part says that the therapist knows how this person feels and has always felt despite active coping efforts. A third part will be to learn with the patient what happened in the course of his or her life that led him to feel this way about him or herself. The central issue brings into the treatment arena both the child who was small and quite helpless when the negative image of the self had its origins, as well as the functioning adult who knows better but cannot help continuing feeling the way the child felt. The discontinuity between one's cognition and what one feels emotionally is brought into immediate striking contrast.

This kind of central issue can be found, formulated and presented to the patient with the expectation of a positive response regardless of the patient's education, race, religion or socioeconomic background. The cultural background of a patient may dictate that symptoms will be expressed in certain ways acceptable to that culture. Thus there may be loud wailing in one group and grim stoicism in another, hysterical symptoms in one and psychosomatic symptoms in another. Nevertheless, listening to a careful history of repetitive painful events in the patient's life (and they are present in every life) to which the patient has automatically responded at a personal symbolic level (as elicited in the mind of the therapist as he or she asks himself what it must have felt like being the patient), will allow the therapist to appreciate that the wailing or the stoicism or the symptoms are, at their core, ways of warding off or of minimizing the devastating negative image of the self.

There is no group anywhere that can claim to have or to experience a variety of feelings or emotions that are unique and special to that group only. All human beings share the same kind and range of emotions. We are different only in the ways we show them or allow them to be seen. The range of emotions available to all of us is remarkably limited. By the same token the ways of expressing to oneself the nature of one's negative self-image is also limited. The ways of feeling good about the self and the ways of feeling bad about the self are subject to the constraints of language in every case. Clinically, this is helpful in that the patient sitting with us can only feel negative about him or herself within what their language will allow. If the patient and therapist speak the same language, cultural and socioeconomic differences between the two will not matter so long as the therapist remains tuned in to the patient's present and chronically endured pain. This is a pain that is felt by and known only to the patient, who as a result may be experienced as bad, unloved, unworthy, incompetent, inadequate, inferior, unwanted, undeserving, controlled and helpless or whatever other word may be used to convey a negative self-state.

Each patient entering psychotherapy seeks the removal of painful affect. In long-term psychotherapy and in psychoanalysis the patient relates the diminution of the pain to the length of treatment. The longer the expected treatment the less trust is there initially. The time limit itself arouses hope based on very early and archaic expectations of wish fulfillment. This mechanism is universal and has its roots in early infancy when the interval between being alone and suffering frustration and helplessness on the one hand, and feeling gratification and infantile omnipotence with mother's arrival on the other, were crucial. It is this interval which profoundly affects later ego development, especially self-esteem, which here refers to the perceived capacity of the self to master present and future threats.

In TLP the rapidity of mother's arrival is felt in the form of the therapist who, by virtue of the central issue with its empathic power, reawakens the infant process and gives rise to an immediate improvement in the patient's self-esteem. This kind of regression is regression in the service of the ego. Boundaries between self and object are blurred temporarily for the purpose of ending a state of helplessness and later through introjection and identification with the positive aspects of the therapist in the termination phase of treatment.

Faced by the approaching loss of the therapist in the final phase of treatment, the patient is again confronted with loss. Regression may be anticipated as in any other kind of psychotherapy or analysis. The time limitation and adherence throughout to any data or feelings that relate directly or indirectly to the central issue serve to limit the end-phase regression to manageable feelings of anger or of sadness or of overt concern about the return of complaints as resistance to the separation.

Once treatment has begun, the therapeutic process in TLP is different from other kinds of psychotherapy in at least two major aspects. One lies in the remarkable telescoping of events and reactions with the release of an enormous amount of information pertinent to the origins of the central issue. A second lies in the adherence by the therapist to the central issue with clarification and interpretations made in terms of that central issue rather than as sexual/aggressive/guilty fantasies about the parents or their representatives. Recognizing these fantasies, especially in unconscious material, the therapist translates them into vivid affective terms of the negative self-image as it has persisted as a maladaptive means of preserving what once was into what is now and is expected to continue into the future. The negative self-image with its deeply unconscious origins defended from intrusion into the preconscious by the patient's automatic maladaptive means has now been brought into full consciousness. Because this is brief psychotherapy more weight is given to clarifications until the termination phase of the last three sessions is reached. In the termination phase interpretations revolve around the role of the central issue in affecting relationships to past significant persons, to persons of importance to the patient and to the therapist within the transference. The effect is to create an *in vivo* rather than an *in vitro* experience for the patient so that the emotional experience becomes intensely felt. The patient is now very much aware of how an attitude of mind toward the self, which arose in childhood, has continued into adult life undisturbed despite a totally changed reality.

The overt difference between TLP and all other varieties of brief psychotherapy is the limit of twelve sessions of treatment following evaluation. Further, the complaints that brought the patient for help are never going to be the central issue. Also, the patient knows from the start when treatment has begun, when the midpoint has been reached and when the end will come. Each of these points has its own characteristics which serve as guidelines for the therapist. It is important to emphasize that the single goal and aim of TLP is to diminish as much as possible the patient's negative self-image. Symptom relief is a by-product of the process and not the aim.

It has given me much pleasure to have been asked by the author of *Time-Limited Psychotherapy in Practice* to write this introductory chapter. Doctor Shefler has been dedicated for many years to the clinical work, the research aspects and the teaching and supervision aspects of TLP. I have had the pleasure of discussing TLP with him in Israel and in the USA on several occasions and was always impressed with his knowledge, his appreciation of the method and his readiness to apply it clinically. His work adds immensely to our information on an important subject which basically has to do with constructing methods of treatment which are brief, clinically effective, cost-effective and provide greater treatment opportunity for a greater number of patients. I am grateful for his contribution.

James Mann, M.D.
Professor of Psychiatry, Emeritus
Boston University School of Medicine
Training and Supervising Analyst, Emeritus
Boston Psychoanalytic Institute.
Waban, July 1991

Chapter 1

Why time-limited psychotherapy?

Brief dynamic therapy typified the psychotherapy arena throughout the final three decades of the previous millenium. The appearance of brief therapies in the 1960s and 1970s stimulated widespread debate regarding their essence and utility, the extent to which they represented a revolution against extended therapies, their advantages and disadvantages as opposed to those of extended therapies, and whether or not they represented an independent therapeutic entity. These debates took place under the shadow of the unquestionable dominance of extended psychodynamic approaches to psychotherapy. The final decade of the millenium witnessed a significant decrease in debates of this sort, alongside dramatic changes in the availability of wide-ranging varieties of mental health care and the changing lifestyles and consumer habits of people in the Western world (and other parts of the world as well). Brief dynamic therapies, including time-limited psychotherapy, constitute widely used and extremely practical instruments found in the toolbox of the modern therapist. By virtue of the fact that they are largely accepted and rarely subjected to debate over their utility, brief therapies have merged into the category of existent, practical and widespread therapies, which need no justification for their use (Messer 2001a).

Scientifically, the status of brief dynamic therapies resembles that of most psychodynamic therapies. Brief therapies have empirically measurable outcomes, though further investigation is still required to understand the mechanisms at work in these therapies. As stated, the relatively new and reasonably secure status of brief therapies was altogether different until very recently. The following three clinical vignettes describe events that took place over twenty years ago. They exemplify and demonstrate the prevailing state of affairs at the time, a state that necessitated the development of time-limited dynamic therapy methods. The identifying details of the patients described in this chapter and throughout the book have been changed to preserve their anonymity and protect their privacy.

The first case involves Joseph, a 33-year-old father of two children. He worked as a scientist in an exact sciences field and sought therapy consequent to feelings of anxiety which began shortly prior to his departure for two years of post-doctoral studies abroad. He felt incapable of settling the various arrangements associated with his travels abroad. He delayed placing his apartment up for rent, put off responding to letters concerning the place to which he was traveling, had trouble completing research papers that were in the process of implementation, and primarily experienced difficulty organizing the division of laboratory duties during his absence among the research assistants and laboratory workers. Joseph sought therapy because he was afraid he would sabotage the implementation of his post-doctoral studies, an undesirable outcome that he very much hoped to prevent.

He requested therapy approximately three and a half months prior to his scheduled departure date. He was under considerable duress and described clear symptoms of anxiety and occasional panic. Physical manifestations of his anxiety included 'butterflies' in his stomach, trembling, sleep disturbances, increased perspiration when thinking of stressful topics, a 'dead end' feeling, and occasional paralysis of all activity, particularly when he had many tasks to implement at once. My clinical impression was that Joseph possessed tremendous potential and was usually successful, yet he currently faced many serious stumbling blocks, which hindered his functioning to the extent of inducing failure. He described similar situations from his past, particularly surrounding times of change and transition (during military service, throughout his higher education, especially around examination periods, and in his relationships with women – consequent to his desire to impress them he repeatedly encountered incidences of impotence and emotional withdrawal).

Though I noted his visible distress, I was able to suggest only two options. The first option was to attempt a crisis intervention approach composed of soothing and supportive components which would continue until just before his departure. I must admit, I had reservations about this option, as I believed Joseph was capable of trying to understand his situation and using his understanding in a more meaningful way to break out of the neurotic cycle in which he was trapped. At the time, I knew of only one way of breaking out of such neurotic cycles – extended psychodynamic therapy. Therefore, the second option at my disposal was to assist in finding a therapist in the city to which Joseph would be traveling, enabling him to begin extended therapy there. Joseph understood my dilemma. He was not interested in supportive therapy and on a rational level appreciated my efforts to find him another therapist. However, on the less rational side, he clearly expressed his disappointment and the feeling that I had rejected him, passed him off to a stranger on the other side of the ocean.

In the second case, Ilana was sent to me under pressure from her parents who insisted 'nothing was right' with her. She was a 19-year-old student at a respectable local college; her functioning and behavior had sharply declined during the previous year. She was an attractive teenager who tried hard to make herself unappealing. She dressed provocatively and cared little about her personal hygiene. Ilana had stopped investing in her studies and consequently her previously high level of academic achievement plummeted. She disappeared from home for hours and refused to tell her parents where she spent her time and with whom. From the little they could ascertain, they believed she was involved with kids who were ill suited to her educational and social level. In Ilana's words, her parents thought she was 'a really bad girl.'

Her blunt and staccato speech contained a disparaging, scornful tone. She emphasized that she only came to therapy under an ultimatum from her parents and insisted she was not troubled by what was happening to her, nor did she understand why her parents were so worried. 'On the contrary, things are finally going my way. I'm doing what I want; it's as if I'm bringing myself to life.' She was troubled, however, by her parents' threat that if she did not alter her behavior, whether on her own or with the help of a therapist, they would apply sanctions, preventing her from maintaining the current lifestyle she enjoyed so much. For example, they would ground her, restrict her telephone usage, and limit her cash flow. Concerned by their threats, she 'gave in' to the pressure and decided to check out therapy.

From the beginning of my encounter with Ilana, I tried to uncover the pain which motivated her attempts to be different, and I found it. To my surprise, in the second session she readily admitted her life was not as fabulous as she claimed. She had painful doubts regarding her identity, who loved her, what would happen if nobody loved her, whom she loved, and to whom she was attracted. She was unsure of what she really wanted from herself nor did she know what she feared. It was relatively easy to recognize Ilana's emotional distress, to express understanding, and to point out the genuine need for therapy.

Satisfied with this breakthrough, I suggested she give therapy a chance. Ilana began asking about how therapy is conducted, what is talked about, how long it lasts, and so forth. The idea of introspection and the sharing of thoughts, feelings, and images appealed to her. She loved to speak, think, and imagine. When I added that it was an extensive process, she asked, 'How long?' I think I anticipated her negative response and consequently stammered a vague and defensive response, 'Uh . . . a year . . . two years.' Ilana leaned back in the armchair and declared, 'No way. I'm not coming here for a year or two years. Why such a long time? How can there be that much to say? There's no way. I'm not crazy.' I was unable to convince Ilana this was the right therapeutic strategy, and she left without scheduling another session. I felt I had missed a potential breakthrough.

The third case centers on Yuval, who at the age of 17½ was referred for treatment by his school guidance counselor. The guidance counselor doubted Yuval's ability to handle his upcoming army service. Although Yuval functioned well and showed no blatant signs of emotional distress, he felt anxious about his immediate future. In the intake session, he raised key issues, such as the struggle with his masculinity. He spoke about his changing body, physical strength, as yet unrealized sexuality, and the influence of his impending army service on these struggles. He mentioned his preoccupation with peer and family relationships and expressed a vague apprehension regarding his ability to form new relationships. Yuval linked these misgivings to his upcoming army service. He appeared aware, open, intelligent, and sensitive, and understood that his difficulties were related to internal emotional processes. Overall, Yuval appeared to be a very pleasant young man.

As I listened to Yuval, my impression was he would benefit from a psychodynamic therapeutic approach. I explained that therapy is an extensive process and Yuval responded, 'I understand, but I'm being recruited into the army in another three and a half months. I hope I'll be able to meet the military demands. I'm not very worried, but even so, I thought I could use some help. That's why I came to you.' There were no signs of a clear emotional or functional crisis, therefore I did not offer him treatment in the form of crisis intervention. Despite his doubts and moderate anxiety, I believed Yuval was competent for military service. On the other hand, I appreciated his willingness to try therapy. I told him I understood his needs, and thought therapy was certainly appropriate. Due to the constraints of reality, however, I recommended he complete his army service, then seek treatment.

Because he had no other option, Yuval unenthusiastically accepted my suggestion, or at least the first part of it. Similar to my experience with Joseph, I felt dissatisfied with my recommendation, yet I was unaware of any alternative at the time.

I am certain many therapists have encountered numerous variations on the situations described in these vignettes. They demonstrate two of the dominant characteristics in the therapy arena during the 1970s: first, the general lack of cumulative clinical knowledge and experience regarding viable therapeutic alternatives to extended psychodynamic psychotherapy, which were especially lacking under those circumstances when real circumstance prevented extensive therapy. Second, the absolute lack of room for consideration of the possibility that an alternative might exist to the widespread and classic option of extended dynamic therapy for every patient.

Situations such as these exist today as well. Many therapists have experienced the problems generated by the encounter between a therapist equipped with an extended dynamic approach and a patient with limited time resources at his or her disposal, as demonstrated in the cases of Yuval and Joseph, or the patient with limited motivation or willingness to invest massive resources in therapy, as in the case of Ilana. Such encounters, like many others in those days, culminated in feelings of helplessness, failure, inability to persuade, and misfortune due to time constraints. Back then, the idea that it might be feasible to attain meaningful achievements in a brief time was alien and associated primarily with crisis intervention, which would potentially evolve into extended therapies. The myth of therapeutic perfection dominated and any thought of therapy limited in time or scope was construed as resistance to in-depth therapy or as a defensive flight into health.

Psychoanalysts and psychotherapists practicing extended therapy today are likely to think similarly. Nonetheless, I have no doubt that today they would know to refer the distressed patient for brief therapy, even if they did not practice this type of therapy themselves. In other words, the former exclusiveness of extended dynamic therapy as the one model suited to every patient under all conditions no longer exists. Even therapists unable, unwilling or untrained in the practice of brief therapy (for which there are various reasons) nevertheless acknowledge its existence and utility as one of the standard therapeutic interventions at our disposal. In the 1970s and 1980s a crucial distinction was drawn between the actual practice of brief therapy, suited for certain therapists but not for others, and the theoretical and conceptual acknowledgement of the importance of these therapies.

Simultaneously, the attitude of therapists practicing brief dynamic therapy underwent significant and steady change in essentially the reverse direction. Like any innovation, brief dynamic therapies contained an element of threat to everything that existed beforehand. Thus, the innovators of brief dynamic therapy methods succeeded in arousing staunch opposition to their very existence, opposition that constituted an exceptionally clear expression of the tremendous threat felt by practitioners of extended therapies. Over time, the rebellious and radical tone of the brief therapy innovators became more moderate. Rather than hailing brief therapy as the new effective treatment for all therapeutic endeavors under all circumstances, it became an additional option suitable for certain situations. Instead of offering brief therapy as the ultimate therapy approach to almost any problem, additional alternatives were incorporated into the store of therapeutic options at the disposal of the therapist and the patient.

Ongoing conflict between alternative approaches to therapy had characterized the middle years of the twentieth century. The great debates between analytical and behavioral approaches and between systemic and individual approaches were characterized by claims of exclusivity. In other words, the essence of the debate was the designation of one approach as the select and singularly effective solution to emotional problems. Toward the 1980s, the pressures and forces of reality coupled with empirical findings led the situation from conflict into eclectic directions, followed by a trend toward therapeutic pluralism. The essence of eclectic thought in mental health care centered upon the search for the optimal treatment composed of the most active and effective elements from different therapy methods. The failure of eclectic psychotherapy models was supported by empirical findings, which showed no meaningful differences in relative efficacy between the various treatment methods. One key variable in ensuring the effectiveness of any particular therapy method was the extent to which therapists adhered to the clear guidelines of the method and performed their duties as therapists as precisely as possible (Barber et al. 1996). In addition, this line of thinking assumed that there were more effective and less effective therapy approaches for various situations. This understanding ended the attack-and-conquer strategy between the different therapy methods, a strategy aimed not only at demonstrating the superiority of a particular therapy method, but proving that other therapy methods were no good at all. Today, the prevailing understanding is that every therapy method possesses unique features which interact well with the unique characteristics of the patients, their diagnoses and clinical conditions.

Previously, as long as the topic of the extended time did not arise directly, then the therapy appeared to continue indefinitely. Frequently, the first mention of the time issue became the pretext for immediate discontinuation of the therapy, or soon thereafter (as in the case of Ilana). Therapists often summarize these experiences of therapy failure by stating: 'The patient was not suited for dynamic psychotherapy.' I view this issue differently and every time I come across this type of statement I think the patient is not ill suited to the therapy, rather the therapy is inappropriate for the patient. The obligation falls upon us, as therapists, to utilize our resources and find the therapy approach best suited to the needs of the patient.

Today, in an era when patients face seemingly endless therapy options, while therapists face economic and legal restraints, the question of suitability between treatment method and patient has grown more critical than ever, for reasons that extend beyond humanistic considerations. In the new age, the model of the authoritarian therapist who dogmatically determines the therapy approach for the perplexed, confused, uninformed patient is no longer acceptable. We are living in an era of information explosion, laws protecting patients' rights, and laws which obligate the therapist to explain the advantages and disadvantages of different therapy methods to the patient. Legitimate questions regarding why the therapist suggests one particular therapy method over

another are typically raised at the beginning of many psychotherapies. Today, patients who are limited in terms of resources yet
goal-oriented individuals intent on achieving clear-cut therapy
results, often unwittingly lean toward time-limited therapies.
Howard, Kopta, Krause and Orlinsky (1986) showed that about
60 per cent of patients had improved after thirteen sessions of
therapy. Similar to this finding, Anderson and Lambert (in press)
found that thirteen sessions on average were necessary to attain
clinically significant change for about 50 per cent of their patients.
Lambert, Hansen and Finch (in press) reported that 50 per cent of a
huge sample of 10 000 patients needed about twenty-one sessions
in order to achieve significant clinical change. In a previous study,
Phillips (1985) concluded that for a wide range of therapies, the
modal number of sessions is one, the median is three to five, and
the mean five to eight sessions. The scientific influences on psychotherapy also promote increased awareness and the consequent
demand for rapid, assessable outcomes.

Freud famously called psychoanalytic therapy 'the pure gold' in
his 1918 Budapest lecture. In certain eras, only those who could
allow themselves the luxury of the 'pure gold' of psychoanalytic
therapy benefited from it. The pure gold metaphor describes more
than the financial resources that over time became an influential
and dominant factor in the accessibility and availability of psychotherapy, both in the private and especially in the public sectors. It
also describes the blend of socio-cultural, developmental,
educational and life conditions that characterize potential patients.
The psychotherapy consumer culture has changed drastically. The
shame once associated with therapy has dwindled and almost
vanished. The cloud of mystery surrounding the therapy process
has evaporated. We have returned to a state in which people seek
psychotherapy because they are experiencing emotional distress,
whether clear and defined or scattered and diffuse. In our clinics,
we come across increasing numbers of clients who know why they
have come for therapy and for what they expect to receive help. It
has become a rare instance in which a patient requests help for a
specific and focused problem and the therapeutic aid offered is an
all-inclusive, comprehensive, multi-dimensional, longer-term
approach. Today, patients and therapists alike know there are
other choices. The option of choosing from among many different
therapy styles is a joint selection process, which takes both the
therapist (according to capability, training, and professional stance)

and the patient (according to resources, capability, and motivation) into consideration.

Brief therapies have appeared in the psychoanalytic clinical literature since its inception. In one of Freud's early works, Katharina (1895), he describes a complete therapeutic process within the duration of one long session. Careful study of this session and of Freud's detailed description of the therapeutic process reveals a complete and highly accurate schematic structure of contemporary brief and time-limited dynamic therapy as we know it, including all of the dimensions which typify the new schools of modern brief dynamic therapy: focus, limited duration, an active and directive therapist, strong motivation for change, a high level of psychological mindedness, and the presence of a clear-cut constellation of conflict in the patient. It is amazing to discover that each of these components, which would one day become the markers of brief dynamic therapy in modern schools of thought, were already detailed in the first analysis described by Freud in 1895. This offers little proof of anything, however, it certainly provides important evidence that the foundations of brief dynamic therapies are based upon the fundamental principles of extended dynamic therapy.

Freud also conducted other very brief therapies, for instance, Bruno Walter whose therapy consisted of two sessions (Sterba 1951) and Gustav Mahler whose therapy consisted of four sessions (Reik 1960). As time passed, interest in and experimentation with active transference (Ferenczi and Rank 1925), controlled termination (Alexander 1951) and focus (Balint in Balint, Ornstein and Balint, 1972) contributed significantly to the development of theory and technique for brief dynamic therapies. Historically, brief psychoanalytic therapies always originated from encounters between patients in distress and therapists seeking a creative, nonconformist solution to which the safe, well-traveled road or 'pure gold' did not lead (Sterba 1951). Over the years, the psychoanalytic movement in its various theoretical streams grappled with the tensions between innovation and rebellion, between conservatism and laying conceptual cornerstones. Freud's students described extremely brief analytic treatments as well: Binswanger (1912) treated a woman with phobias in six months. Tannenbaum (1913) described an eight-week therapy. Oberndorf (1947) presented a one-year therapy for use with severely disturbed patients.

Without exception, all brief dynamic therapy methods developed consequent to the emotional distress of patients of the types I have described above and of additional types. All of the various methods clearly state the difficulties faced by therapists when offering these therapies, for they represent patient-oriented compromises. Nonetheless, they all emphasize the need and obligation to seek a solution for patients whose needs are not met by classical, extended in-depth therapy. For as much as we value its practice, study, research, and instruction, TLP does not meet the needs of every patient, whether due to time issues or other reasons. In every time period, innovative and creative thought within the various streams of psychoanalysis originated with analysts who did not seek to fortify the analytic method, but who struggled with its limitations when faced with patients whose pain and suffering were not relieved by the analytic approach. Therapy length, especially one of very extended duration, was not considered a crucial element in the classical definition of psychoanalytic therapy. It was a dimension that was later incorporated into the psychoanalytic method and rapidly became one of its most prominent features. Theoretical justifications for the extended duration of therapy did not tarry in their arrival (Shefler 1988).

If we return to the question of why time-limited psychotherapy, the simple answer would be that it is feasible, reasonable, and often the most natural and obvious solution to cases such as those presented at the beginning of this chapter and in many similar cases. Nevertheless, as we will see throughout this chapter, for many of the years during which dynamic psychotherapy developed, not only was it impossible to ask, 'Why brief and time-limited therapy?' but there was no chance of receiving a positive response to the question. Back then, the considerations and answers given usually alluded to condemnation of the patient who opted for a 'flight into health,' or of the therapist who was perceived as emotionally and practically incapable of containing and creating a holding environment for the patient and the patient's desires, difficulties, and wishes.

During more than one hundred years of existence, dynamic psychotherapy and psychoanalysis have not only changed in terms of technique, theory, and their theoretical and clinical purposes. First and foremost, the fundamental goals of these therapies have undergone profound transformation.

Freud began practicing psychodynamic therapy out of curiosity and a profound aspiration to treat patients who had not been helped by previous treatments. He was unconcerned with the method, other than as a means for healing his patients. Even the question of what is considered psychological healing has undergone transformation and modification over those hundred years and has developed in varying directions. In this context, it is important to remember that Freud was a neurologist and as such he conducted his first therapies under the framework of the medical model. In other words, the patient sought therapy in order to relieve, cure, or to alter a condition from which he or she suffered. Furthermore, in its early years, the therapy focused on the visible markers of suffering (i.e., the symptoms) and tried to uproot them directly through interpretation of their symbolic meaning.

Over the years, the length of psychoanalytic therapy increased for many reasons. These are summarized and discussed by Malan (1963). According to Malan, the leading factor in the elongation of analytic therapy was the recognition of repression in psychoanalytic theory as a camouflage mechanism central to the development of mental health or illness. This recognition highlighted the significance of and need for extensive time, necessary for the process of raising repressed material anew from the unconscious. A second factor requiring considerable time for processing is that of resistance to uncovering memories, events, fantasies, part objects, introjects, and so forth. The processing and overcoming of resistance comprise a substantial proportion of the psychoanalytic therapeutic process, a process that, as stated, requires time.

The third theoretical factor that influenced the lengthening of analytic therapies was that of regression, the psychic process of emotional reversion to early developmental periods. Irrespective of the debate over its importance, this process requires considerable time resources to enable the search for repressed and hidden contents.

The over-determination of symptoms indicative of emotional disorders necessitates an ongoing search for additional explanations of the meaning of the presenting symptom. Therefore, the therapist does not settle for providing a single meaning for a symptom, thus ending the process of interpretation and insight. Instead, after reaching one particular understanding of the situation, the therapist continues digging for additional forms of understanding. The centrality of transference and countertransference processes in psychoanalytic therapy also contributes to the extension of therapy. Although initiation of the transference neurosis and its ultimate resolution, attained by repetitiously working through the transference, deepen the shared understanding between patient and therapist, these processes also require additional time.

The experience of timelessness must be added to the afore-mentioned therapy elements as another fundamental experience in analytic therapy, an experience that is supposed to reconstruct the early development of the patient under therapeutic conditions of full protection and understanding. The experience of timelessness was presented as a high-ranking element in analytic therapy within which the patient would not have to fear separation or even think about it for a considerable amount of time. This experience brought to light an additional concept characteristic of analytic therapy in the 1950s and 1960s – the myth of perfection. The essence of this myth was that analytic exploration and investigation, which lasted as long as possible, could elicit a perfect outcome. More than any other concept, the myth of perfection contributed to the belief that the longer therapies lasted the more successful they were considered to be, regardless of the actual clinical and emotional phenomena that occurred within the therapy.

The vague nature of therapy goals, the forms of change, and the definitions of therapeutic interventions and roles each contributed to the lengthening of therapy. Though it originated as a focused, concentrated experience, medical in nature, with clearly defined curative goals, psychoanalysis, and subsequently analytic psycho-therapy, developed into a long, extensive process that never reaches a designated conclusion. As long as this process material-izes under conditions of mutual consent based upon free choice on the part of both patient and therapist, it is more than acceptable. The patient and therapist can select freely the alternatives most suited to them. Problems arise, however, when the patient neither chooses this therapy method nor possesses the capacities to make such a choice.

After World War II, several issues emerged and stimulated the need for abbreviated therapy options. The beginning of World War II forced the recruitment of the professional mental health care community, including psychoanalysts, for the task of quickly returning shell-shocked soldiers to a state of fitness. The well-known works of Grinker and Spiegel (1944) indicated that under certain conditions it was possible to perform important analytic work in a brief time, yielding meaningful and enduring results. Another influential factor was the appearance of non-psycho-analytic psychological treatments. First introduced by Wolpe in

1958, the behaviorist therapy approach, based upon the use of learned conditioning, produced therapies of brief duration. The behaviorist approach and subsequently the paradoxical and cognitive approaches created a situation in which the therapist tried a particular therapy method, presuming changes and results would appear within a limited amount of time. Therapists adhering to this particular method accepted the absence of change as a mismatch between the specific therapy method and the patient, leading to the termination of the therapy and another attempt using a different therapy method, and so on. Psychoanalytic thought views such a stance as alien, maintaining that failure to produce change is not necessarily due to the unsuitability of the therapy method. Rather, lack of change indicates therapist and patient have yet to decipher and comprehend the roots of the emotional problem that led the patient to seek therapy or that they have yet to penetrate the emotional realm in which change will transpire. As a result of this professional stance, many psychotherapies are likely to last for a considerable time, not for reasons or goals which are clear to the therapist and patient but because both members of the therapeutic dyad are immersed in exploration for its own sake.

A third factor that significantly altered the perception of dynamic psychotherapy approaches was the appearance of psychotropic medications. The discovery of these medications revolutionized the lives of severely mentally ill patients. In addition, the appearance of other new groups of medications induced rapid effects upon more common, yet nevertheless difficult, emotional conditions such as anxiety and depression. Recently, the tremendous expansion of research on psychiatric medication has prompted increased functional specification for these medications, accompanied by decreases in their side-effects. Thus, medication has become an accessible, convenient, and generally rapid remedy for a respectable proportion of the problems that bring people to seek psychotherapy.

The fourth factor that massively influenced the development of brief and psychoanalytic psychotherapies relates to the major impact of community psychology and psychiatry in the 1960s and '70s. In years past, the existence of psychotherapy was shrouded by a veil of secrecy and isolation from all other human activity. This was also true during much earlier periods in human history when care of the mentally ill was influenced by moral or religious views as well as during the time when the transition was made to medical approaches for care of the mentally ill. The community approach began as a form of fierce opposition to institutional psychiatry. Adherents to this stream of thought firmly opposed institutions, which they described as totalitarian in every respect, and establishments, which were perceived as all-powerful. The wide-open expanses of the community replaced the walls of the closed institution. To a large extent, the role of mental health caretaker was transferred to social agents, replacing the cold and distant stance of the professional therapist. This held true in cases of acute primary care, but even more so in cases of secondary and tertiary preventive care. Thus, important roles in mental health care were assigned to religious authorities, teachers, general practitioners, educators, and often the legal authorities and police. Of course, there were also non-professional volunteers who underwent training and supervision prior to fulfilling their positions.

The community movement in mental health care impacted considerably upon several realms, ranging from the status of patients and therapists in mental health care and in society at large to the management of and control over financial and political resources in the mental health service industry throughout the world. The community approach is most relevant to our topic of interest in its impact upon the lifting of the veil of secrecy and mystery surrounding psychotherapy. Consequent to increased acknowledgement of therapy and actual descriptions of therapy in the media and arts milieu, the general public gradually gained a greater awareness of the benefits of psychotherapy, in contrast to the former veil of shame and aversion to these types of therapies. Generally speaking, this phenomenon contributed to a drastic rise in the demand for therapy and consequently an increased need for therapy methods that economize on time.

The fifth and final influence upon the direction taken by modern schools of brief dynamic therapy was the aspiration of health insurance companies to reduce expenditure related to extended mental health care. Initially in the United States, and subsequently in Europe, these companies encouraged research endeavors focused on demonstrating that brief therapy was as effective as extended therapy. In fact, the lack of difference in outcome indicated the unmistakable economic advantage of brief therapies.

Simultaneously, an additional phenomenon occurred in the therapy arena, relating to the goals of therapy and indirectly to its duration. As time passed, the various types of dynamic therapy and analysis splintered into several groups, according to their goals, under the divergent cultural influences in Europe and especially in the United States where therapy become a fashionable status symbol. The first group consisted of those therapies aimed at curing and providing relief. Both analysis and psychotherapy were intended to provide release from emotional distress, not using the focused, direct method practiced in the past yet with the clear goal of changing and curing the suffering patient. Even today, therapists in both public and private practice adopt this approach. This group of therapies clearly rests upon the medical model of treatment. That is, it assumes the presence of emotional distress and illness in the patient, while the therapist possesses knowledge of how to enact change. These types of therapies have a singular goal: the eradication of distress and the abatement of emotional pain from which the patient suffers.

The second group of patients view therapy as a means for exploration and introspection and for expanding their familiarity with the depths of their emotional worlds, even though therapy might have begun with the goal of relieving suffering and emotional distress. Patients and therapists in this group do not necessarily work toward the goal of reaching a particular clinical destination. Rather, they aim toward a deeper understanding of the patient's personality and personal history. Change occurs but not necessarily according to the formulation of the medical model, which seeks to achieve positive change and decreased suffering.

The third group consists of patients who are themselves therapists and who have opted for therapy within the framework of professional training, due to personal distress, or a combination of both. Similar to the second group, one often finds a lack of specific suffering destined to change subsequent to therapy among these patients. This group approaches therapy as a broad and in-depth journey into the depths of the soul and personality, such that change occurs even though the directions and trends of change might be unexpected, unknown, and are often not subject to quantification or assessment.

These assertions should include mention of changes in the prevailing attitude toward the referral to and acceptance of medical treatments in general and mental health care in particular. In recent decades, the atmosphere within which medical services are provided has shifted from an authoritarian system providing service to a community reliant upon its service network and accepting it without protest, to a highly regulated system required to fulfill the demands placed upon it by its patrons. Inherent to the current situation is that a much greater emphasis is placed upon the wishes and rights of the patient in the therapy framework and there is more room for the patient to influence the nature, length, cost, and desired outcome of therapy. Under the previous model of the patient-therapist relationship, the disappearance of symptoms following a brief intervention was routinely declared a 'flight into health' on the part of the patient. In the past, therapists perceived this flight into health as an expression of patients' lack of will or resistance to coping with the deepest layers of their disturbances.

Today, in an age when patient-therapist relations are characterized by the patient's right to choose the type of therapy and its framework, the choice of symptomatic relief is certainly a legitimate one, even if the therapist has significant objections regarding the implications of the patient's choice. The therapist can voice these objections but cannot force the patient to accept them. Furthermore, the impact of process theories has intensified. These theories explain intrapsychic change as a succession of meaningful, centralized, and focused experiences from which the patient can continue to work independently on change processes, rather than as a continuous succession of therapeutic experiences. In recent decades, the more widespread therapy becomes, the more questions arise regarding its funding and implementation in the public health system.

Alongside medical developments and the increased economic demands of many therapies, the question of the economic efficiency of therapy has been revisited. This question arose primarily due to the long duration and frequent difficulty in demonstrating effective and enduring therapy outcomes. Inherent to all forms of psychotherapy, these difficulties served as a primary impetus for the development of brief therapies geared toward meeting the changing needs of a society that has grown increasingly more aware of emotional difficulties and limitations, while also becoming more conscious of the cost of therapy, its utility, and the responsibility for funding it. Thus, medical insurance companies, for example, promptly discontinued their funding of analytic and psychodynamic therapies by defining very strict therapy goals and refusing to accept extended therapies, conducted as a way of life, as an economically worthwhile type of medical treatment under any circumstance. Toward the end of the 1960s a clear distinction was drawn between therapies designed to relieve emotional emergencies, distresses, and dangers, and therapies aimed toward enabling people to become better acquainted with themselves and ·their personalities.

This distinction between therapy types was made more difficult by the fact that novice therapists-in-training needed to continue practicing extended therapies in the public sector. I will address this issue and the problems it raises more thoroughly in a later chapter. In short, public mental health clinics face the challenge of negotiating the administrative demands placed upon them by the increased quantity of people seeking mental health care on the one hand and by the need to train new therapists entering the mental health care system on the other. Public health clinics must simultaneously minimize the number of therapy hours given to an individual patient, reducing therapy to the relief of the most immediate emotional distress, while co-operating with institutes of higher education and professional training, professional unions, and therapist licensing bylaws that require training in extended therapy for neophyte therapists. Therefore, the best candidates for the training of novice therapists appear to be patients from the second group described above.

Let us return to the question of 'why time-limited therapy?' The answer is implicit in the brief historical description outlined above: therapists must aspire to conduct brief therapies due to limitations in time and financial resources. Furthermore, throughout the final six decades of the twentieth century, therapy has become more widespread and familiar, it arouses less social resistance and scorn, and it is no longer instantly associated with the stigma of deviance and abnormality. Therapy has become a highly demanded commodity while the ability of the establishment to supply this commodity to all of its consumers is dwindling (a fact which Freud alluded to in his analytic gold quotation of 1918).

Partial solutions to the problematic circumstances I have outlined are linked to alternative allocations of therapy time. James Mann (1973) described this equation regarding therapy resources very well when he related the challenges he confronted as director of the Boston Psychiatric Clinic. Mann (and, later, Mann and Goldman 1982) described the demand placed upon him to provide more therapy to greater numbers of people. It was a political demand. He translated this political demand into the restriction of time resources allocated for each therapy.

At this point, I would like to assert my central position regarding brief therapies on the whole, including time-limited therapies. Brief therapy is not the therapy of choice for all circumstances, nor for all patients. Nevertheless, it is suitable for a segment of the population classified as the first type of patient group above. It can reasonably be estimated that brief therapy presents a viable option for the 20–30 per cent of mental health patients willing to accept it in lieu of extended therapy, in addition to another 20 per cent of patients unwilling to commit to extended therapies or unable to receive extended therapies (such as the cases of Ilana and Joseph, respectively). The combined total of these two groups indicates that brief therapy provides a therapeutic solution for a reasonable portion of the population, but not for the total therapy-seeking population.

We should be honest and remind ourselves that the same state of affairs exists for the many varieties of extended therapy. Whereas one type of therapy was once considered suitable for all therapeutic needs, this situation no longer exists in practice. It is increasingly recognized that emotional states are unique, come in many varieties, and are highly specific to the personality structure and life circumstances of the individual. This understanding has broadened the range of viable therapeutic responses for any particular therapy case and relieved the sting of controversy between divergent therapeutic positions within the field of psychodynamic psychotherapy, such as extended and brief analytic therapies. Of course, this viewpoint holds true in regard to other therapy approaches as well. Contemporary debates regarding the relative effectiveness of therapies in various circumstances are no longer characterized by lethal competition aimed at discovering the most effective therapy while declaring all other therapies substandard. Instead, these debates utilize clearer definitions and draw sharper distinctions regarding the suitability of a particular therapy in a specific situation, in comparison to an alternative therapy in a different situation.

Given that brief therapies developed in response to administrative and economic pressures, they have become a compromise between the therapeutic ideal and the constraints of reality. In practical terms, taking a broad view of brief therapy over the years reveals its role as a complement to extended therapy, appropriate for certain types of people who can be helped by it and inappropriate for others unlikely to benefit from it. A third group exists as well. This group is capable of benefiting from either brief or extended therapy and can therefore choose either. Likewise, the therapist has the leeway to offer either type of therapy.

As we near the conclusion of this chapter, I want to emphasize that today brief therapies should not be perceived as revolutions or rebellions against extended therapy approaches. Rather, they ought to be viewed as a complementary, supportive, and strengthening component of the therapeutic choices offered to patients by professionals who believe in and are knowledgeable about psychodynamic psychotherapy approaches.

Several historical surveys of the development of various brief therapies (Crits-Christoph and Barber 1991; Messer and Warren 1995, Messer and Warren 2001) raise a variety of needs, which ultimately lead to the recognition that dynamic therapy can be brief and yet still be effective. Among the brief therapies, time-limited psychotherapy (TLP) exemplifies an entirely different line of thinking, according to which brief therapy is more than simply a means for adjusting to and compromising with reality. It is also an appropriate and effective exploitation of a realistic need. As will be described in greater detail in the next chapter, Mann (1973) emphasized that the time limitation created by administrative needs and compulsions stimulated his creative thinking and led him to a profound understanding of inadequately processed separation processes and their influence on the development of neurotic emotional distress. Ultimately, this thought process brought to fruition a therapeutic model in which time and its limitation exert a curative effect on the therapeutic model and the change processes elicited by the model. This is an outstanding example of how circumstance begets creative development. Like many other analysts who practice brief therapies, Mann maintained that in many clinical cases, classical analysis or extended dynamic therapy is still the treatment of choice. On the other hand, he identified situations and assembled an array of diagnoses for which, in his opinion, time-limited therapy can be very beneficial.

Empirical support for the effectiveness of these treatments further influences the answers given to the question of why time-limited therapy (Barber and Ellman 1996; Crits-Christoph 1992; Shefler et al. 1995). Unlike extended analytic therapies, brief dynamic therapies have been continuously researched, as has almost every new psychotherapeutic treatment introduced after the mid-1960s. Despite the presence of serious difficulties in the implementation of research on both brief and extended dynamic therapies, brief dynamic therapies enable easier and more effective investigation of issues such as efficacy and endurance than extended dynamic therapies. The research difficulties will be discussed at greater length in Chapter 11 of this book. Empirical findings regarding comparisons between types of brief therapy as well as comparisons between the outcomes of brief and extended dynamic therapies generally indicate the high efficacy of brief therapy methods, including time-limited psychotherapy. In addition to the scientific value of these findings, they have quite a bit of political impact upon policy makers involved in bureaucratic aspects of mental health care. We can summarize by saying that time-limited therapy provides an extremely suitable solution to the most frequent distresses of many patients, especially in an era when time is considered an exceptionally precious resource and aspirations for rapid and profound change have become widespread.

The question of why TLP naturally evokes a second question on this topic: toward whom is TLP geared? Who can be helped by TLP? I can provide a clear answer by revisiting the three groups of therapy patients presented above within the context of this second question. Time-limited therapy cannot be the optimal therapy for individuals interested in expanding their self-knowledge and delving deeply into the inner workings of their psyche. It is also not the therapy of choice for therapists seeking their own therapy in order to improve and deepen self-awareness. These types of therapeutic activities require generous and often unlimited allocations of time. Furthermore, they should only be conducted based upon freedom of choice and patients' autonomous decisions to allocate their resources in this manner.

As such, the time-limited therapy under discussion is designed to provide relief for the patient particularly in need of it. This is the patient suffering from chronic, enduring pain, likely to break out under certain circumstances and appear in the form of a recognized disorder, an accumulation of symptoms, or a general sense of distress. Alongside these characteristics, it is important for patients selected for time-limited therapy to possess the emotional strength that will enable them to achieve maximum benefit from this therapy. The relevant personality strengths for patients suited to time-limited psychotherapy are a good ability for interpersonal attachment, readily available emotional ability, strong motivation for change, and a satisfactory level of psychological mindedness.

These are the main criteria for patient suitability to time-limited therapy, which describe the basic personality structure and the raw potential contained within it. The next chapter is dedicated to a detailed description of the clinical model of time-limited therapy. The diagnostic and personality traits of patients suited to this type of therapy will be discussed in clinical terms.

In addition to these traits, and the presence of emotional distress, it is very important to note that the question of time-limited therapy is also a question of informed selection of this option. The patient might choose time-limited therapy due to time constraints, limited funds, or limited willingness to make a long-term emotional investment. Likewise, the mental health care provider might choose the time-limited option due to considerations such as the need to provide service to a large number of people, shortage of available professional staff, etc. It seems to me that educated discussion of whether to choose or reject the option of brief therapy hinges upon the familiarity of patients, therapists, and policy-makers with the potential and limitations of this type of therapy. Therefore, brief therapies, including time-limited dynamic therapy, are not competitors to non-time-limited extended therapy. They simply provide another option, a potential alternative for certain people and situations. I believe this understanding of the time-limited therapy option ought to precede the use and implementation of brief therapy methods. Moreover, it does not arouse strong resistance resulting from the fear of competition nor does it threaten the existence of extended dynamic therapy approaches.

Time-limited dynamic therapies arouse fierce resistance among therapists who practice extended therapy approaches (Messer and Warren 1995; Witztum and Dasberg 1986). However, their strong objection is based upon a misunderstanding of the place of these therapies in the array of possible therapies offered to patients. Their view of brief dynamic therapy as a threat to the existence of extended therapies is erroneous.

The therapist adopting a traditional and extended psychody-namic approach must understand that the focused, time-limited, and brief approaches are not a source of upheaval within the field of psychodynamic therapy and likewise do not pose a danger or a threat to the existence of non-time-limited psychodynamic approaches. On the contrary, brief therapy provides an additional therapeutic tool, suited to particular populations and circumstances. Modern therapy perspectives compel therapists to relate to the realities of their patients' circumstances as well as to the alternatives demanded by their patients.

Who are the therapists most suited to the practice of TLP? In addition to dynamic understanding and at least a minimum of experience with extended dynamic therapy, there are certain personality features that characterize the therapist likely to succeed in the use of TLP. It appears to me that the first definitive trait of the optimal TLP therapist should be immense curiosity regarding emotional phenomena. In addition, the therapist must possess abilities for attachment and expression coupled with a good ability for separation. The therapist well suited to this type of work must be sensitive to the emotional pain felt by people when they turn to therapy and must be prepared to hone swiftly in upon the pain and attempt to assuage it. Furthermore, the therapist should not hesitate to try and rapidly formulate conscious and unconscious understandings of the patient's and the therapist's emotional processes in service of the focused and brief nature of the therapy. A frequently asked question is whether brief therapy is appropriate for novice therapists or if a broad base of experience is required in order to practice this therapy method. I will respond to this question at length in the chapter dealing with supervision and instruction of time-limited dynamic therapy (Chapter 12).

Alongside the modern understanding of the important role played by brief therapy, it is vital to reduce the fundamental resistance to this type of therapy by developing training and educational programs for brief and time-limited therapy approaches. Training programs geared toward experienced therapists, skilled in extended dynamic therapy techniques, must include components aimed toward overcoming traditional and personal resistance to brief therapies.

At the same time, brief therapy training programs for neophyte therapists must address their specific needs, which are entirely different from the needs of experienced therapists. Beginning therapists face difficulties centered around their lack of clinical experience and the consequent lack of self-confidence when it comes to adopting clear stances regarding focal points and interventions in brief therapy. The time-limited therapy developed by James Mann is unique in the clarity of its clinical model, which includes clear instructions for patient selection, formulation of the central issue, and administration of the therapy. This lucidity undoubtedly encourages and motivates novice therapists to acquire the skills and abilities utilized in this type of therapy. It is relatively easy to learn and in my experience can serve as a model for the implementation of focused interventions, even without the desire or intention to choose the arbitrary and circumscribed time framework.

In many aspects, TLP is a therapy well suited to the third millenium. It is effective, brief, focused, and can be taught relatively easily. At the same time, it rests upon the foundations of in-depth psychoanalytic therapy and is sustained by its tradition and long history. The innovation of TLP attains its greatest expression in the choice granted to the patient and the freedom allowed for the therapist to conceptualize radical means and approaches to therapy. The next chapter contains descriptions of the therapeutic model as well as the theoretical basis and patient selection criteria for the time-limited dynamic therapy developed by James Mann.

Chapter 2

Time-limited psychotherapy

Fundamental principles and the therapeutic model

In time-limited psychotherapy, a brief dynamic therapy method established by James Mann (1973), the operational mechanism is planned and built upon a rapid and intensive emotional connection between patient and therapist, via a focused central issue, followed shortly thereafter by separation. In this chapter, I describe the theoretical foundations upon which Mann set down his therapeutic model, and the therapy model itself. In this chapter, I intend to explicate Mann's basic assumptions, the principles behind his practical concepts regarding the therapy model and its suggested guidelines, while integrating my experiences and the lessons I have learned over years of clinical practice in the application and supervision of this model. Although I have presented the main points in considerable detail, I want to strongly encourage any therapist aspiring to deepen his or her understanding of time-limited psychotherapy to read Mann's (1973) original book and the casebook published by Mann and Goldman (1982). Both books are exemplary theoretical, ideational, clinical, and humanistic works.

Time and separation

Time and separation are two intimately linked concepts. In psychotherapy and psychoanalysis, where the therapeutic setting includes sufficiently stringent time limitations, these two concepts are even more profoundly tied to one another. Every patient, as well as every therapist, is familiar with the vibrant experiential and emotional tones at the close of the therapy hour, the conclusion of a therapy hour prior to a vacation or weekend, and of course, the emotional turbulence that typifies the full termination of dynamic psychotherapy, or psychoanalysis.

Separations can be small or large, long or short, temporary or eternal, and from more or less significant figures. Alongside their intrinsically painful and traumatic dimension, separations of any kind contain one of the most fundamental components of psychological and emotional development in humans. Coping with loss involves processing the difficult emotions of sorrow and anger that characterize the condition. The individual attempts, at times with outside help, to convert these emotions to feelings of compassion and love, through the development of autonomy and reliance upon internal psychological resources.

As its name suggests, time-limited dynamic psychotherapy is not just one of a series of brief dynamic therapies in which the constraints of reality force the limitation of time resources allocated for therapy, while concurrently circumscribing the goals of therapy. In most brief therapies, once the patient's problems are identified, a focal problem is selected upon which the therapeutic dyad concentrate their emotionally intensive and centralized efforts. The same is true of time-limited therapy. According to this method, however, the time limitation means the separation is preordained immediately at the beginning of the road, thus explicitly establishing the crux of the method: the focus on separation and its implications for the emotional and psychological life of the patient. As with any therapy method, it is important to specify the theoretical basis used for understanding the development of psychological problems and, subsequently, to try to adapt the theory behind the therapeutic technique accordingly.

Four psychological theories of psychoanalysis

The theoretical basis for time-limited therapy is connected to the four psychoanalytic theories later described by Pine (1989). The structural theory describes the presence of innate sexual and aggressive drives, conflicts between the different domains of the ego, and their impact upon the development of symptomatic conditions. Closely linked to the drive theory, ego theory proposes a mechanism for control and mediation between the drives and the social and cultural demands of reality. Object theory describes the development of relationships by means of introjection and identification with early object representations. Finally, self theory relates to the development of the experience of selfness, placing emphasis upon early narcissistic development.

Mann and Goldman (1982) base the theoretical model of TLP upon these four psychoanalytic theories, highlighting the mutual and complementary relationships between the four theories. Their wording differs slightly from Pines, and they prefer the use of the term developmental theory, rather than ego theory. Their starting point is the structural model described by Freud (1913, 1914), according to which the conflict between various domains of the ego serves as the developmental source of symptoms and psychological disorders. This model, however, does not provide adequate explanations for the etiologies of the wide range of personality disorders and psychotic conditions. The psychoanalysis of the self, particularly Kohut's (1971, 1977) contribution to this field, enabled better understanding of the impact of the narcissistic position upon the development of non-psychotic conditions. Mann and Goldman endorse the complementary relationship between these two theories, which may appear contradictory (due primarily to significant differences in therapeutic technique, rather than theoretical contradictions). In addition, the environment in which the newborn is reared, as described by object relations theory, bears heavy influence upon the development of psychological health or pathology. Mann and Goldman underscore the impact of early relations with the mother upon the development of self-esteem and each individual's attitude toward himself or herself. Everyone has been hurt by the relational failures of the primary object, and one of the primary goals of healing through transference is the repair of these injuries. The developmental perspective of psychoanalysis adds the final dimension to the integrative psychoanalytic understanding of Mann and Goldman. Utilizing the concepts of regression and development broadens the psychopathological view of the patient and expands the pathways of curative processes, based upon processes of regression and development that transpire within the therapeutic process and occur naturally throughout the everyday life of the patient.

Integration

This integrative model, composed of the four complementary psychoanalytic approaches, forms the theoretical basis for Mann's TLP. As a result of psychotherapy, change can occur in different psychological realms and in accordance with various theoretical concepts. Change can be effected in the realm of early emotional experience with a significant figure, and self-image can be altered. Unprocessed emotions of rejection experienced during a separation can be examined, and the yearning for an endless connection with a benign figure can be felt. The perception of oneself as weak and helpless can be revised, and the strength that seems to be at the disposal of the individual can be evaluated as realistic or as a defensive illusion.

The working assumption held by all brief dynamic therapies, including TLP, is that elimination of a specific difficulty, such as those described above, stimulates additional processes of change. This assumption is rooted in the fundamental theories of change in psychotherapy. Are change processes point-by-point processes, throughout which specific points change as they are treated directly, one by one? Or is the system of psychotherapeutic change and modification a broader one, influenced not by specific therapeutic acts, but by the overall framework of the therapeutic process coupled with events occurring over the course of the patient's past, present, and future life? The integrative model described above supports the latter view.

Perceptions and modalities of the experience of time

In addition to proposing an incisive, extensive, and integrative analytic understanding as the theoretical basis for TLP, Mann made another innovative and important theoretical contribution by accentuating the relationship between time and separation as two fundamental components of the process of change in therapy. Through his development of the concepts of two modalities for experiencing time, Mann showed us the role time plays in the human development of psychological health or illness. The newborn is equipped with a modality for experiencing time which Mann labeled *infantile time*. As long as its basic needs (satiation, warmth, soothing, holding, painlessness, lack of extreme stimulation) are met, the infant has no experience of time. In other words, when the infant experiences a pleasant and harmonious state of total satisfaction, in which it feels soothed and satiated, as far as it is concerned, there is no reason to alter this state. This is the perception of endless time – infantile time – remnants of which are experienced by every adult, especially at moments of gratification and satisfaction. The sensation often accompanying such pleasant and harmonious experiences, occasionally spoken but more often only thought, that the experience should be everlasting and eternal, is a remnant of the endless sensation of infantile time. As long as no internal need for change arises and the wish for the pleasurable state to last forever remains, the infant feels omnipotent, experiencing its desire for the situation to remain unchanging as having come true.

The internal reality of the infant changes, however, as does its external reality later on. Often, while in a state of total satisfaction, the infant is also physically bonded with its mother, held by her, supported, and warmed by her body heat. A change in this state heralds the conclusion of endless time and imminent separation from the mother. The infant becomes hungry, its skin burns or itches, and the harmony is upset. Then the need arises for rapid, instantaneous, and immediate change, aimed at reinstating the previous state of tranquility. The infant expects to be fed, bathed, and soothed. With time, as the infant develops, it learns to rely upon sources of help and gradually internalizes the ability to delay gratification of its basic needs, partially because it learns not to become anxious that the lack of immediate gratification implies its needs will never be gratified. The incorporation of additional sensory and emotional components into its repertoire, along with the rapid developments of physical and mental functions, reduce to a certain extent the primacy of the basic needs and their fulfillment in the totality of the infant's life. These processes contribute to the development of an additional modality of time experience, which Mann called *calendar time*.

The calendar modality of time experience is a more mature modality that sets the pace of reality in motion. It is finite and contains concepts of separation. There are similarities between the modality of calendar time and the reality principle that Freud discussed within the context of the psychosexual developmental processes of the infant. The experience of calendar time and its programmed, certain, and predictable components transform separation into a programmed and predictable experience. The more solid the sense of calendar time in the individual, the more lucidly he or she understands the processes of separation on a deep level. The understanding of the inevitability of separation, inherent in every relationship along the continuum of time, forms one of the foundations of the existential pain, experienced by every one of us, in one form or another. Separations contain the potential for damage when they are experienced as sudden or unmeditated, and when they leave the individual feeling wounded, injured, or deficient. Internal processing of the separation, recognition of the remaining part-object introjects after separation from a love object, and encountering the diversity of emotions connected with separation can transform separation into an experience that contains not only the pain of loss, but the potential for growth and development, and for autonomy and independence.

Winnicott (1955) described the depressive position as a normal developmental state, dependent upon the development of the sense of time. This sense is responsible for the child's developing ability to throw away objects, to relinquish things, and to hide. Later derivatives of this sense of time include development of the ability to distinguish between fantasy and reality, and the emotional capacity for sadness and mourning. The assimilation of these emotions with benign introjects and positive memories enables the developing child to overcome mourning and grief in the long run. According to Winnicott, the development of the sense of time is crucial to the development of the individual's ability to cope with loss and mourning throughout life.

The brief therapy experience is designed to cope with the fear that time is running out, even in approaches that did not emphasize the time limitation in their initial development. This type of therapy generates a re-experiencing of all significant past experiences, figures, and relationships. It brings to life conflicts between wishes for eternal life, timelessness, and omnipotent infantile fantasies versus finite time, reality, and death. Thus, TLP intensely connects the most important psychological and emotional motives. Immediately upon the commencement of therapy and throughout the entire therapy, these motives are encountered on an emotional-experiential level, in the struggle with the contradictory expectations that the patient brings to therapy. On a conscious level, the patient seeks a brief and effective therapy. Unconsciously, the patient seeks an infinite bond with a containing, supportive figure. The therapist's proposal of brief and time-limited therapy opens up an additional expectation for the fulfillment of this wish. The intense experience of this expectation in TLP provides one of the sources of momentum for the therapy. Ongoing elucidation of these wishes in an empathic atmosphere, the patient's expectations of the therapist, and disappointments generated in the early stage of therapy all contain formidable healing powers. The main source of healing power, however, derives from the processing of the tensions surrounding the rapid coping with separation from another significant object, this time a transference object, and the attempts to transform this separation into a non-painful separation. As Mann (1973) stated:

> If we undertake psychotherapy of limited duration, it would be wise to begin where the patient is; namely, that as soon as he learns that the amount of time for help is limited, he is actively subject to the magical, timeless, omnipotent fantasies of childhood, and his expectations in respect to the treatment arise from them as he lives them now. It is on the basis of this meaning of a real-unreal, conscious-unconscious now that we move into active consideration of the treatment itself.
>
> (1973: 11)

In the context of inevitable separation and its consequences, which are likely to be painful, we must consider the fact that in many extensive psychodynamic therapies, separation from the therapist is repeatedly delayed. Thus, the patient often avoids separation due to his or her fears, doubts, and dependence upon the therapist. Sometimes, however, the therapist avoids separation as an expression of his or her own difficulties with separation. The processes of separation-individuation according to Margaret Mahler and, later, according to Winnicott, are fundamental and critical processes for normal psychological development. The ability to cope with separation and loss is one of the most blatant universal expressions of psychological health.

The circumstances leading to the development of TLP

Even with his theoretical and conceptual interest in the concepts of time and separation, and the development of conscious and unconscious modalities for the experience of time, Mann still continued practicing the traditional psychoanalytic approach. Until the mid-1960s, that is, when he was appointed Director of Psychiatric Education at the Boston School of Medicine. There he encountered a familiar situation, found in psychiatric clinics throughout the world, even today: the relatively limited number of patients in extensive therapies and an additional number of patients whose therapists changed each year. For the most part, clinic therapists are psychiatric or clinical psychology residents with a high turnover due to the requirements of their clinical rotations, typically a long process that takes several years, composed of brief, finite periods. Although patients attain a certain achievement by the end of therapy, they repeatedly regress, as each regression culminates in another separation. On the other hand, there is the constant pressure of the long waiting list of patients anxious to begin psychotherapy, even though there are not enough therapists available to accept them. In no uncertain terms, Mann faced the demands of the municipal administration, which ran the clinic in conjunction with the Boston School of Medicine, to alter the reality described above. He understood the future of the clinic was uncertain unless a fundamental change took place in its functioning.

Termination of therapy and TLP

This realistic need led Mann to combine his understanding and development of the concepts of time modalities with the clinical observations and impressions familiar to many therapists regarding the termination process of extensive therapy. According to these observations the most significant changes and processes occur toward the termination of therapy. Often, there is a sense that immediately subsequent to the declaration or scheduling of therapy termination, the slowed-down therapy process (the slowing of which also leads to the consideration of termination) suddenly accelerates markedly. The conclusion of therapy is also characterized by a return of the phenomena that initially occurred in the therapy in the form of symptoms, distress, and difficult feelings. Often, the patient (and occasionally the therapist as well) experiences a generally heightened state of emotion toward the end of the therapy and the upcoming separation, accompanied by a sense that the therapeutic work has become more vigorous and effective. Not infrequently, this sense stimulates thoughts of further postponing the termination in order to take advantage of the current acceleration, especially after a period of decreased excitement and momentum. This phenomenon is commonly interpreted as the patient's sophisticated resistance to concluding therapy, seemingly creating a situation in which there is once again something to work upon in therapy. Most methods of postponing the termination of therapy, such as extending the session by a few minutes, are first and foremost manifestations of separation difficulties between therapist and patient, whether they occur within the confines of the therapy hour or in the broader format of the total therapeutic relationship. Separation difficulties are expressed in the language and concepts of infantile time, which seeks to preserve an imagined state of eternal closeness in reality: 'Don't leave me, don't abandon me, I need more.' The actualization of separation makes the statement and expresses the feeling that it is possible to exist separately, while preserving the experience of wholeness. These two central topics, time and separation, are intimately linked. The differentiation and development between infantile time and calendar time elucidate these relationships even better.

Knowing, from an administrative perspective, that he must shorten the duration of therapy, Mann recognized that from a theoretical-practical point of view he could select only one specific aspect of therapy. When internally debating the question of which segment of therapy to select, Mann relied upon his understanding of the meaning of time in the psychological life of the patient, and upon his observations of the intense and accelerated processes occurring toward the end of therapy. Initially in experimental form, and later more systematically, Mann began conducting therapies that lasted for twelve sessions.

The fundamental rationale behind Mann's approach was that if he did not have the time and means to travel the full distance, then it was necessary, and worthwhile, to offer patients therapies composed essentially of termination, or separation. Mann created a certain paradox. He confronted the patient with the problem of separation at the beginning of therapy, and tried to bring the patient to a state of independence by the end, so he or she could separate from the therapy and the therapist in a benign fashion. Mann held as true his principle assumption that brief, time-limited therapies are characterized by their intensity and profound emotional depth. Over time, he observed the strength of the time-limitation factor as a therapeutic mechanism, and found his therapy approach was appropriate and effective, even under other circumstances which did not involve time pressures or the limitation of other resources.

Schematization

In order to cope with human emotional complexity rapidly, and within a brief time, Mann understood the need to develop conceptual-schematic means for helping the therapist to obtain a quick impression, identify problematic foci, and diagnose the strengths and limitations of the patient relatively swiftly. Mann proposed two such conceptual systems, based upon two fundamental principles in psychoanalytic theory. One was the patient's system of intrapsychic conflicts, and the other was the affective system. Mann proposed different ways of utilizing each of these two conceptual systems.

Universal conflict situations

As specified above, separations are a normal part of the life cycle, from the beginning through to the end. Some separations are tremendously significant and painful. Furthermore, countless events occurring throughout our lives reawaken the painful and anxiety-provoking crises experienced during the early process of separation-individuation, as described by Margaret Mahler (1972). Losses of prestige, money, status, etc. are derivatives of anxieties linked to separation-individuation, and sensitivity to these processes typifies most human beings. Notwithstanding individual behavioral, symbolic, and social differences, failure to control these separation anxieties generates four basic universal conflicts:

a independence versus dependence;
b activity versus passivity;
c adequate self-esteem versus diminished (or loss of) self-esteem;
d unresolved or delayed grief or mourning.

These conflicts arise in response to states of separation and separateness. Every individual reacts differently to separation and loss. There is a wide range of response and action modalities. The divergence in reactions relates to the prominence of one conflict over the others in each individual and, of course, to the position of the individual within the conflict, the position adopted when struggling with it. The conflicts represent closely linked emotional aspects and, in many cases, all four conflicts surface within the patient over the course of therapy.

Among people who suffer neurotic distress or psychological complaints, active entrenchment in a state of conflict yields extremely painful effects. The conflict defines the central axis of the patient's psychological activity. Furthermore, in many cases, the patient leans more toward one pole of the conflict than the other, whether temporarily or for a longer duration. Clear identification of the patient's stance within the conflict elucidates for the therapist the emotional modalities by which the patient functions. The modalities in which the therapist works often stem from this understanding of the patient. For example, a patient struggling with a conflict between dependence and independence, with a tendency toward dependence, will dictate completely different relational modes for the therapist in comparison to a patient struggling with a conflict between self-esteem and a tendency toward diminished self-esteem. It should be emphasized that identifying the central conflict does not usually commit the therapist to any particular mode of activity. It does, however, enable the therapist more easily, and schematically, to ascertain the psychological make-up of the patient, honing in on the particular form in which the patient experiences, and functions within, the sharpest pain, throughout his or her narrative. Individuals suffering from neurotic disturbances or reporting psychological complaints often appear similar to one another, especially when diagnosed according to a system of nosological diagnosis, such as the ICD or DSM. The personal history of each patient, and the quality of the unique relationship formed with the therapist, transform the stories and events into emotional phenomena and unique patient-therapist interactions which are, ultimately, extremely personal.

The basic affects

In their second book, Mann and Goldman (1982) describe an alternative method for achieving a focused and schematic characterization of the patient's psyche, based upon the affective network of the patient. A substantial proportion of psychological responses are affective in nature, and swift affective diagnosis holds considerable weight in the diagnosis of the overall psychological state. Toward the goal of expediting the diagnosis, Mann proposed a model which schematically divides the broad range of human emotions into five basic, fundamental affects. The wide array of emotional, and experiential, diversity can be described by means of these affects and their various combinations. The intent behind the schematic reduction to five affects is not to diminish the value of the human affective system. Rather, this schematization creates salient and discernible reference points that can, and ought to be, utilized when the amount of time at the therapist's disposal is brief and limited.

Mann discussed five basic human affects, from which a broad array of modalities of human emotion can be derived:

a   sad – its derivatives include anhedonia, depression, grief, feeling undesirable, despair, pessimism, hopelessness, dissatisfaction, etc.;
b   mad – its derivatives include anger, distress, fury, extreme anger, aggression, violence, etc.;
c   glad – its derivatives include altruism, love, optimism, happiness, euphoria, peace, feeling desirable, satisfaction, etc.;
d   frightened – its derivatives include anxiety, nervousness, tension, restlessness, fear, avoidance, etc.;
e   guilty – its derivatives include worry, discomfort, shame, etc.

Other emotions are viewed as variations or combinations of these basic affects.

One should be cautioned against mistakenly considering Mann's opinions and outlook simplistic, as if humans were not complex beings or as if he believed it was possible to discern indiscriminate common foundations among all people. As a model and as a tool, Mann's approach enables the therapist to conceptualize the fundamental components comprising the patient's life story. The establishment of four conflicts or five basic affects must not be perceived as a diminished appreciation of psychological complexity. Rather, it should be viewed as a purposeful description of the human psyche according to a conceptual model, or simple scheme, providing for a firm grasp of the patient and supplying tools for active coping with complicated psychological problems in an extremely short time.

Using these conceptual systems, which incorporate the four psychological theories of psychoanalysis, an original view on time and separation, conscious and unconscious perceptions of time, four universal conflicts, and five basic affects, Mann proposed a model for brief and time-limited dynamic therapy, the components and stages of which are described below.

THE THERAPY MODEL

The assessment stage

Prior to beginning treatment, the designated patient must undergo assessment, a process lasting one to two hours. (This depends partially upon the skill of the interviewer, the complexity of the problems, and the developmental history of the patient.) The assessment process is of the utmost importance for the treatment process and its success. During the assessment, the therapist asks to hear the recent history of the patient's life, and the circumstances and events that led the patient to decide to seek therapy. Then the therapist asks the patient to tell his or her life story and personal history in a detailed, narrative, and associative fashion.

Identifying the pain

Using his or her empathic abilities, the therapist listens attentively to the patient's story and attempts to identify the chronic and enduring pain from which the patient suffers today, when seeking treatment, and has essentially suffered throughout life. The distress experienced by the patient developed along an axis formed by the particular sense of pain, and the therapeutic focus will be aimed toward this same axis, as will be elaborated later in the chapter. Mann began with the basic understanding that regardless of the nature of the complaint, the personality type of the patient, the duration of the problem, etc., the individual seeking treatment feels distressed and pained. Mann claimed this pain has been embedded within the patient for years, and was most likely reawakened in response to a stressful or painful event. Over the course of his or her psychological and emotional development, the patient tried to soothe, alleviate, and assuage the sense of pain, and apparently succeeded in most instances, or at least very often. When the individual comes to recognize the need for therapy, for help from another person, it is only because the pain has become overwhelming, whether temporarily or over an extended period.

The interviewer hears the life story and developmental history of the patient, from childhood to the present, listening attentively and empathically, and remaining particularly attuned to the chronic and enduring pain felt by the patient throughout life, and in current meaningful situations. The interviewer endeavors to locate this pain, or its derivatives, in the present, as well as in the assessment situation through observation of the evolving connection between the interviewer and the patient. As stated, the evaluator relies upon empathic listening more than any other clinical tool, listening carefully for the pain the patient has felt throughout life and still feels today. Of course, Mann spoke about psychological pain as a metaphor, not as a tangible sensation. During this intensive assessment process, the therapist is greatly assisted by the presupposition of the existence of pain, whereupon his or her role is to uncover and understand the pain, thus anchoring him or herself in the chronicles of the patient's development. This way, the therapist and patient form an initial alliance, supported by a mutual understanding of their shared goal as the uncovering and understanding of the source of the current acute pain, the early roots of which lie in the patient's past. Finding and diagnosing the focal pain comprise important steps toward building the central issue, in essence, the therapist's central and fundamental interpretation of the patient's condition.

As stated previously, identification of the universal conflict that characterizes the patient, and the patient's specific position along the axis of conflict, facilitates the therapist's swift detection and delineation of the operative modes of psychological functioning in the patient. The assessment process has two clear goals: one is to *determine the suitability of TLP for the particular patient*. The topic of TLP suitability and criteria for patient selection is discussed at length toward the end of this chapter. Once the evaluator decides TLP is indicated for a patient, the second goal is to *formulate the central issue*.

Time requirements for assessment

An additional question related to the assessment stage concerns the amount of time required for this process. Many patients can be assessed within a single session. Other patients require two sessions. In my experience, it seems preferable in any case to conduct the assessment process over the course of two hours, separated by a week or several days, for several reasons. One reason relates to the actual diagnostic process, for which it is advantageous to examine the treatment candidate at a minimum of two points in time, in order to obtain an impression of processes occurring over a certain stretch. An additional reason concerns the selection and formulation of the central issue. It appears that conducting two assessment hours, with a break in between them, enables the interviewer to process the material gathered from the first interview during the time between the two sessions. This strategy is especially helpful if the interviewer lacks experience in TLP. It also enables the therapist to correct, improve, and fine-tune questions and hypotheses that arise during the first interview.

A small segment of patients might feel offended by the rapidity with which the essence of their problems can be diagnosed and assessed. This can generate such strong resistance that they drop out of therapy. For all of the reasons cited above, I recommend conducting the assessment process over two sessions. As we will see in the continuation of the chapter, the instructions for selecting and formulating the central issue are very explicit, and can even be stated in a standardized format. If a skilled evaluator, or a closely supervised novice therapist, cannot find a central issue within two sessions, or three at most, it should raise questions regarding the suitability of TLP for the particular patient.

Assessment by the therapist or an independent evaluator

At this point, we shall consider the question of whether the assessment is best performed by the therapist or by an independent evaluator. In psychodynamic therapy, the therapist typically conducts the intake, even though situations may arise in which somebody other than the therapist conducts the intake. This type of scenario usually arises for two reasons:

1   In some public clinics, senior personnel conduct the assessment process and then transfer patients, along with their treatment recommendations, to the treatment personnel. This approach has both advantages and disadvantages. The obvious advantage is the examination of the patient by more than one person, which can be useful in deepening understanding of the patient and providing a more diversified view of the patient and his or

her problems. On the other hand, patients may feel overly exposed or embarrassed about sharing their life stories with more than one other person, or they may find themselves making inevitable comparisons between the evaluator and the therapist. These types of comparisons often create difficulties for the patient during the initial acclimatization to therapy or over the course of the therapeutic work.

2   Some treatment centers are affiliated with universities or research institutes. These centers may conduct research in psychotherapy in which the research design requires clinical assessment of patients independently of their therapists. As we will see in the chapter dedicated to research in the field of TLP (Chapter 11), objective assessment of patients prior to and following treatment demands a division between therapists and evaluators. Though this may inconvenience the patient, it is of supreme importance that the evaluator has no connection to the treatment before, and especially after, the conclusion of the therapy.

TLP lends itself to empirical investigation relatively easily, therefore when we selected it as a subject for research, we based our assessments upon evaluators who were independent of the therapists. We found the defined, semi-structured, almost formulaic process of psychodynamic interviewing, geared toward early developmental processes along the primary axes of functioning (motor, affective, cognitive, social, and sexual), contributed to the evaluators' ability to rapidly absorb the life story told by the patient.

Even when the assessment was carried out by an evaluator other than the designated therapist, the emphasis placed upon empathic and accepting listening by the evaluator accelerated the rapid establishment of a pleasant atmosphere and the development of a therapeutic alliance. The quality of the therapeutic alliance itself serves as one of the indications of patient suitability to TLP. The assessment interviews were recorded and fully transcribed, word for word, and then given to the prospective therapist who read the transcript or listened to the tape. Our experience showed that after reading or listening to the assessment interview, the therapists required an additional hour's assessment before beginning treatment, so that they could enter into an intensive psychodynamic interaction with the patient. The therapist used this hour to ask questions not asked during the intake. The hour also enabled the therapist to receive an unmediated impression of the patient's personality and to confirm the impressions of the previous evaluator. Because the therapist had obtained a significant portion of the anamnestic information regarding the patient beforehand (from the interview transcripts), the therapist was more perceptive of experiential elements within the clinical examination. In hindsight, we found this method of independent evaluation not only contributed to the research design, but it provided a sound basis for a more thorough evaluation of the patient. As stated above, from a clinical perspective, a comparison of the emotional experiences of two professionals within a short time provided a solid means for validating decisions regarding the suitability of TLP for the patient in question. As we shall see toward the end of this chapter in the discussion regarding patients likely to benefit from TLP, the patient's ability to form a rapid attachment is one of the most significant measures of patient suitability. Unequivocally, double examination of this measure contributes significantly to the initial decision-making process in TLP. Although assessments conducted by independent evaluators are most common at centers for psychotherapy research, a more comprehensive and in-depth assessment seems best carried out by an independent evaluator. Of course, in the typical public clinic scenario, and especially in a private clinic, the assessment interviews used to determine the degree to which TLP is suitable for the particular patient can be conducted by the therapist assigned to the patient.

Selection and formulation of the central issue

Like any brief dynamic therapy, TLP is also a focused therapy. The focus in TLP hinges upon the formulation of the central issue. The formulation of the central issue, its schematic structure, and its distinctive role as a central process factor in TLP were developed extensively by Mann and Goldman (1982). The brief duration of the therapy does not allow for treatment of defense mechanisms, therefore the central issue must bypass the resistances and touch upon the anxieties of the patient, while contributing to the swift formation of a work alliance and rapid positive transference relations. During the assessment process, the patient is directed by the therapist to relate his or her life story, including the recurrent pains and frustrations.

The effectiveness of the central issue as a healing factor, as formulated in TLP, is directly linked to the time limitations. Lack of change is attributed to a lack of a sense of time, a blurring of past, present, and future. In contrast, clear delimitation of the time dimension stimulates the conscious and unconscious meanings of time for the patient, within the context of the patient's self-perception and the potential and likelihood of altering this view. Granting the patient a time-limited opportunity for introspection is likely to elicit change, even if the change is only due to the powerful wish for deviation from the chronic cycle of preservation and eternalization.

Locating the pain

The central issue relates to affective developments across the timeline of the patient's life. When gathering the patient's anamnestic personal history, the therapist repeatedly and empathically tries to contemplate, 'How does this patient feel right now, and how did he or she feel in the past, during each given incident?' The therapist asks these questions while incorporating the developmental schema of the universal conflicts and relating to the basic affects. When the therapist directs these questions toward the patient, it touches upon personal and private experiences and memories, which the patient may have never previously shared or articulated. The pain related to these emotions represents a remarkably valid and reliable emotional affirmation of the patient's current and past feelings, in the context of the particular experience being recalled and elevated to various levels of consciousness. In a manner familiar to all human beings, the pain experienced mediates between a past event and its emotional impact. Pain forever describes a feeling of injury, victimization, and affront. These difficult emotions are denied and repressed over the course of emotional development, though they often reverberate internally and generate severe neurotic cores. The patient seeking therapy first and foremost seeks recognition of his or her maltreatment at the hands of others, irrelevant of any objectivity regarding the actual events. At moments like these and throughout the intake, during which the therapist adopts an active, directive, and empathic stance, the location of the patient's chronic pain is experienced as an actualization of the wish for acknowledgment of his or her suffering. Patients generally desire such acknowledgment from their primary care-taking objects, their parents, and in psychotherapy the desire recurs through transference processes. The formulation of the central issue does not include conflictual relationships with primary objects. Rather, it focuses upon self-perception, the individual's reflection upon and appraisal of himself or herself, the patient's self-esteem, as vital to his or her existence. Humans employ various forms of coping as a means of overcoming their hurts and anxieties. The treatment aims to strengthen the patient as much as possible, reduce the chronic and enduring pain, and alter the negative self-perception. From the patient's perspective, this goal is accomplished through talking freely and recounting his or her life story. The therapist listens vigilantly and empathically, pinpoints painful junctions in the story (often connected to experiences of separation and change), and formulates the central issue for the patient, which touches upon the development of a negative and judgmental sense of self.

The central issue as clarification and interpretation

Although the central issue is seemingly formulated as a clarification, it actually comprises a strikingly profound understanding of the patient's very early and damaging emotional experiences. Rooted in the search for the patient's deepest pain as an expression of lifelong difficult feelings, the therapist's theoretical understanding leads the patient to reveal these feelings quite rapidly (if the patient is suited to this type of therapy). Not only is this swift exposure not damaging, but it also provides the patient with a transference experience of an early figure genuinely interested in knowing all about who he or she is, everything that troubles and preoccupies him or her – in essence, a mother. It should be emphasized that in the dynamic therapeutic situation, which is typically vague and undefined, the patient grabs on to any clear statement made by the therapist and transforms it into an exceedingly important anchor. Based upon this anchor, regression occurs for a brief and limited duration, contributing to some of the changes that take place within the patient. The central issue is, in effect, a central interpretation based upon the link between time, affect, and diminished self-esteem.

Table 2.1 The different elements of the central issue

The central issue	Central issue elements
You are a woman with strengths, but today and throughout your life, you've felt your efforts have gone unappreciated,	Supportive component Time component Self-esteem component
and therefore you feel, and have always felt, bitter and angry.	Affective component

The structure of the central issue

Practically speaking, once the therapist is ready to formulate the central issue for the patient, Mann (1973, 1991) instructs the therapist to identify three basic components used to build the central issue for the specific patient. These components include time, affect, and the patient's attitude toward himself or herself (self-esteem). Though it only appeared on an implicit level in Mann and Goldman's book (1982), the element of therapist support and recognition of the patient's strengths and abilities was later incorporated as a crucial fourth component of the central issue. The therapist combines the components selected from the life story of the patient into a single highly empathic statement. This statement is presented to the patient at the conclusion of the assessment process, which occurs during the first therapy hour. In order to clarify Mann's approach, an example of a complete central issue, including all its components, is presented in Table 2.1. The central issue, presented to the patient as a cohesive statement, appears on the left side of the table. For the sake of didactic presentation and elucidation, the central issue is divided into its four components, displayed in the right-hand column.

Patient reactions to the central issue

Based upon Mann's reports and our clinical experience, when the central issue is accurate and hits upon the affective state of the patient, presenting it to the patient in a concise and well-formulated way elicits emotional reactions similar to those elicited in patients who have been given an accurate interpretation. These reactions are typically strong (crying, silence, sudden laughter, profound reflection, etc.) or an arousal of associations, the rise of significant material from the preconscious or subconscious memory. These emotional responses induce the initial formation of the emotional basis for the therapeutic alliance, as an expression of the sense of relief experienced by any patient who feels understood. The accuracy of the central issue means the therapist was sensitive enough to find and select the primary concerns currently preoccupying the patient and engendering pain, now and throughout his or her life.

At this juncture, a warning is in order. During the early stages of study and training, the rather simple schematic structure of the central issue arouses strong feelings of ambivalence among TLP trainees. On the one hand, they perceive a shallowness and seemingly automatic uniformity in the formulation of the central issue, while on the other hand, they experience anxiety about failing to pinpoint and formulate a comprehensive and successful central issue. In regard to this point, it is important to remember that despite the schematic structure to which they aspire, the psychodynamic interaction between patient and therapist imbues each therapy with its own highly individualized qualities. When coupled with the unique personalities of the therapist and patient, this gives rise to a wide variety of central issues.

In one investigation of this question (Shefler and Tishby, 1998), three skilled TLP therapists were given transcripts from tape-recorded assessment sessions and asked to formulate a central issue for each patient. We hypothesized the three central issues would be formulated identically, or at least very similarly. Our results showed the central issues were quite different at the most overt level of their formulations. However, when we broke down the central issues into their four components and conducted technical analyses upon them, we found they all contained the same foundations, but to an extent the selection of these foundations varied between therapists. Here are a few examples of central issues selected for patients:

a   You are a capable young man, highly motivated to succeed and progress. Nonetheless, throughout your life, you've felt you've failed because you're not in the right place for yourself, and then you feel worthless and depressed.

In this case, the conflict relates to self-esteem and the affect is sadness.

b   Even though you have made the effort to achieve adulthood
and independence, you have always felt anxious inside
because you believe you are alone and not important to
anyone, and that pain prevents you from changing things and
moving on.

In this case, the conflict is between dependence and independence
and the affect is anxiety.

c   Though you've succeeded in many things, two conditions are
very important to you: to be your own master and for others to
agree with you. When one of these conditions doesn't exist,
you feel hurt and angry.

In this example, the conflict is between dependence and independence and the affect is anger.

d   Though you have attained significant achievements in your life,
every time you have to make a decision connected to change
and commitment, you retreat, feel trapped and helpless, and
flee.

In this example, the conflict is between activity and passivity and
the affect is anxiety.

The formulation of the central issue constitutes one of the
primary sources of anxiety for TLP therapists. Many therapists,
especially novice therapists, are frightened by what appears to be
an intellectual challenge requiring an accumulation of vast clinical
experience in order to construct the central issue. Many residents
and trainees sense this is the point at which the therapist's ability,
experience, and skill are funneled into the formation of a meaningful concept. Furthermore, it cannot be ignored that in extended
dynamic therapy, the therapist is not expected to provide a precise
and substantial formulation of the essence of the patient's life after
an hour or two. It is even more difficult to do so in the presence of
the patient during the therapy hour. It is impossible to overlook the
test-like nature of the situation prior to the formulation and presentation of the central issue. The therapist indubitably scrutinizes
the success of his or her understanding of the essence of the
patient's emotional life, i.e., of the central issue (which is soon
enough scrutinized by the patient as well). Tests of this nature

inevitably generate stress and tension. Therapists conducting TLP should remember they are working in a fashion not dissimilar to the way they have worked until now. They employ empathic listening, make an intensive attempt to understand the events, and focus upon the few components most relevant to the formulation of the central issue. The explicit and public formulation, subject to the judgment of the patient, is an unfamiliar experience, which must be dealt with during the course of training and supervision.

It is true that practice, supervision, and cumulative experience are of tremendous importance in the formulation of the central issue. Nevertheless, the instructional, almost manual-like guidelines for the formulation of the central issue combined with the dynamic understanding of the special non-technical role played by the TLP therapist, make it nearly impossible to err in the selection and formulation of the central issue. If the therapist does not have malicious intentions or an overpowering resistance to TLP, the patient has a focused problem, and they share an understanding manifested in fruitful dialogue during the assessment process, then the situation readily lends itself to the formulation of a central issue. In the event that the situation does not readily lend itself to the formulation of a central issue, then TLP is most likely not indicated for the patient. Supervision and training are crucial at this stage and can assist in the formulation of the central issue, as well as preventing the treatment from getting stuck as it progresses.

The transition from assessment to treatment: the therapeutic contract

As stated, the assessment process takes approximately two sessions, each of forty-five to fifty minutes duration. At the conclusion of these sessions, the therapist defines and formulates the central issue, which will be presented to the patient in the following hour. This third session will be considered the first therapy hour. During the first third of the third session, the therapist presents the central issue to the patient. The therapist then waits for the patient's response. As discussed above, the patient might respond in two basic fashions: either the central issue speaks to him, or it does not. In the former case, the patient responds as if to an interpretation that strikes a chord: it either brings an emotional reaction, the introduction of new associative or narrative material, or profound reflection in an attempt to understand and process the central issue through dialogue with the therapist. In the latter case (which typically strikes fear into the heart of any TLP therapist), the patient does not understand the central issue or does not feel it resonates within (either because it is inappropriate, or TLP is not a suitable treatment, according to the criteria detailed later in this chapter). The patient then responds by misunderstanding, closing up, asking blunt and shallow questions, or shutting down emotionally and distancing from the therapist. As emphasized earlier, an appropriate central issue generates a profound psychological response, emotional release, and the elevation of associative content or renewed memories, in effect deepening the affective therapeutic process already in progress. At this stage, the patient's reactions are treated psychodynamically in every respect.

Linking assessment to the beginning of therapy

In my opinion and in my experience, the problem facing the therapist at this juncture is one of the most difficult faced by the TLP therapist. The patient has entered into therapy, even though the setting, terms, framework, etc. have not yet been established. The presentation of a meaningful central issue serves as a condition for the formation of a deep and meaningful connection between patient and therapist. Only in this scenario do the declaration and predetermination of separation take on meaning. Therefore, only now, after the transformation into a significant object for the patient, should the therapist navigate the remainder of the first hour toward the explicit establishment of the therapeutic contract and the termination date. In addition, the therapist should explain the terms related to the therapeutic setting in detail: cancellations, rescheduling, a clear termination date, and a clear establishment of the number of therapy hours. As I emphasized beforehand, the presentation of the central issue is one of the most meaningful statements in the treatment process. With this statement, the therapist transforms himself or herself into a meaningful, powerful, and precious figure for the patient. With this statement, the therapist enters into the inner, hidden, painful world of the patient and becomes a significant object. Now, the separation from the therapist will be significant as well. Therefore, the procedural order – assessment, central issue selection, central issue presentation, and then the establishment of the therapeutic contract – is not simply a straightforward administrative requirement, but the essential and crucial therapeutic sequence around which the treatment rationale is built. This sequence forms a meaningful link between the central issue and the time limitation, enabling the therapist to become a significant object for attachment and separation over the course of therapy.

At this stage, the therapist arranges an absolutely clear-cut therapeutic contract with the patient. The contract is usually based upon twelve treatment sessions, of fifty minutes each. In most cases, the sessions are held once a week, at a fixed time and location. Mann (1973, 1991) heavily emphasized the termination and the actual date of the final therapy session. This fact is of paramount conceptual importance in this treatment method. Using Mann's conceptualization, the individual endlessly struggles with the drive and tendency to view time (subjectively) as everlasting versus the (objective) perception of time as transient and finite. Therapy is quintessentially a concentrated struggle with this fundamental issue. The countdown toward the termination session and its imminent approach places the experience of an everlasting bond with the therapist (expressed through the depths attained in the relationship and the patient-therapist interactions) in direct contention with a concrete manifestation of the 'calendar' nature (the realistic facet) of time. This experience occurs whether the patient is aware of it or not.

Mann proposed a twelve-hour therapy model (not including the two assessment hours). The specific number of hours does not contain any special meaning, as long as the framework of the beginning and ending of therapy is maintained. This obligates TLP therapists to come prepared with their calendars and work schedules and to know their plans in advance. TLP requires a relatively large degree of commitment on behalf of the therapist, and some therapists find this difficult. In the formulation of the therapeutic contract, the therapist has the opportunity to highlight the importance of time as a psychological resource.

It is important to point out that concurrent with the attention to the structural and technical arrangements, the therapist must be a person who views time as important and meaningful. I do not mean time must have a compulsive meaning for the therapist, but he or she should possess a solid internal stance toward time that is mature and realistic. Respect for time, a clear sense of time, recognition of time as a meaningful resource, and good time-management are all essential attributes for the therapist choosing to practice time-limited therapy.

The question of why twelve sessions has been asked repeatedly. There have been mystical speculations regarding the number, around such ideas as twelve astrological signs, twelve tribes of Israel, and twelve months in the year. James Mann (1973) related to this question, but did not provide a clear answer. Over the course of my work, I have thought often about this particular length of time, its symbolic meaning, and its practical aspects. In my meetings with Mann during the years 1984–1993, I asked many questions regarding the number of sessions. Mann had nothing to say about the symbolic or mystical meanings he might have considered when he proposed this number, therefore, I did not attempt to find a symbolic interpretation either. The principle of time limitation shares no direct connection with the number twelve.

TLP can be conducted in eleven hours or in fifteen hours, as long as its length is arranged at the beginning and maintained. When considering the twelve therapy hours at the standard TLP pace of one hour per week, the duration of the therapy spans three months. When we conclude an extensive analytical therapy of several years duration, we do so gradually. (I am talking about termination, not about breaks in the therapy.) Often the patient and therapist share the thought or even reach an agreement that 'therapy will end next year,' or, alternatively, 'it seems this is the last year of therapy.' During the year, therapist and patient may decide, 'we'll end therapy in the spring or summer.' Thus, the patient and therapist designate the time span in a more specific manner, but it is not yet clearly defined. The specific date for termination of the therapy is usually set two to four months prior to the scheduled date.

As I understand it, the choice of twelve sessions is not based upon a mystical number, but upon a reasonable estimation of the time needed for the work to be accomplished. It is a reasonable segment of time for a person to perform a significant amount of inner emotional work, while simultaneously looking ahead, anticipating, and feeling the preplanned separation. In reviewing the question of the optimal duration for TLP, I see no particular reason not to adhere to the length of twelve sessions, although, as long as the principle of predetermined and limited time is understood, the framework can be set anywhere between ten and twenty sessions. This leaves room for the therapist's assessment of the patient's, and his or her own, abilities to perform meaningful work within the allotted time frame. If the therapist believes it is possible to accomplish within fifteen treatment hours what could not be accomplished within twelve hours, the choice is left to him or her. Free choice in this area is likely to reduce therapist resistance to entering into a limiting and laborious therapeutic system.

From an empirical perspective, several studies support the time framework proposed by Mann. Howard, Kopta, Krause, and Orlinsky (1986) demonstrated improvement in an average of 60 per cent of patients after thirteen treatment hours. Anderson and Lambert (in press) also showed that thirteen treatment hours is on average the number required to achieve reasonable and stable outcomes from dynamic psychotherapy.

Many therapists center their objections to brief therapy upon the time limitation and the arbitrary fixing of a number, which immediately raises the question of why exactly twelve or thirteen sessions? In this context, I would like to describe an interesting anecdote from my institutional experience. Over the several years during which we conducted the TLP research project, it was clear that every treatment must take precisely twelve hours. Common refrains heard in our staff meetings included, 'Somebody so damaged deserves more than twelve treatment hours,' or, 'This is a complicated case. I don't believe I can treat it in twelve sessions. Maybe fifteen to seventeen sessions would be more helpful.' Alternatively, 'What do you mean twelve hours? I'm sure we'll take care of everything within six to ten hours.' As team leader, my unswerving task was to steer each of these objections back to the main agenda: 'We are studying the classic model of TLP, therefore every therapy conducted within this framework will be for a duration of twelve hours. If that doesn't suit you, treat the patient outside of this particular framework.' It is important to emphasize that this dogmatic stance was influenced primarily by our research design. When we finished the research project and the group of therapists asked what our next undertaking would be, how we would proceed with our work, I thought of studying TLP conducted for lengths of time which deviated from the standard twelve hours. I proposed my idea to the group and they accepted the basic suggestion. It was interesting that in every instance when the suggestion arose to either add to or decrease treatment hours, the therapist's response was, typically, 'Why? Twelve hours seem to be exactly what's needed.'

When just starting out, I recommend studying and gaining experience in the classic twelve-hour model. Once a therapist acquires the basic skills, he or she can decide autonomously whether more or less time is needed for processing the specific central issue for any given patient. Furthermore, situations might arise in which the patient (or therapist) does not have time for twelve weeks of therapy, yet TLP can still be considered. Based on my experience, as long as the therapist possesses a clear understanding of the necessity to maintain whatever framework is selected (for each individual patient), then TLP can be offered for any duration of between ten and twenty hours, according to the needs, terms, and desires of both therapist and patient.

While clarifying the therapeutic contract, the therapist should emphasize the terms for schedule changes and making up sessions cancelled by either therapist or patient. It should be very clear to the therapist that the treatment will end on the scheduled date, which is not subject to change. To a large extent, this dictates the way in which therapist and patient handle unexpected and potential changes during therapy. For example, it would be unwise to reschedule a cancelled session for one week after the scheduled termination date, in other words, to postpone the termination of therapy by a week. This would provide a tempting opening for the patient, and sometimes for the therapist, which is better avoided, in the understanding that it would constitute a severe rupture to the therapeutic setting and the treatment rationale.

Sledge, Moras, Hartley, and Levine (1990) found that patient attrition among new patients in TLP was approximately half of the expected rate for brief, but not time-limited, dynamic therapy or extended dynamic therapy. One of the conclusions reached by these researchers was that predetermination of the duration of therapy positively affected the staying power of patients in TLP, alongside other factors such as therapist activity, development of the positive therapeutic alliance, and interpretations focused upon the central issue.

Due to the importance of continuity in the treatment, it is vital that the therapist be aware of and attentive to his or her calendar. It is preferable not to begin TLP during certain periods of the year, such as just before the therapist's extended vacation or reserve duty, around the holidays, etc. Likewise, the TLP therapist's sensitivity to the issue of time should prompt an inquiry regarding the patient's plans for the upcoming months, so as to be certain both of them can dedicate the three or four months required for TLP. It is important to be cognizant of this issue prior to beginning treatment in order to prevent mishaps, which would contain tremendous emotional meaning because of the structure and rationale of the therapy.

The procedure and phases of therapy

TLP is distinct in its integration between the time limitation and the unique, patient-specific formulation and presentation of the central issue. Within a brief space of time, the therapist crystallizes a deep, emphatic, and meaningful understanding of the patient, instilling within the patient the sense that the therapist will not recoil from, be frightened off by, or lessen his or her willingness to treat the patient. This unique stance taken by the therapist is critical to the formation of the therapeutic alliance between therapist and patient. The therapist's choice to treat the patient within a brief time period and to adopt an active stance impact heavily upon the developing atmosphere and the feeling of optimism. After all, it is impossible not to feel optimistic when a highly capable and powerful person penetrates and comprehends the very essence of the patient, presents that understanding in a lucid manner, and is willing to accompany the patient through the process of examining and processing the central issue. In contrast to other brief dynamic therapies, the extremely well-defined structure of TLP derives from the visible nature of both its beginning and its end. Between these two easily discernible points, an entire therapeutic process takes place.

At the conclusion of the assessment process, following the presentation of the central issue, it appears the therapist has developed a basic understanding of the patient's focused problem and passed on this understanding to the patient in an empathic manner. At the same time, the therapist has created an infrastructure for the development of basic trust and a minimum work alliance. The patient responds to the central issue and the therapist begins interpreting, keeping the interpretations focused upon the components of the central issue, using the technique of 'selective attention and selective neglect'. In other words, the therapist responds to material that touches upon the central issue, or derivations of it, while ignoring material unrelated to it. From the moment the central issue is presented and the therapeutic contract is established, the therapist's role is to keep the therapy developing and revolving around the central issue. Mann described three phases that typify therapy.

Phase one: 'the honeymoon'

During the first phase, called the 'honeymoon phase' by Mann (1975), the patient becomes absorbed in a euphoric cloud of hopeful optimism, believing all of his or her problems and heartaches will be solved by the promising new therapy relationship that has come his or her way. At this phase, the patient treats therapy as if it were a wondrous act of magic, and clings to the omnipotent thought that therapy will rescue him or her from all distresses experienced up to this point. Meanwhile, the therapist is concerned with cultivating the therapeutic alliance and preserving the central issue through active, attentive listening, along with selective responsiveness and intentional neglect, two of the concepts used by Deutsch (1949) and Deutsch and Murphy (1955) to describe the psychoanalytic process. The therapist ignores anything not connected to the focal point. This is no easy task, as the therapist must first repeatedly verify that the selected central issue is in fact relevant to the patient and his or her condition. Second, the therapist faces the tremendous, and often hard to resist, temptation of delving into other issues from the patient's life and inner being.

This first phase usually lasts for the first three or four treatment hours. The overpowering sense of optimism engendered by the opportunity to solve problems in such a short time, i.e., the positive transference, alongside the warm emotional responses to the therapist's empathic efforts, color the first phase of therapy in positive, optimistic, and occasionally idealized tones. At this stage, crucial work is performed on the rapid development of a strong therapeutic alliance. The first phase of TLP is also the stage at which the patient and therapist are furthest from the termination of treatment. Thus, the atmosphere of infantile time occupies a central position.

Phase two: ambivalence

Mann (1973) called the second phase 'the ambivalent stage.' The patient realizes the honeymoon is not eternal. The patient and therapist must cope with severe doubts arising in the patient regarding the likelihood of changing anything in his life. The patient feels that not everything raised is discussed or treated. The initial euphoria, typified by the overpowering sense that everything will fall into place, dims in contrast to the small yet meaningful experiences of disappointment, frustration, misunderstanding, and the encounter with elements of calendar time. Some, and usually all, patients are cognizant of the sense that time is running out, which contributes to the ambivalence characteristic of this stage, lasting from the fifth through the ninth therapy hours.

At this stage, the therapist's maintenance of the pace and structure of the therapy is of utmost importance. The therapist must not succumb to the blatant hints dropped by the patient suggesting there is not much point to what they are doing if nothing is going to work out anyway. The encounter with these frustrations arouses a desire in the patient and, on occasion, this desire gets acted out in the form of tardiness or absences from therapy. The therapist must avoid identifying with the patient's growing distress. Therefore, the therapist should not attempt to compensate the patient by making up sessions or postponing the termination date in response to guilt feelings over the distress seemingly initiated and caused by the therapist and the circumscribed nature of the therapy. This is the phase at which the universal conflicts alternate rapidly and during which most of the patient's affective modalities are usually most marked. The therapist must adhere to the central issue and anchor his or her interventions in contradistinction to the patient's claims, using the material from which the central issue was built. The therapist bears responsibility for the serious task of avoiding the pitfalls of negative transference reactions.

Phase three: separation

The third and final phase of therapy is the 'separation phase.' Whether conducted in a honeymoon atmosphere or in an ambivalent and difficult atmosphere, the treatment continually progresses toward termination. The termination elicits complex, though not necessarily difficult, emotions from previous separations experienced by the patient (and by the therapist as well). At this stage, the therapist confronts the patient with the pain and difficulty of separating from the therapy and from the therapist. The patient encounters memories of other significant separations and abandonments from the past. Again, the therapist takes an extremely empathic position and, as the separation grows nearer, actively participates in the feeling of pain experienced by the patient. For some patients, unprocessed separations lie at the foundations of their central conflicts and form the cornerstones of their central issue. For others, the central issue concerns another basic conflict, and the separation from the therapy and therapist become central only toward the concluding stages of therapy. The separation stage typically occurs over the course of the four final treatment sessions.

The transition from phase to phase and the differences between the phases, in terms of the contents and tasks facing the therapist, are described in the case studies presented in the following chapters of the book.

Mann emphasized, and our experience supports his position, that these phases ought to be viewed as the most frequently found, or as a common model, but in no way a hard and fast rule. The duration of four therapy hours per stage is also not an absolute, but a common finding that can differ from one therapy to the next. In our research (Wiseman and Shefler 1993), we found some patients progressed through Mann's therapy phases in the proposed order and within the appropriate amount of time. Other patients, however, progress through the phases in a different order, unlike Mann's descriptions, or do not even exhibit all of the phases in their treatment. In many respects, the progression of treatment hours is reminiscent of treatment hours in non-time-limited dynamic therapies. At both the beginning and the end of treatment, the sessions are 'colored' by the clarity and the uniqueness involved in the rapid construction of the therapeutic relationship (the first stage) or intensive separation (the final phase). As explained in Chapter 1, the therapeutic technique and the principles of therapeutic processes are essentially the same across the various approaches to brief dynamic therapy. Furthermore, despite their differences from extensive dynamic therapies, brief dynamic therapies contain most of the fundamental components of psychodynamic therapy.

Messer and Warren summarized the theory of change used in Mann's therapy method:

> The theory of change in time-limited psychotherapy, then, includes an integration of several elements, including *induced*

hope and optimism stemming from the time-limit and the therapist's show of confidence in the patient's ability to master conflict; *insight* derived from clarifications and interpretations around the central issue and its relation to separation anxiety, as well as insight about defenses against feeling; *incorporation of a more benign interject*, brought about by the kind of relationship established by the therapist; and patients' *use of the therapist as a self-object* thereby enhancing their self regard.

(1995: 205)

Post-termination follow-up

Brief dynamic therapies commonly include one or more follow-up sessions, held after the termination of the therapy. The purpose of the follow-up is to examine the outcome of the therapy. Typically conducted by means of a session initiated by the therapist, when it is impossible to hold a session or the patient objects, the follow-up can be conducted over the telephone or by mail. This type of follow-up can be initiated and scheduled in advance if, at the time of termination, the therapist informs the patient he or she will be invited to a follow-up meeting. Otherwise, it can be done *ad hoc*. This issue is largely determined by the nature of the separation process between the particular patient and therapist. If the therapist senses the process is especially difficult, it is preferable not to raise the issue of follow-up, due to the risk of unconsciously encouraging hopes for an additional meeting, which may bypass the difficulties inherent within the separation from therapy. The optimal time for conducting this type of follow-up is three to four months after the termination of therapy. Often the follow-up hour is not only used for clarifying the actual clinical state of the patient, but as a means for accelerating or propelling the continuation of the brief and time-limited therapeutic process.

In the context of following-up on therapy outcome, the question arises of why therapists conducting brief therapy insist upon follow-up sessions. Alternatively, what prevents a therapist conducting extended therapy from holding follow-up sessions of this type? I believe the answers to these questions are influenced by three factors: first, because brief therapies were considered innovative therapy methods (even though historically, as we saw, the only therapies were brief dynamic therapies), there was often an intertwining of uncertainty and curiosity regarding the outcomes of

these interventions. The only way of verifying the various hypotheses that arose regarding brief therapy processes was through
direct follow-up of their outcomes. A second answer stems from
the continuation of this line of thought: innovative fields of therapy
are generally accompanied by validation studies of their efficacy
and stability. The way to examine the efficacy and stability of
therapy outcome is through following-up the course of events in
the patient's life subsequent to the termination of therapy. A third
factor influencing the existence of follow-up as an accepted
routine in brief therapy is the patient-oriented nature of the treatments. As such, they stimulate the natural human, and empirical,
curiosities of therapists to follow-up on the outcomes of their
therapeutic activities. When therapists vehemently oppose any
type of follow-up after therapy termination, it indicates a defensive
element.

It should be reiterated that our treatment procedure served as
the foundation for empirical study, and the evaluators were not the
therapists themselves. The evaluators, however, implemented the
follow-up procedures. In terms of the impact of follow-up meetings on the separation process, the use of evaluators who were not
the therapists held a clear advantage. We have already pointed out
the potential impact of an evaluator who is not the therapist. The
same is true for follow-up. We have no doubt that utilizing objective evaluators provided a better, more balanced means of hearing
the patients during the follow-up sessions and assessing whether
or not their conditions had improved. Indubitably, the transference
effects differ, and are severely limited, during a follow-up session
held with someone other than the therapist. By virtue of diminishing the transference effects, the use of an independent evaluator
thus significantly impacts upon the nature of the follow-up and its
goal, which is to obtain as objective a picture as possible of the
clinical state of the patient following the termination of therapy.

Which patients benefit from time-limited dynamic therapy?

The establishment of definitive criteria for patient selection for a
particular therapy method is an ever-growing demand in the field
of psychological treatment today. Beyond a broad agreement on
the necessity for these types of criteria, it is difficult to pinpoint and
formulate them, because these criteria vary greatly, depending on

whether they are formulated by therapists or by insurance company medical directors. In extreme or severe cases, there is usually no difficulty in determining the treatment of choice. The state of affairs differs, however, in regard to the more moderate clinical conditions. Like most dynamic psychotherapy methods, TLP is not intended for the treatment of severe or extreme conditions (those that are easily diagnosed). On the contrary, TLP is meant for more moderate clinical conditions. The ambiguity that typifies neurotic conditions and the initial reactive states, or, alternatively, the initial reaction in the relationship with the therapist or the diagnostic clinician, make it difficult to reach a definitive match between the treatment and the individual.

Like all brief dynamic therapies, TLP necessitates and places considerable weight upon reaching a positive decision at the beginning of therapy as to the suitability of TLP to the patient. TLP, like other brief dynamic therapy methods, is based upon an intensive emotional experience that must be appraised and recognized as reasonable by both the therapist and the patient. Brief dynamic therapies do not belong in the category of explorative therapies, in which the therapy process allows slow exposure, along with increasingly in-depth (and sometimes surprising) knowledge of the patient and his or her psychological abilities.

Since the initial formation of brief dynamic therapy, therapists have asked themselves which patients are the most suitable for this type of therapy. Sifneos (1972, 1979) attempted to establish a set of criteria for patient selection for brief therapy. He emphasized ego strengths manifested in academic and professional achievement, a significant relationship with any one person throughout the life of the patient, the ability to become engaged in the interaction with the intake clinician, expression of affect during the intake interview, and the presence of a focused complaint. Furthermore, strong motivation for change was considered essential to the success of the treatment. Mann (1973) added that these criteria can be used to rule out the differential diagnosis of borderline personality disorder.

After many years of recurrent and ongoing struggles with the difficulties of choosing clear-cut and infallible criteria for patient selection (or patient rejection) and thoughts about various procedures that could help determine these criteria, I want to propose a multi-dimensional system for assessing patient suitability for TLP. As stated, this system was developed upon the basis of daily clinical fieldwork and provides a clear, convenient, clinical and practical means by which the evaluator or therapist can make appropriate decisions regarding patient selection for TLP.

The system consists of four interrelated dimensions. Over the course of the assessment interviews at the beginning of treatment, however, the dimensions vary in their degrees of accessibility and transparency for the evaluator. The four dimensions are:

a   quality and degree of ego strengths;
b   nosological diagnosis;
c   ability to pinpoint and propose a meaningful central issue;
d   reality-based considerations.

a   Quality and degree of ego strengths

Mann (1973, 1991) and Mann and Goldman (1982) vastly expanded the spectrum of patients suited to TLP and posited that solid ego strengths, expressed in the ability to cope with loss, offer an important general indication of suitability to this type of treatment. The ability to cope does not mean coping is free from difficulty or pain. The opposite is true. It refers to coping that does not entail sinking into despair and destructiveness, or giving up and withdrawing into depression. According to Mann, the willingness to invest emotional resources in attachments to others is considered another ego strength. Evaluation of ego strengths across several areas simplifies the assessment process and enables the therapist to obtain a fuller picture of the patient's personality, in light of the ego strengths. When assessing these strengths for psychodynamic therapy of any kind, we usually look at the following five areas:

1   ability to form relationships;
2   availability and activity of the affective system;
3   achievements;
4   high motivation for change;
5   psychological mindedness.

Before expounding upon these areas, it is important to emphasize the use of a weighted sums approach to assessment, that is, consideration of the relative weight of each element in making the final decision whether or not to treat the particular patient using TLP. Some people have more limited relational abilities but very strong motivation for change, whereas other people possess diminished psychological mindedness but very active affective systems. In order to reach the appropriate decision, the evaluator or therapist should know how to weight these traits for each patient.

1 Ability to form relationships

In any dynamic therapy, the interpersonal relationship between therapist and patient is decisively important, and all the more so in time-limited therapy. Critics will justifiably argue that there are those who seek psychotherapy precisely because they have difficulty forming relationships. Patients suffering psychological distress in this area (primarily diagnoses of depression, severe enough to disturb communication, or schizoid and avoidant personality disorders) will not manage in such a brief period of time, to form an emotional relationship with the therapist through which profound change can occur. Despite patient resistance along the way, extensive treatments enable slower development of the relationship, at the pace best suited to the patient. The ability to form relationships is largely related to the willingness of the patient to form this type of relationship, despite the potential hardships. The assessment measure used in this area is the combination of ability and willingness manifested in the personal history of the patient and the nature of the emotional events occurring between the evaluator, or therapist, and the patient, throughout the assessment sessions. It is important that the narrative related by the patient during the assessment process provide evidence of significant relationships, in both the past and the present. Significant relationships mean relationships containing emotional depth and the ability for intimate and sexual relationships, appropriate to the patient's age and developmental stage. It is important that the quality of this relationship gains expression in the therapist's experience during the assessment sessions. Thus, this essential ability is validated during the assessment by both the emotional content and the quality of attachment between the interviewer, or therapist, and the patient. The ability to form relationships with others is also a manifestation of the patient's willingness to invest emotionally in human objects.

In brief therapy, the ability to form emotional relationships is a critical factor in the success of the treatment. In time-limited therapy, the rapid development of a therapeutic alliance forms the basis of the assessment and, subsequently, provides the foundation for the development of the central issue.

2   Availability and activity of the affective system

In continuation of the first aspect of the formula, the primary essence of the relationship formed is its emotional essence. Individuals seeking psychotherapy can be damaged in different areas and zones of their psyche. Because time-limited therapy is based upon a very intensive emotional relationship between patient and therapist, the patient ought to be capable of forming a relationship of this nature. The patient's ability depends upon the availability of his emotional system in the service of forming relationships. For example, during the initial phase of a severe depressive state, any type of communication with the patient is impossible, including emotional communication. There is no point in attempting time-limited therapy in those types of situation. The emotional system can be distorted, turbulent, damaged, etc. In time-limited dynamic therapy, emotional activity is of prime significance. Primitive defenses such as splitting, denial, and isolation of affect, distance the individual from his or her direct emotional systems, thus restricting their availability in the service of the patient. As described earlier (pp. 40–41), Mann postulated the separation-individuation process as the overriding motive for psychological development, a process that presents significant emotional challenges to all human beings struggling with its consequences and, as a result, with psychological development.

3   Achievements

One of the clearest indications of the presence of solid ego strengths available in the service of the patient is the degree to which he or she can point out successful functioning in different areas: scholastic, career, artistic achievements, athletics, social, and other successes. Achievements offer proof that the patient basically possesses solid ego strengths which at a certain stage, arrested, failed, were delayed, or the like. Highlighting achievements serves as one of the basic components in the formulation of the central issue and as the basis for evaluating the ability of the patient, currently in a state of crisis or delay, to return to normal functioning and activity. Sometimes we come across patients whose actual achievements are not especially impressive, yet they demonstrate adequate ambition for future achievements. These can also be included in the set of resources unique to ego strengths.

4   High motivation for change

Any therapeutic process intended to achieve internal change relies heavily upon the patient's motivation to undergo change, invest resources of time, money and emotional energy, forgo freedom, etc. The motivation for change occurs on a conscious level. It is the conscious willingness of the designated patient to support the process of change. This does not refer to unconscious processes of resistance to change. The degree of motivation for change is elucidated on two levels: one is the patient's verbal declaration of motivation for change and the other is the direct and indirect degree to which the patient is genuinely willing to invest in the said change. In this context, I am often reminded of a patient who came to me for brief therapy. When I offered him a time for the first session, he immediately claimed the time was inconvenient for him. The same thing happened with the other four alternative hours I offered. The obvious conclusion was that despite the patient's desire for therapy, his motivation for investing the energy and time required for the process of change was severely limited. Whether conscious or unconscious and latent, the lack of internal motivation for change presents a serious obstacle to TLP.

5   Psychological mindedness

For a considerable number of patients in extensive therapy, their ego strengths grow and develop. Brief dynamic therapy requires the patient a priori to possess the strength and potential embedded in psychological mindedness. This concept relates to the patient's ability for introspection and to locate and experience psychological features within this introspection. Through introspection, the patient can expand his or her self-understanding and reach the roots of his or her psychological problems. The ability for psychological mindedness assumes the presence of the potential for symbolization, the ability to see different motifs as symbolic representations of internal psychological processes. Thus, for example, the patient's ability to view a physical sign or symptom as an expression of tension, conflict, or psychological difficulty indicates a high level of psychological mindedness. Good verbal ability is usually, but not always, connected with psychological mindedness. In contrast, seeing exteriors as definitive and others as responsible for one's own distress, along with the inability to recognize internal sources of problems, are signs of diminished psychological mindedness.

These five elements actually describe an extremely broad range of psychopathologies. As every reader probably realizes, I have not discussed levels or degrees of psychopathological severity. My focus is upon basic abilities, likely to be damaged at the time the patient seeks therapy. Nevertheless, the presence of these five indicators can serve as the basis for positive selection of patients for time-limited therapy. The range of psychopathology can be described using nosological diagnoses as well. The absolute, or nearly absolute, lack of these ego and personality strengths within the patient will transform any dynamic therapy, including TLP, into an ineffective and inappropriate treatment.

b Nosological diagnosis

Nosological diagnosis, the diagnosis of syndromes and symptoms, concerns mainly the labeling and naming of the compilation of clinical symptoms. In some patients, the markers are clear and sharp and, therefore, more easily diagnosed. For therapists and evaluators more experienced in clinical interview and observation, the markers appear more readily and far more clearly. The assignment of a diagnosis situates the diagnosed individual on a familiar axis, using language shared with other professionals. For some more experienced evaluators, the process of nosological diagnosis is uncomplicated, and its findings are very helpful when deciding whether or not to offer dynamic therapy of any kind, and TLP in particular.

In regard to the diagnoses of neurotic and personality states suited to TLP, four large groups of patients are suitable for TLP: people suffering from various types of adjustment crises, people suffering neurotic disturbances, young people undergoing transitional and developmental crises, and people with mild personality disorders. As long as they are not overly defensive, TLP can help these patients. Borderline personality disorders, suffered by many people seeking or referred to psychotherapy, present a more complicated diagnostic problem. It appears the levels of personality organization proposed by Kernberg (1975) enable the acceptance of patients into TLP who are diagnosed with borderline disorder, yet who show a high level of personality organization. (In terms of the above-mentioned levels for patient selection, these would be patients diagnosed with borderline personality disorder but who exhibit solid ego strengths for coping.) People with severe psychosomatic conditions are often overly entwined in rigid defenses. Therefore, they would have difficulty benefiting from TLP.

The nosological, or symptomatic, diagnosis greatly facilitates the identification of contraindications for TLP. People in psychotic states will experience difficulty in coping with the transition from infantile to calendar time and handling the frustration of the rapidly approaching ending of intimacy. People in moderate to severe states of depression will not co-operate with the therapy process and will be unable to form verbal or emotional relationships with the therapist. People suffering from schizoid or avoidant personality disorders will be unable to connect quickly enough within the intensive therapeutic relationship. People with toxic or organic deficits, who exhibit obvious cognitive rigidity and diminished abilities for abstract thought and psychological mindedness, are not suited to TLP. Patients with severe compulsive disorders, characterized by rigid defense mechanisms, will be unable to benefit in the brief time offered, and people with severe narcissistic disorders are apt to be offended by the proposition of a limited treatment for problems they perceive as paramount and severe. People with dependent personalities are prone to feeling hurt by the rapid separation from the therapist and can be damaged by TLP.

c Ability to pinpoint and propose a meaningful central issue

In his first book, Mann (1973) stated that any patient for whom a suitable central issue can be found, can be treated with TLP. In other words, the mere ability of the patient to present himself or herself in a focused fashion to the assessment interviewer and to engage the ability of the evaluator to formulate a meaningful central issue serves as a criterion for patient suitability to this type of treatment. In the same book, Mann struggled with the question of which is the better indicator of suitability for TLP: quick, successful location of the central issue or precise nosological diagnosis. I see no need for a debate of this kind. For some patients, the decision will be based upon the nosological diagnosis, if there is one, while for others, the deciding factor will be the selection of the central issue or the strength of ego functioning. In some clinical situations, the complex psychological essence of the chronicles of the patient's life are elucidated without reaching an exact nosological diagnosis, and sometimes even without a systematic and detailed assessment of the ego strengths. The establishment of a meaningful central issue itself can serve as an indication for successful patient selection in TLP, even without detailed diagnoses. The central issue is a type of diagnosis and, though idiosyncratic, it contains meaning for patient and therapist alike.

d Reality-based considerations

The selection of TLP is not only a scientific and medical question, but a reality-based question. Two especially clear reality-based dimensions frequently constitute the deciding factor in the selection of this type of therapy:

1   The objective dimension: lack of external time and money resources. Today, many people seek brief therapy, including TLP, generally due to time and financial constraints. In many instances, these constraints positively affect the patient's ability to focus and summarize their problems, generally leading them to the formulation of a central issue.
2   The subjective dimension: the desire of the patient to undergo focused psychotherapy. Sometimes, although patients have the resources at their disposal, they have no desire to invest extensive resources in therapy. This might be due to the understanding that they only need help with a circumscribed aspect, or, alternatively, it might be due to previous frustrating therapy experiences. As explained at length in the previous chapter, we live in a consumer's era. As such, the consumer and his or her choices considerably influence the type and nature of the selected therapy.

With that said, remember that a lack of means and/or lack of desire for extensive therapy are not in themselves indications for brief therapy. They serve as a basis for therapy selection by the patient, on the condition that the therapist deems this type of treatment appropriate. In the clinical reality, many patients, from a wide variety of populations, find TLP appealing. A considerable number of patients do not understand, nor are they familiar with, the considerations involved in determining the suitability of TLP to a particular patient. (Neither are nonprofessionals *expected* to know the indications and contraindications for any type of therapy.) Nevertheless, TLP inherently appeals to the person on the street: it is focused, brief, sounds effective, cannot be too expensive, and, in short, contains all the advantages any therapy can have. Based upon their impressions from things they have heard or read, many people seek out and request TLP, primarily from skilled therapists with reputations in this specific field. In these cases, the therapist should state up front that together they can examine the extent to which TLP suits the patient's problems, and, if TLP is not appropriate, the therapist should explain the reasons to the patient.

It seems this multidimensional system enables the evaluator or therapist to reach sufficiently clear conclusions regarding the suitability or unsuitability of the patient for TLP in nearly every case, wherein the determinant of any decision might be one dimension or another. Based on everything stated above, it is easy to apprehend the multidimensionality of TLP in its integration of the problems with the abilities of the patient. In many situations, the fact of a clear nosological diagnosis serves as an indication for, or contraindication against, offering TLP to the patient. In other situations, the appraisal of ego strengths, coupled with the demands of reality and the lack of contraindications, determine whether or not the therapist chooses to offer TLP to the patient. In still other situations, the therapist may have difficulty assigning a precise diagnosis or reaching a clear assessment of the patient's strengths, yet the therapist finds a meaningful central issue for the patient. This is another possible situation that can lead to a positive decision to offer TLP to the patient. The idea behind a multidimensional model to facilitate the process of making decisions regarding the match between TLP and any given patient was to unburden the therapist struggling with the adoption of an unusual or uncomfortable stance, in which he or she must actively reach a rapid decision. In a situation of this sort, the four decision pathways are likely to help the therapist, especially the less experienced therapist.

In conclusion of this discussion on the suitability of TLP to patients and patient selection for TLP, I want to discuss the dilemma of whether extensive psychotherapy for a particular patient is ever preferable over TLP, or vice versa, whether TLP is ever preferable to extensive psychotherapy. Study of each of the selection dimensions presented above unequivocally elucidates the fact that any patient suited to TLP can, in theory, also receive extensive dynamic therapy. With this assertion, I intend to claim that from a strictly clinical perspective, regardless of realistic and practical considerations concerning time and money resources, whether they are the private patient's concerns or the public institution's concerns, any patient suited to brief therapy is also suited to extensive therapy. I do not discount a priori the objective conditions of the individual or the mental health care system, and I believe, today, these should be viewed as an integral part of patient-related considerations, taken into account when selecting the psychotherapeutic approach.

From a strictly theoretical and clinical perspective, it is difficult to imagine a situation in which TLP is preferable to extensive psychotherapy. Nowadays, however, clinical decisions are rarely made in a theoretical vacuum but are heavily influenced by the availability of resources.

In conclusion, TLP is a focused and time-limited psychodynamic therapy method. The focus, in the form of a central issue and the preset time limitation, following an assessment procedure, creates a powerful dynamic momentum between patient and therapist. Because the therapist becomes a significant object for the patient as a result of the understanding formulated and presented in the central issue, the anticipated separation forms a parallel axis to the axis of the central issue selected for the treatment. Along these two dynamic axes (which occasionally unite, for example, in cases of patients whose chronic and enduring pain relates to traumatic separations in their past), the therapist and patient process the emotional and experiential wealth that develops between them as a consequence of entering into the above-described situation. The process finally draws to a conclusion through the means of a follow-up session, held a few months after the termination of therapy. This session enables additional clarification of the patient's clinical state following therapy, as well as a bolstering of the therapeutic effect through additional elucidation of the central issue, with the added perspective of time.

In every brief dynamic therapy, including TLP, the therapeutic task involves rapid penetration into a circumscribed realm of the patient's psychological depths, enactment of swift and focused change, and a quick exit. All of this, with a minimum or none of the potential damage likely to occur as the result of rapid entrances and exits. In order to execute these tasks, detailed instructions for the therapy method are extremely crucial.

Chapter 3

Adolescence

The capacity to choose what to be

At his request, Ofer (aged 17½) was referred for therapy by his parents following their consultation with his teacher. Though he could not specify what it was, Ofer felt something was not right with him; something was not working for him. The referral was prompted by a decline in his ability to concentrate and his fears regarding his upcoming army service.[1] The following background information was gathered during a preliminary session held with Ofer's parents.

Ofer was the middle of three children. His older brother, Eyal, was 23 years old, and his younger sister, Sigi, was 14 years old. Ofer's father, Reuven was a 47-year-old construction engineer and a senior officer in the army reserves. Born into the seventh generation of his family in Israel, he grew up in Jerusalem and was educated in the public school system. Reuven served in a combat unit in the army. He was lightly wounded in the Six Day War, but continued his regular service for another two years. Following his army service, he studied construction engineering at the Technion Institute. After graduation, he and a friend started a company that grew into a thriving business. Reuven was charismatic and assertive. Although he was not particularly pleasant, he was extremely honest.

---

1 In Israel the army service is compulsory and has become the norm. Almost all healthy young adolescents aged 18 have to do it. It is the melting pot of Israeli society, and especially for boys in the process of becoming men. In many families and sub-societies, pressures are put on the boy towards joining certain élite units, following in the footsteps of their fathers or brothers, and sometimes their own unfulfilled ambitions. In many cases, the moratorium needed for a quiet process of working-through of the adolescent developmental predicament, is charged with stress caused by these norms and standards of masculinity..

Ofer's mother, Dina, was a 46-year-old native Israeli born to Holocaust survivors who met in Israel after they both emigrated from Europe. Despite the grim background, she reported a happy childhood: 'We tried not to pay attention to it . . . My parents made every effort not to create a "holocaust home." I don't know if we succeeded. I think so, but I don't really know.'

Dina was a good student and was accepted socially. She did not recall any particular problems. She served as an inspector in the Air Force and met Reuven on a rigorous hiking trip in which they both participated. He was her first serious boyfriend and, after dating for two years, they married when she was 22 years old. Neither of them described tensions or feelings of exaltation in the early years of their relationship. Dina studied at a teachers' college and, after graduating, began working in the educational system. Today she is the vice-principal of her school. Over the years, she completed a Master's degree and planned to begin doctoral studies. She was a very warm, sensitive, pleasant woman. She projected ease and optimism as well as the ability for depth.

Ofer's older brother, Eyal, served in an élite military unit. He had been an excellent student at his prestigious high school, the same school Ofer currently attended. Eyal was successful in every respect. He was strong, attractive, masculine, accepted, and knew what he wanted. Reuven could not conceal his pride when he said, 'He never had even the slightest problem.' Eyal was his father's buddy; they were the two men in the household. Reuven loved Eyal's successes and his unfaltering masculinity.

Ofer's parents described him as a typical middle child. He was vulnerable, uncertain of his position in the family, and perhaps outside of the family as well. They considered him talented and saw no reason for him to fall short of reaching the same achievements as Eyal. 'Everything we gave to Eyal, we also gave to Ofer.' Ofer and Eyal had a very good relationship.

Ofer felt close to Eyal, identifying with and imitating him. Dina was not sure that Ofer possessed the same strengths as Eyal, whereas Reuven believed that, 'If he wants to, he can be exactly the same.' Both parents treated the decline in Ofer's functioning as an ambiguous signal of distress that they understood as transient. 'We have to get him back on track,' said Reuven. 'Just so problems won't suddenly appear when he goes into the army.' When I asked Reuven what he meant, he replied immediately, 'So he won't wind up in some low-profile job.' Dina was not sure it was so simple, but she could not explain further. She sensed something: not danger, but distress.

At the end of the session with Ofer's parents, I suggested Ofer call me to arrange a session. Reuven responded, 'Just tell me when and he'll be there. He'll adapt himself to you. You can count on me.' I replied I was certain he would pass along the message to Ofer that he should call me to arrange a session.

The following day, Ofer called, and in a hesitant voice asked if I was Dr Shefler. I heard his father in the background saying, 'Whenever he wants you to come, say yes. He's very busy.' Ofer sounded embarrassed. He told me he had heard about my session with his parents and he wanted to set up an appointment with me. I asked how urgent it was and he answered that he did not want to delay it. I suggested an appointment two days later. He sounded hesitant and repeated the date and hour over and over while he weighed it in his own mind. Then, he asked if there was another possible time.

I asked what was wrong with the time I suggested. He explained that he had made plans with a friend and it would be difficult for him to explain why he needed to cancel their plans. I suggested an alternative time and he accepted it without hesitation. When I offered directions to my office, he responded, 'I'll find it myself.' From this short telephone call I could already identify two important issues: Ofer's struggle for independence, and his motivation for treatment.

Ofer arrived on time. In the doorway, I greeted a tall, attractive, broad, swarthy, muscular, modestly dressed young man. I reached out to shake his hand and was amazed at his soft, sweaty touch and limp handshake. Before we exchanged a word, I pondered the meaning of the contradiction between Ofer's solid appearance and his soft touch. (I thought to myself: if it is so obvious, it must be meaningful.)

Ofer entered the room, sat down, looked at me, and smiled. He seemed somewhat embarrassed. I asked what brought him to seek therapy. He replied, 'I wanted counseling. Counseling about something, but I don't know what . . . I don't know what isn't working for me, but something is not right and I think it might have to do with the army. Maybe. Do you think that could be it?'

I asked Ofer to describe what he felt, what was happening to him. He said that he felt tense, distracted, 'But not anything so serious. I'm just not calm. I'm also doing less well in school. Not really on my grades, because I already have the grades I need. I'm having trouble concentrating and I'm nervous about the matriculation exams that are starting soon.'

Ofer answered my questions openly, willingly, and accurately. I asked him to tell me his life story as it came to mind. He sunk into the armchair, and into himself. Then he began to recall his life in quite a bit of detail. I felt comfortable with the sense of quick emergence of a working alliance. His early childhood was wonderful and he could not think of anything negative. He nostalgically recalled his home, pre-school, and neighborhood as warm, pleasant environments. Ofer enjoyed sharing his memories. He loved his kindergarten teacher very much and fondly described her motivational tactics. She would ask, 'Children, who knows how to dance as nicely as I do? Who are the children who eat as nicely and quietly as Shula?' (I felt annoyed by this description.) Ofer did not remember having a difficult transition from kindergarten to elementary school or, later, from elementary to middle school.

Ofer remembered wanting to grow up quickly. He wanted to go to school, 'like Eyal.' He also wanted to learn judo, 'like Eyal.' He did not have any recollection of being jealous of Eyal, because he always received the same things from his parents as Eyal did. Ofer was a good student and socially well adjusted. In all he did, Ofer marched faithfully in the shadow of his brother.

I observed, 'Eyal was very influential on you as a child.'

Ofer validated my observation with a story: 'When my sister was born, my aunt asked, "So Ofer, are you ready for the baby to come home?" I answered, "I don't want her to come home, but Eyal said it would be fun, so she should come home already."'

Throughout his life, Eyal had a clear opinion about every aspect of Ofer's life from his clothes, friends, girlfriends, and how his bedroom was arranged, to the positions he held in their youth movement.

Ofer was very close with his childhood school friends, especially Yaniv and Omri. He spent extensive time with them, in school, in their youth movement, and just hanging out. Yaniv was very similar to Eyal. He was strong, extremely masculine, and wanted to join a combat unit in the army. Omri, on the other hand, was a young man with a host of problems.

Ofer described his parents as warm, loving, giving people. 'I don't lack anything.' He was pleased with his physical appearance and liked his face and his body. 'I'm good-looking, so they say, and I know it.'

Ofer had experience with girls. At the age of 16, he had sexual relations with a girl who had a reputation for being sexually promiscuous. 'I didn't want to, but she puts out for everyone and then she tells everyone how each guy was.'

THERAPIST   How did you feel?
OFER   Trapped. I was scared to death but at the same time I felt desire. She was disgusting – fat, repulsive, but she knew how to do what everyone wanted and dreamed of. She just put out without any problem. If she told everyone that I didn't sleep with her, I would get a reputation for being gay. That would be the worst.
THER.   Why?
OFER   Because that's what they say about Omri [*the second friend*]. He's not like that at all, but they say he is.
THER.   And what they say matters so much.
OFER   Right. It matters a lot. It's everything.

Ofer was involved with a girl his age, Merav, although they were not in a steady relationship. They spoke often, spent time together, and went on trips together. They 'fooled around' with each other, but were not sleeping together.

OFER   Eyal keeps asking, 'So . . .?' I don't want to yet. Sometimes I masturbate and think about her. I like that, but Eyal says, 'You're not a man.' And then sometimes I get frightened that maybe Eyal is right. How is it that Omri is my friend? So, I decide not to see him anymore, that I don't need him. But, he's a good friend and a really nice kid. We're friends. We really like talking and laughing together. And then I get together with him again. But don't think that I have a sexual thing for him.
THER.   Why would I think that? Because that's what Eyal said?
OFER   How did you know? Eyal says he's seen him with all sorts of characters. And also, there's the way he looks at me. But that's him. And so what? He's a good friend of mine.

The conclusion of the first session surprised me.

OFER It's already over? We didn't get to everything and the time flew by.

THER. It's hard to leave something so pleasant.

We arranged another session for the following week.

Second session

After a short silence, I began (aiming to direct Ofer to the affective climate of the first session):

THER. How did you feel about our session last week?

OFER So so.

THER. Can you say more about that?

OFER Look, it's uncomfortable to talk about these things. I don't know how this can help. What can possibly happen? You have experience and you'll tell me things, but so what?

THER. I hear your concern that you'll have to please me and be what I tell you to be.

OFER [*Smiles.*] Yeah. My father asked me, 'So, what did he say? You should listen to him. He's not me; he knows.'

THER. And you want to think about what *you* say, what you think, and, mainly, what you want.

OFER [*Looks at me as if he did not understand what I said.*] I'm not at all sure what I want. Everything's so confusing. I have this. I don't have that. I don't have any direction, and everyone says yes to this, no to that. I don't know what I want, especially right now.

THER. What do you mean?

OFER For example, I'm not very interested in school. But everyone says it's very, very important – school determines my future. I get anxious before exams. Even though I feel pressured, I somehow manage to pull myself together and I usually get high grades. It doesn't make me feel particularly good. I study because it's supposed to be important for the future, but I don't get satisfaction from my success in school.

THER. And what are your feelings about going into the army?

OFER You've hit on the major problem. I don't know. Eyal's stories are very stimulating, but scary. I'm afraid of being wounded, getting injured. I work out and I'm strong, but the thought of getting hurt, that my body can be torn apart, broken, terrifies me.

THER.   You're afraid that, like Eyal, you must serve in a place or a position in which you're likely to be physically injured.

OFER   Yeah, something like that, but I'm not a weakling or a coward. I'm not afraid of dying. I'm afraid of getting hurt.

THER.   I see you're strong, but I hear you saying, 'Look, what I have is valuable. I'm not sure I'm willing to run the risk of ruining it.'

Ofer had a very interesting approach to the army. He understood that he had no choice. He had an obligation to serve in the army, but he was unsure whether he wanted to be with his friends, or to do something that interested him like electronic warfare or anti-aircraft operation, or to go with the typical combat choice, 'like Eyal.'

OFER   Do you understand? I'm the good boy who does what's expected of him. [*He shares a memory from sixth grade.*] There was an exam that I hadn't studied for. I got my paper and wrote on it, 'I can't write anything, because I don't know anything, because I didn't study.' The teacher was so nice. She said to me, 'Ofer, I don't understand what happened to you. Sit and study right now. You can take the test tomorrow.' I didn't want to, so she said to me, 'Fine. Tomorrow, I'll test you on the material.' I didn't want to. I wanted to fail. I don't even know why, but that's what I wanted. But she completely ran me over. And what do you think happened in the end? I studied at home, and the next day I did what she wanted. [*Ofer burst into bitter tears.*]

THER.   It's so painful when you have your own will and it gets run over.

[*Ofer listened, and calmed down within a few minutes.*]

THER.   And what do you really want to do?

OFER   I don't know.

THER.   That's very confusing.

And indeed, the process of formulating the central issue is also confusing. I found it very helpful to discuss Ofer's central issue with a group of TLP therapists. The intake is presented by the therapist, and each of the participants suggest what seems to be central for him or her, regarding the four elements of the central issue: the recognition of the patient's abilities, strengths, and accomplishments, the time factor, the dominant emotion in the patient's life, and the patient's emotional self-perception. The group discussion on each of the elements, as well as the formulation of the central issue, clarifies the relative weight of each of them to the therapist, and helps the therapist to come to the optimal choice.

In this case I selected a central issue focused on the dependence-independence conflict and the emotional experience of anxiety, which causes Ofer to experience himself as weak and unconfident. At the same time, I made a conscious choice not to focus on other aspects of Ofer, such as the struggle with his sexual identity and depressive features.

Presentation of the central issue

Although you are a healthy, strong young man, throughout your whole life you have been preoccupied with the question of whether you are allowed to be what you want to be. You are very uncertain and every time you decide to be yourself, you are filled with anxiety and doubt your abilities.

Ofer sank into the armchair, listened intently, wiped his face, cried a little, and thought. After a few minutes of silence, he spoke:

OFER   I was afraid you'd say something else.

THER.   What did you think I would say?

OFER   That I need to understand that my father and Eyal just want what's best for me. That they are more experienced. My father told me that whatever you say, it's the truth. He also said that I would see he is right. Eyal has experience, but my father has even more. They know what somebody like me needs and what's right for me. That's what they said about you, that you'd know what I need.

THER.   Everyone else knows what you want and what you need. What about you?

   [*This interpretation stems directly from the central issue.*]

OFER   I dream about what I want, but I don't believe in it and I don't share it with anyone. I do what I'm supposed to do; that's what they want from me. But it's not really so far from what I want.

THER.   [*Taking a directive role.*] You're coming around the bend now. What do you really want?

OFER   [*Embarrassed.*] You'll laugh at me. I don't have an answer. As okay as I am, I don't know the answer to such a simple question.

THER.   Simple question? I told you before, I think it's a central and frightening question for you.

OFER   How do you know these things?

THER.   I listen to you and feel what you are experiencing.

OFER   And what does that matter?

THER.   At the moment, what matters most is what's happening to you, what you want.

OFER   I have a lot of stories like those ones. My whole life has been like that. But I don't feel pathetic.

THER.   You're not pathetic. You're strong, virile, and you don't know yet how to please yourself.

OFER   What can be done?

THER.   In therapy, we'll try to figure that out together, how you came to experience yourself so that you don't let yourself want anything without feeling uncomfortable by the fact of your wanting. We'll focus the therapy on that.

I offered a twelve-session therapeutic contract. I wanted to finish the treatment by the end of spring, before Ofer's matriculation exams began. Because Ofer had planned a vacation previously, we scheduled ten sessions and set a clear termination date.

OFER   How do you know that will be enough?

THER.   Does that worry you?

OFER   It doesn't worry me. I'm just not sure . . .

THER.   It's hard to imagine that we've barely begun and you already have to think about ending.

OFER   I'm not worried. I'm just asking.

Rather than provide a detailed description of the treatment, I will briefly describe the process. Ofer got into the therapy quite easily. He was optimistic, and he enjoyed talking and sharing. It was easy going and pleasant for both of us. Ofer found a non-threatening adult who did not demand he please him and who encouraged him to think independently. In Ofer's imagination, as well as in the therapeutic reality, I was there for him and took him seriously. I enjoyed his youthfulness, charm, and rapid response to therapy, as is typical during the initial honeymoon phase.

Ofer shared memories revolving around the same theme: he was not allowed to please himself; he could only please others. At first, he spoke about his wishes enthusiastically. Then, he grew angry as he delved into the pain of his unfulfilled wishes. Ofer was most interested in his relationship with Merav. He asked me about love, saying he would listen to me but would decide alone. He tried to get close to her, but she didn't want to be any closer. He felt vulnerable and angry both with her and me. He said that I misled him because talking did not help. He discovered that not everything he wanted could happen, and returned to the idea that perhaps it was preferable not to want anything for himself. That way he would avoid disappointment. Ofer continued thinking about what he wanted from Merav. He realized that, like her, he was not ready for full sexual intimacy. Though he was embarrassed by this realization, he was not ashamed to discuss it with me. He may have felt protected by the focus on his ability to please rather than the hidden content behind that ability, such as his desires . . .

Ofer decided not to join an élite combat unit, and whatever would happen, so be it. He described a conversation with his friend Yaniv, in which Yaniv remarked, 'We've been together such a long time and now you're leaving me?' Ofer retreated and thought perhaps he would join an élite unit, but then realized he did not want to. He stood up to Yaniv and said, 'You want to be in the [élite] unit and that's right for you. I don't. It's not right for me. Believe me, it's not. But we're friends and there are the weekends and after the army.' Yaniv replied, 'If you're afraid, I'm with you. I'll help you get over it.' Ofer answered, 'I'm not afraid. I just don't want to do it. If you want to be with me, come with me to anti-aircraft.'

OFER Computers are so interesting – missiles and all sorts of serious things, and they don't destroy you in the unit. It has double meaning. I told you – I'm afraid of being injured and I want to do something in electronics. Besides that, I have the feeling you don't think about the army the same way as my father does.

THER. Now you have to start thinking like me.

Ofer laughed, and I added that it was hard for him to accept that I wanted what he wanted for himself. At this point, Ofer felt tense about the break planned after the fifth session.

OFER   I'm used to coming here and I enjoy it. If I don't come, it's like I'll get weaker.
THER.   Does the same thought come to mind when you think about what will happen after the therapy is over? Is this reinforcement only temporary and when we finish therapy and separate, you'll feel differently?
OFER   I can always continue coming, can't I?
THER.   I know it's hard to see yourself alone, without me.

The combination of a strong therapeutic alliance and the awakening separation anxiety aroused the ambivalence usually present at the second stage of therapy.

OFER   I think I'll miss you, but I'll call to consult with you.
THER.   You'll miss having the advice or the closeness with someone who does not tell you what you should want, but lets you feel free to choose for yourself.
OFER   I'm slowly becoming my own advisor.

In the final sessions, Ofer appeared to have solved his problems. He had chosen a military framework. He also found the appropriate distance to keep from Omri. That distance contained a level of closeness that was not threatening and did not arouse suspicion, yet did not entail too great a distance from someone he loved. He realized that even with Omri's problems, he did not want to lose the friendship. Ofer discovered that not everything had a definitive solution, but that there was a middle ground.

At the same time, Ofer began to take interest in another girl, but did not know how to break off his relationship with Merav. He did not know what to tell her, what she would think of him if he told her the truth, or what she wanted. Parallel to his romantic interests, Ofer spoke about the possibility of continuing his relationship with me by telephone after he was drafted. Separation is difficult, even if it is what you want, and it is even more difficult when you don't know what you want. Ofer was flooded by thoughts of separation, in his everyday life and in his therapy.

Toward the end, Ofer's mood varied from session to session. He brought a booklet for me to one session, and in another session he asked what I would buy him when he was drafted. He wondered what we had done in therapy and suddenly paid attention to the cost. He was disappointed at having to pay for therapy, as if that made it less genuine. A few minutes later, he stated that he did not know why, but he felt close and comfortable with me. 'You're like a friend, but you're not a friend; you're like a father, but you're not my father; you're like Eyal, but you're not Eyal; you're like Merav, but you're not Merav.' I asked what it meant for him that I was like everyone else, but not like anyone else. Ofer responded, 'Maybe that I'm more with myself. It's clearer to me.'

Ofer appeared festive in the last session. He entered the room confidently, looked around, and soaked in everything. He conducted a very deep and moving summary of what had transpired in therapy. He pointed out various shades of emotion and problems that had troubled him, as well as those that still troubled him. I felt truly sorry to terminate a therapy that had been so beneficial, clear-cut, and fun with such an endearing and responsive youth. I would have continued therapy with him had it been possible. It seemed that he would have made the same choice. I both desired and mourned the separation from Ofer. I was pleased with his increased confidence, freedom of choice, and autonomous desires. He was planning and taking action in all areas of his life. Ofer's parting handshake was firm and strong.

Follow-up

I phoned Ofer three months post-termination. Dina informed me that he was in the army and would return my call during his weekend leave. He called two weeks later. He did not think he would manage to see me, but he said he would be happy to speak on the telephone. He was in basic training in the anti-aircraft framework. 'The guys' were great; he felt accepted and was interested in what he was learning. He felt no existential threat.

'I think of you sometimes. When I don't know what I want, I play a game: what would Gaby say? And then my imagination starts working and whatever I imagine seems to be what I want. It's getting easier, like we spoke about in therapy.'

Ofer was in a new relationship and felt they loved each other as adults do. It felt natural to him. He had not yet told Eyal about the relationship.

'I need to speak to you about something serious. Omri needs therapy. He's having trouble. I convinced him he needs therapy. I said I'd find him an excellent therapist, someone he can count on. He's willing to see you and I promised him I'd speak to you about it.'

I was touched by the thought, but I did not think it was appropriate or practical. Perhaps it was Ofer's way of continuing therapy with me, through Omri.

I answered, 'I don't think that's the best idea, for you or for Omri. It's preferable that he see someone uninvolved, who will be just for him.'

Ofer responded, 'Maybe you're right. And that way, you stay mine.'

The above case demonstrates how psychodynamic therapy can be limited by selecting a focus and adhering to it throughout the treatment. Ofer's emotional state improved during the therapy and the improvement was maintained throughout the period until the follow-up. Clearly, there were other important issues that were not addressed in the therapy, and that is the price of choosing a focus. In contrast to the therapeutic costs, Ofer's more organized and positive self-concept were invaluable gains for him.

Discussion

Many people would argue that Ofer did not need psychotherapy. He was healthy, functional, strong, came from a supportive family, and possessed superior physical and emotional potential. Ofer's transient and sophisticated functional difficulties could be viewed as the response to natural developmental processes typical of adolescents (Meeks 1971). Some societies place greater ethical, cultural, and functional burdens upon their adolescents than others. Israeli society is an example of such a society, where the entry into adulthood occurs with the very heavy pledge of obligatory military service, lasting two years for females and three years for males. This service is a normal part of life for every Israeli teenager and brings up different issues for each individual. There are adolescents who fulfill their hearts' desires through their military service (and often their fathers' dreams), while for others their service becomes a source of conflict in regard to the values of the society in which they were raised. Some young men avoid military service on ideological grounds, while others view their service as a test of their independence, masculinity, and coping ability. The society that imposes cultural burdens upon its adolescent youth ought to provide them with a solution when difficulties arise in their coping with those imposed tasks (Erikson 1968). From this viewpoint, it seems to me that Ofer received precisely the dosage of therapy he needed. The therapy did not label him as sick, strange, or crazy. Rather, it paralleled his natural growth processes and enabled him to see things not just as threatening, but to view them constructively.

Ofer possessed the personality features of the ideal brief therapy patient. He was capable of interpersonal relationships, possessed very good emotional ability and a strong ability for insight, and demonstrated a sincere and serious motivation for change. Furthermore, Ofer requested help with his struggles once he felt unable to cope on his own. Thus, in effect, he invited me to join a process already in motion.

The non-threatening experience felt by Ofer in therapy represented not only a means for achieving his immediate transient goals, but made him capable of obtaining help in the future. We learn this from the fact that he referred his good friend for therapy. One might claim that Ofer would have coped just as well with his problems without therapy. Quite possibly. There is no way of proving otherwise. Nevertheless, the far from excessive effort invested in his therapy by both Ofer and the therapist absolutely justifies the option of therapy as an accompaniment to developmental challenges for Ofer and similar adolescents. This type of therapy eliminates overly piercing demands regarding the cost, required investment, or the placement of a limitation upon the adolescent for an extended time period, demands likely to drive the adolescent away from therapy.

Regarding the questions of curative factors in Ofer's therapy, it seems to me that the foremost factor was his ability to discuss his problems in a revealing, open, and enabling manner with a sensitive, empathic adult who accepted the relative difficulties of the adolescent and took them completely seriously. As a typical teenager who did not allow himself to choose what he wanted to be, the highly relevant focus, within the secure conditions of therapy, enabled Ofer to gain a better understanding of the processes of emotional development he was undergoing and assisted in the consolidation of his identity, in a manner which was directed yet non-pressurizing, enabling but not coercive.

These differences in the adult's treatment of the adolescent are critical, and therefore can elicit significant change, as illustrated in the treatment of Ofer. Over the course of Ofer's therapy, it was easy to detect areas that remained untreated, such as the conflict between activity and passivity, the question of sexual identity, Ofer's competitive relationships with other men, and the narcissistic features in his personality. These selective neglects can frustrate the therapist and sometimes the patient. Let's not mistake the omission of these issues for their insignificance for Ofer. The fact that they did not arise in a pressing way does not minimize their potential future impact upon Ofer. They were not treated in the current therapy because it was focused and time-limited. One of the difficulties of this type of therapy with this type of patient, with whom there was a positive and enabling therapeutic alliance, is the temptation to continue and address more and more questions as they arise. The time limitation, initially compelled by reality, became an emotional framework in the selected therapy model, which provided the impetus for Ofer's attachment to me. The mere fact that Ofer and I upheld the task we took upon ourselves, and reached an emotional level that enabled a meaningful separation, contributed to the positive outcome of the therapy.

Chapter 4

Obsessive personality

Coping with perfectionist tendencies

In his writings on client selection, Mann (1973, 1981) designated the client's ego strength and ability for rapid emotional involvement as the most important selection variable for time-limited dynamic therapy. In addition, he emphasized the client's emotional capacity to withstand separation, that is, acceptance of the loss that is intrinsic to separation. Both variables must be well assessed in the selection process. According to Mann, neurotic clients who present with obsessive-compulsive features and who depend heavily on the defenses of isolation and intellectualization, are limited in their ability to express emotion and are, therefore, unable to commit themselves to the therapeutic relationship early enough in the therapeutic process. Nonetheless, these clients may possess the ability to cope with loss, although they lack the overall emotional involvement whose function is twofold – to provide therapeutically meaningful material and to engender a fuller experience of the loss.

Identifying features

Samuel was the first born in an observant Jewish family. At the time of treatment, he was 25 years old, living in his parents' home and completing a teaching certification course.

Presenting complaint

Samuel presented with complaints of internal tension and stress, a lack of confidence, and a sense that he was not actualizing his full potential, primarily in terms of his studies and interpersonal relationships. From an early age, he had felt pressured to achieve the maximum in all areas of his life. He feared making erroneous choices, and consequently agonized over, and often avoided, making decisions to an excessive degree. When he sought treatment, Samuel had nearly completed his teaching certification requirements, although he felt dissatisfied and wanted to pursue a different profession.

Additionally, Samuel was preoccupied with self-image issues, focusing on both how he viewed himself and how others viewed him. A few weeks prior to seeking treatment, a woman with whom he had a short romance ended the relationship. She claimed that she did not know how Samuel felt about her nor did she know what he generally felt about things, leaving Samuel feeling hurt and rejected.

Personal history

Samuel's mother, a classroom teacher, was a dominant and hyper-critical woman who judged people, particularly her own children, according to her high standards. She was very demanding and often doled out unsolicited advice. According to Samuel, he inherited his tendencies toward order, cleanliness, and pedantic behavior from his mother. Samuel's father, a gentle and attentive man, was a good-hearted and loving father who showed greater consideration for his children's individual abilities and needs. Samuel's parents told him that they spoiled him as a child and took very good care of him.

Samuel had always been introverted and never enjoyed playing as other children did. His mother, however, always pushed him toward the activities that she deemed important. From an early age, if Samuel did not like a particular school subject, his mother would sit with him, attempt to explain the lesson, and then holler at him for not grasping it. He attributed his fears of failure and ignorance to those childhood interactions. In Samuel's own words, 'Since then I have always wanted to prove myself.' As the eldest sibling, he was looked up to; however, the admiration he received always included the perceived burden of serving as an example to his siblings. He felt simultaneously loved, yet pressured and criticized by his family.

At the age of 13, Samuel left home for a well-respected *yeshiva* high school (institute of intense Jewish study). At the time, the decision was made by his parents. However, now he supposed that he would have made the same decision. Leaving home was difficult; he missed it and returned often. Ultimately, Samuel felt good that he had risen to the challenge and performed well in his studies. He dedicated most of his time to succeeding in school and did not invest in social relationships. Consequently, Samuel did not make many friends.

When treatment began, Samuel was studying education and had nearly completed the teaching certification requirements. Although he had not yet reconciled himself to teaching, he continued studying for the purpose of acquiring a profession. He was grappling with the dilemma of which direction to proceed in and what to study further, if at all. He had turned to various professionals who could advise and guide him. In the interpersonal realm, Samuel was preoccupied with marriage and the search for a spouse, a pursuit that predominantly precipitated feelings of anxiety and failure. He felt that he had not yet realized his potential and that time was running out. He felt generally dissatisfied with his decisions and believed that others were equally dissatisfied with him.

Samuel was diagnosed as suffering from adjustment problems with obsessive-compulsive features. Furthermore, he appeared to have self-image difficulties as well as problems with issues of dependence and independence. He impressed us as a highly intelligent young man who was motivated for therapy. Samuel claimed that he hoped to understand why it was so difficult for him to make decisions about himself and his life, without feeling pressured to acquiesce in the opinions of others. He wanted to comprehend better the seemingly unattainable pinnacle to which he continuously strove, and to feel content with himself and his life choices.

Course of treatment

Following the preliminary assessment, we debated the degree to which Samuel was suited to Mann's method of time-limited therapy. Our doubt centered on the extent to which Samuel would be able to work with his emotions. Finally, we decided to attempt treatment by this method, a decision that we regarded as questionable. The central issue, presented to Samuel in the first session (post-intake), was as follows:

Although you are a talented and capable young man, you are continually plagued by self-doubt and self-criticism. You have set personal standards for yourself that are discordant with your true desires. This leads to feelings of disappointment and failure.

Samuel agreed and added, 'When I am unable to live up to the standards that I set for myself and that others expect from me, I feel worthless.'

Mann labeled the first stage of treatment, 'the honeymoon.' In Samuel's case, the first four sessions were characterized by the unrealistic expectation that he would receive explicit advice on how he should lead his life and would be directed toward a specific path. With this guidance, he hoped to reach the distant apex to which he aspired. Samuel began each session by asking if the therapist had reached any particular conclusions based on the data provided in the previous session. Each time that the therapist explained that he would not receive explicit advice from her, he felt uncertain that he would achieve anything in therapy. The therapist interpreted Samuel's behavior with statements such as, 'You expect me to tell you what to do and how to behave just as your mother has always done.'

Samuel consistently arrived late to the sessions, repeatedly attributing his tardiness to concrete reasons. The therapist interpreted the late arrivals in light of the central issue: you don't feel confident that you will reach that high point you are always striving toward; therefore, you avoid fully committing yourself to the therapy by coming late. Furthermore, when you come late, you feel pressured to accomplish more than you possibly can. The time inevitably runs out, leaving you feeling frustrated and disappointed, even though the control still remains in your hands.

Over the course of these four sessions, Samuel spoke at length, trying to cover as much ground as possible in hopes of achieving the maximal results. His preoccupation with saying everything possible prevented him from relaxing and going into greater depth. It was very difficult for the therapist to intervene because Samuel did not allow her to get close to him. For the most part, he asked questions and answered them himself since he thought he already knew what the therapist would say. He relied heavily on intellectualization, and generally spoke about 'knowing and understanding,' rather than 'sensing and feeling,' patterns upon which the therapist consistently reflected.

Samuel arrived to the third and fourth sessions with a memo pad on which he had listed the complaints and problems that he experienced as well as those that others had noticed. It was difficult for him to express himself spontaneously because he was afraid that if he spoke at random, he would not express himself as clearly and completely as he felt he should. Samuel had difficulty handling uncertainty and the unexpected, fearing that he would not uphold the high standards that he set for himself. This fear created a pervasive sense of failure, leaving Samuel feeling unworthy and inferior. The therapist adhered to the central issue in her inter-pretations: you experience frustration and failure because you set standards that are not suitable for you, but that you think others expect from you.

Samuel began to explore his feelings toward his parents and family, yet still very cautiously. He was angry at them but feared expressing this anger because he felt that he must respect his parents. After all, they had raised him and took care of him. He felt compelled to compensate for their shortcomings, even though he harbored much resentment toward them. In this context, an apt metaphor was that Samuel felt like a pawn in a game of chess being maneuvered by his parents, the king and queen. This metaphor proved useful in terms of his relationship with the therapist as well. He felt angry when she directed him toward experiencing his emotions when he preferred to remain on a cognitive, analytical level. 'What's wrong with that?' he asked. 'Aren't my thoughts important enough? It's hard for me to share what I am feeling with you.' In response to the therapist's question, 'What is hard?' Samuel explained that in his family, where he should have experienced closeness, instead he felt strange and alone. Likewise, he felt emotionally isolated in the world outside his family.

Samuel held most of his emotions inside, preferring to cope independently. Even when his parents tried to get close to him, the expectation that they would be critical rather than understanding stifled the expression of his feelings toward them – he just couldn't trust them. Samuel felt that he had coped alone his whole life and did not know how to share his difficulties with others. This point was emphasized in therapy when Samuel said that he was not sure that the therapist understood him, pointing out concrete 'barriers,' such as her lack of religious observance and her young age.

The first four sessions were characterized by slow and intensive work revolving around the central issue. The therapist ascribed to this stage the metaphor of carving stone in which she attempted to peel away layers of intellectual understanding until she reached the strata of emotion. For the most part, Samuel did not respond easily to her attempts. As a result, the therapist felt that the therapy was extremely difficult and tiring. She wondered whether the treatment would succeed and what would happen as it progressed.

The treatment process continued throughout the next four sessions (the fifth through the eighth), however, greater emphasis was placed on clarification of the central conflict. With this goal in mind, the therapist used interventions such as, 'If I tell you what to do and how to behave, I will be just another person to whose expectations you must submit. It will be just like the relationships with your parents and with others in your life that leave you feeling frustrated and disappointed. In our therapy sessions, you have an opportunity to be yourself and to proceed at the pace that you choose, even though you waver between wanting and resisting that independence.

Samuel delved more deeply into this dilemma with which he had contended for years. 'You expect me to reach my own conclusions, independently,' he said. 'But I'm not sure I'll succeed, so I pass off the responsibility to somebody else. It's hard for me to be in a framework where I'm not told what to do, yet when I am told what to do, I feel held back and unable to make decisions for myself. Maybe what you are saying is that just like I am so tightly tied to my mother's apron strings in terms of what she thinks of me, what others think of me has also become very important.'

Seeing that Samuel was beginning to go more into depth, the therapist pressed him to express more emotion. Samuel responded to her pressure by saying, 'I blame my mother for always pressuring me and making demands based on her concerns rather than according to my wishes and abilities. She never gave me the permission to fail, yet she predetermined what I was capable of achieving. 'You won't achieve anything more, so come to terms with what you are. After all, you're the son of simple people.' She always admired successful people and I was very jealous of them. I always wished she would appreciate me as I was and my accomplishments. I feel so much anger toward my mother for that, but I'm afraid to express it. It's difficult to speak about feelings in general, but anger is the most difficult to express. I'm frightened by the threat that it might get out of control. It's like what happened to an uncle that my mother always compared me to.'

Samuel was ashamed that his parents were not more highly educated and the topic of them being 'simple people' arose repeatedly throughout this stage of therapy. As a child, he was ashamed of his father's work as a manual laborer. Since then, Samuel wished he were somebody else, somebody who did not feel inferior to others. Accordingly, he contemplated studying one of the subjects that would procure him a higher social status, while deep down he knew that he was not cut out for those professions nor did they really interest him.

Samuel continued to arrive late to all of the sessions, until the seventh. Each time, the therapist interpreted his recurring tardiness as Samuel acting out his need for control and his fear of becoming dependent on the therapy as he began to reveal his emotions. She equated this pattern to Samuel's tendency to reduce the feeling of dependence upon his parents by not sharing his emotions with them. As a result of the intensive attention paid to the issue of tardiness, Samuel arrived to the subsequent sessions on time.

In the seventh and eighth sessions, Samuel discussed his relationships with women, attempting to understand why the women he dated would conclude so quickly that they did not have feelings for him and end the relationship. He realized that 'It's not enough just to give them the impression that I'm a successful person and to demand that the women I date be successful, too. Now I understand that I need to let them in on an emotional level, even though I still think that being emotional means being weak, not masculine.'

In the ninth session, Samuel remarked that only four sessions remained; however, he did not address the conclusion of the treatment nor the impending separation. In contrast to the early sessions, he felt less pressured and was less concerned with pleasing the therapist, who sensed that Samuel preferred to prolong the feeling of not being pressed for time rather then experience the feelings associated with termination. Samuel also needed more time to continue expressing clear feelings of anger toward his parents, both in the therapy sessions and directly toward them, something he had never done before.

Samuel stated, 'It seems to me that everything I've gone through stems from the way I've been treated at home. My mother exerts such complete control over me that despite the fact that I'm an adult and I have my own opinions, I feel bound to her. Whenever she saw that I wasn't succeeding, she called me names like jerk, ignoramus, or dense. It was really insulting and humiliating, and, since then, I've had to prove that really the opposite is true. My father is a loving and understanding person, but he always remained neutral, never intervening when my mother came down on me. Where was he? I'm so mad at him for not being there when I needed him.'

By this point, the therapist felt that Samuel was generally more relaxed and better able to express his emotions, although he still had not expressed his feelings toward her nor toward the fact that they would be terminating the treatment very soon. Each time the therapist attempted to raise the issues of termination and separation through other topics that Samuel brought up, Samuel insisted that he had nothing to say about the upcoming conclusion of therapy other than that he preferred to deal with it when it happened. He added that he did not think it necessary to verbalize every emotion he felt for the therapist since there are other ways of expressing emotion. The therapist persevered in her attempts to raise the issue of separation, but to no avail.

For the eleventh session, Samuel had prepared a quasi-summary of his achievements in therapy on his own initiative:

> Previously, I didn't allow any space for my emotions, the most important thing was to live up to the expectations of others. When I was unable to achieve something, I immediately blamed myself and I considered any expression of emotion to be a sign of weakness. Now I realize that it's okay, and it's better that I do things according to my personal capabilities, not according to what others expect from me. At first, I expected to become a different Samuel. I thought that you would change me, but now I know that it doesn't work that way.

The therapist continued trying to focus Samuel's attention on the separation issue, on how he felt just one session before the conclusion of the therapy. This aroused an array of emotions. Samuel responded, 'That's true. I kept wondering why there are only twelve sessions. Who said that would be enough? I figured, though, that if you decided on twelve sessions, then you must have thought that was what I needed, but I don't feel that way now.'

When the therapist inquired, 'What do you feel now?' Samuel answered, 'Anger, a lot of anger. You brought out emotions that I had never revealed and I don't know how I will continue on my own. Not knowing what will happen after the therapy is over really stresses me out. Like I told you, ambiguity and uncertainty have always been hard, although I'm already trying to look beyond the half-empty glass at what I gained here in therapy.' The therapist observed a significant change: for the first time, Samuel had shared what he was feeling toward her.

The final session serves as a microcosm of the full treatment process. Samuel began the session by commenting that it was the last session, then immediately switched to another topic: the new subjects that he intended to study the following year. He had decided to pursue the subject areas that interested him, even though other people might look down upon those subjects. Although, he added, 'the reality' was hard for him to accept. When the therapist asked what he was referring to as 'the reality,' Samuel answered, 'Everything.'

'And what about the current reality, the conclusion of our relationship?' continued the therapist. Samuel responded, 'Yes, it's difficult for me, but I already told you everything last week. All week long, I've been thinking about what will happen afterwards, about how I'll cope. I'm afraid that I've changed. I'm more sensitive and I feel like I want to do things differently, but I don't know if I'll succeed. I must try to believe in myself.'

The therapist concluded by wishing Samuel well on his continuing journey, trying to reinforce his personal strengths, both those that he had always possessed as well as those he had acquired in therapy. Samuel felt good that for the first time someone had confidence in him and that he was finally able to remove his protective mask and just be himself. In his characteristically serious and reserved manner, Samuel thanked the therapist and the treatment process was terminated.

Follow-up

Samuel was part of the control group in an empirical study on time-limited therapy (see Chapter 11). Therefore he had to wait three months after the intake session before treatment began.

Consequently, Samuel's first follow-up session was after the intake session and prior to beginning treatment, at the end of the waiting period. The second follow-up session was held two weeks after the termination of therapy, the third was held six months after the termination of therapy, and the fourth, one year after termination. Below are summaries of the four follow-up sessions.

First follow-up: post-waiting period and pre-treatment

Samuel appeared tense, describing his situation as more or less static. He recapitulated his career dilemmas in obsessive detail and reported that he was still very troubled by the tensions within his family and the difficulty in finding a suitable spouse. Subsequent to the waiting period, there was no notable increase in the level of pervasive stress Samuel experienced, whereas the motivation for change had been transferred on to the treatment.

Second follow-up: two weeks post-termination

Samuel appeared relatively relaxed and reported that he felt well. He believed that he had accomplished something and had embarked on the right track to organizing his life anew. Even though he was just at the beginning, he felt confident. Samuel said he had learned from therapy that 'there isn't any hocus pocus.' He understood that his dependent relationship with his parents, and with his mother in particular, led him to aspire to unrealistic heights, yet caused him to feel depressed and unsuccessful when he failed to meet those high standards. 'The therapy enabled me to take my life into my own hands, to do what I choose, even if it's not what others would choose for me and even if I don't reach any great heights of achievement.'

The first step in actualizing this principle was Samuel's decision to move out of his parents' house and into a dormitory situation. He was still unsure which occupational direction he should take, but he was leaning toward continuing his academic studies. Socially, he felt at ease and more open in his friendships. In his relationships with women, Samuel showed a budding ability to withstand 'failures.' He proudly recalled that in his most recent romantic relationship, the woman expressed appreciation for him as he enjoyed the process of getting acquainted and the overall encounter with her. The fact that they ultimately decided that they were not a suitable match was perceived neither as a failure nor as a disappointment.

Third follow-up: six months post-termination

Samuel appeared liberated. He arrived early to the session, explaining his punctuality as an expression of the change that had come over him. Previously, he had resigned himself to the belief that, 'I'll be late no matter what, or I won't succeed in any case,' and easily gave up, making failure inevitable. Whereas now he told himself, 'If you try, you will succeed,' and was able to perform better.

Samuel reported three additional meaningful changes in his life:

a   He decided he would begin teaching upon completion of his studies so that he could be independent, while postponing the pursuit of further academic study. He realized that the aspiration for higher education derived primarily from his desire to win the admiration of others, which now seemed less important to him. He intended to cultivate his other areas of interest extracurricularly.

b   Samuel reported that although he still had a tendency to delay performing anxiety-arousing tasks that involved a threat of failure, such as studying for an examination or writing papers, he had found a way to cope better. He began taking planned breaks, such as a short trip or a musical break, then returned to his studies with increased vigor.

c   In his relationships with women, he allowed himself to ponder the relationships without feeling pressured to reach an immediate decision. He felt increased confidence and gained greater pleasure from dating, and even maintained several dating relationships at once.

Fourth follow-up: one year post-termination of therapy

Samuel announced that he had got married about one month prior to the session. He married a woman who had finished studying and was prepared to support them financially until he finished his studies. This would enable him to complete his study requirements without pressure and to dedicate time to other important activities.

Samuel felt that his wife accepted and supported him. He was proud of his ability to create a healthy, open relationship despite the imminent hardships of a new marriage. Subsequent to his marriage, change began to occur in Samuel's social relationships: he and his wife received invitations from their friends and hosted guests in their new home.

Samuel's relationship with his parents had also improved, even against the backdrop of his marriage. They respected his decisions, supporting the couple to the extent that they were capable. In addition, Samuel worked with his father in his free time.

Samuel observed that he felt relaxed. He recalled the therapy as beneficial and considered it the prime stimulus for the positive change that had occurred in his life. He still found it difficult to meet the requirements of his teaching course and to keep up with the time schedule. Nonetheless, he no longer experienced the tension and sense of failure that he had felt prior to therapy. Instead, Samuel felt optimistic that he would succeed in coping with his problems in the future.

Discussion

Samuel was a young man with an obsessive personality who presented with complaints of internal stress and pressure. Furthermore, he described himself as continuously feeling a lack of self-actualization in the areas of education and interpersonal relationships. This description concurs with David Shapiro's (1965) description of the obsessive-compulsive condition, which he described using three dimensions: rigidity, the mode of activity and distortion of the experience of autonomy, and the loss of reality. The obsessive personality features, along with the emotional constriction felt during the assessment sessions, served as contraindications for brief therapy. Mann and Goldman (1982) explain that the affective deficit prevents the individual with an obsessive personality or neurosis from emotionally connecting in a rapid and in-depth fashion.

After weighing the indications, the high motivation for change and the evaluation of reasonable ego strengths found in Samuel, tipped the scale in favor of trying TLP. This provides an additional example of the complexity of the selection process involved in TLP. Samuel's therapy exemplifies the principle that patient selection does not necessarily require the presence of all the criteria in support of brief therapy, alongside the absolute absence of contraindications. A situation might arise (and Samuel's therapy provides a fine example) in which during the final consideration, the therapist might find that despite the presence of contraindications or the lack of all of the positive indicators, it is worthwhile trying TLP.

Samuel's emotional difficulties became manifested in the transference in his unequivocal expectation to receive and obey directions from the therapist. Over the course of therapy, and especially during the final phase, this attitude was to some extent transformed into a more mutual form of acceptance, trust, and a sense of security.

During the follow-up sessions, held until one year after termination, there was a visible improvement in Samuel's life and in his feelings toward himself. In his own words, the therapy represented 'the primary motivation for a change for the better that occurred' in his overall state. He felt freer, did not give up on himself, and took responsibility. He reported changes in his relationships with his parents and friends, and even got married. The conflict defined as central in Samuel's life when he sought therapy was 'dependence versus independence.' The specific components of his personality were obsession and rigidity. An important additional component related to the basis of his model for relationships with women. Samuel dealt with every female figure in his life as if he were coping with an authoritative, active, and decisive figure – precisely the way he dealt with the figure of his mother. As required by this type of therapy, his therapist was authoritative to a certain extent (defining the type of therapy, establishing the setting, selecting the central issue, and fixing the termination date), yet she also represented hope through her active stance and emotional understanding (focus-definition of his enduring pain). As such, she provided Samuel with an encounter that was at once familiar to him from his relationship with his mother, yet different because, as in any dynamic therapy, it contained personal space – enabling, accepting, and empathic – which was sorely lacking in his life. Paradoxically, this combination constituted an impetus for relatively swift engagement with the therapist and a more rapid than expected change in a young man with a personality like his. Using Shapiro's (1965) conceptual system, the change in Samuel can be viewed as a modification of his rigidity. Because this type of change occurred, his sense of reality on the one hand (including, for example, relationships with significant figures) and modes of experiencing autonomy and selfhood on the other, were altered.

As far as can be predicted in regards to long-term dynamic therapy, in which the therapist adopts a less active and directive stance, it is safe to presume that Samuel, who was not at all used to this type of stance, would have required a long time in order to find ways of coping and forming an attachment. He almost certainly would have responded with resistance and perhaps avoidance. Going through a stage of that nature might have been meaningful and important for Samuel. Nonetheless, based upon our acquaintance with him, Samuel exhibited a tendency toward meticulous and exhausting repetition along with increased anxiety in unclear situations. These tendencies indicated there was a risk that he would not have withstood the ambiguity and the feeling of 'stuckness' characteristic of these sorts of situations in extensive therapy, and would have dropped out of therapy.

Notwithstanding Samuel's vigorous efforts toward perfectionism due to the nature of his personality, the very clarity and focus of the treatment, by definition, enabled him to perceive the essence of the therapy and continue 'working on himself' in an aware and almost behaviorist-like manner, even subsequent to its termination. This combination contributed to his feeling of competence and aided his progress. One of the often-heard claims aimed at TLP therapists is that they tend toward obsessive-compulsive activity by virtue of their abandonment of associative attention and their adoption of selective listening techniques – selective attention and selective neglect – and by virtue of their persistent adherence to the focal issue. As seen in the case of Samuel, however, it is quite likely that the focusing (yet constricting) limitation of TLP was a blessing in that it enabled the formation of a relationship for a person with such limited interrelational capacities.

Chapter 5

Transition and the narcissistic personality

The following case study highlights the developmental aspects of time-limited psychotherapy. When a client has difficulty advancing from one developmental stage to the next, TLP may be the treatment of choice due to two of its principal components: the objective time limitation and the empathic central issue that together provide the impetus for growth.

Both theorists and clinicians have examined short-term therapy in a developmental context. Shefler (1988a) concluded that the majority of short-term therapies include one, or both, of the following goals: (a) the removal of obstructions to the client's normal developmental process, or (b) the reattainment of previously established, but currently arrested, emotional equilibrium through reinforcement of the client's existent intrapsychic strengths.

Witzum and Chen (1989) described a model that construes the client as continually undergoing a process of growth and development and possessing various change-inducing strengths. This model contrasts an alternative model proposed by Bennett (1984), who describes change as the overcoming of resistance. According to Bennett's model, the therapist's function is to accelerate the growth of healthy resources within the client, thus overcoming impediments to normal growth.

Mann (1973; Mann and Goldman 1982), Bennett (1984), and Colarusso and Namiroff (1979, 1987) debate the clinical implications of adult developmental theories. White et al. (1981) suggest that unresolved childhood conflicts re-emerge at every stage of adulthood and present a formula for choosing the optimal type of short-term therapy for each developmental stage in adulthood. They designate Mann's model (1973, 1981; Mann and Goldman 1982) as particularly suited to the late adolescent stage, characterized by the separation-individuation conflict. Based upon interpretation of the Oedipal conflict, Sifneos's (1972, 1979) model is highly appropriate at the stage of early adulthood characterized by the search for a mate. Similar to Mann, Goldberg's (1973) therapeutic model is based upon empathy and is suited for the stage of settling down during which narcissistic and other related features arise. White et al. (1981) emphasize the importance of a developmental diagnosis in treatment selection.

Based upon Kohutian self-psychology theory, Goldberg (1973) relies upon techniques developed through the psychoanalysis of narcissistic problems, focusing on the self-object transference. According to this model, the therapist does not attempt to induce personality change in the client. Rather, the therapist aspires to achieve renewed intrapsychic equilibrium.

The fundamental principles of Kohut's (1968, 1978) self-psychology are especially relevant in cases involving self-image problems, such as the case presented in this chapter. Familiarity with these principles can increase the therapist's understanding of the therapeutic process involved in such cases. Kohut differentiates between self-object and object, describing a group of self-object needs that must be met for the development of self-esteem to occur. Whereas other separate individuals are worthy of esteem in their own right as autonomous objects, or 'independent centers of initiative,' the value of self-objects lie in the internal functions and emotional stability they provide.

The self-object needs include:

a   *mirroring*: essential to healthy development, parents' complementary responses to a child reflect and validate feelings of self-worth. In addition, these responses build self-respect. Parental responses of indifference, hostility, and excessive criticism reflect low self-worth and hinder the development of assertiveness. In a generally positive and responsive environment, optimal failures facilitate the development of internal mechanisms for maintaining self-esteem, enduring failure, and taking initiative. The child's self-object needs develop from archaic demands for endless attention into healthy self-object needs for occasional admiration and social acknowledgment.

b   *idealizing needs*: children desire unification with someone who helps them feel secure and at ease. The idealizing need begins with the desire for unification with the 'idealized parent image' and develops into a desire for closeness to that source of power. The intensity of the need decreases as the child develops self-soothing mechanisms when feeling upset or over-stimulated. Minor failures to satisfy the idealizing need facilitate the development of internal structures. Simultaneously, basic success in satisfying the need creates an environment safe enough for growth to occur.

c   *alter ego needs*: because they need to feel similar to others, children imitate their parents in a variety of daily activities. For example, a boy might imitate his father shaving or a girl may imitate her mother attending to the baby or cooking. These experiences instill in children the sense that they are like others, part of the human community.

Parents' empathic failures in meeting their children's self-object needs obstruct the development of intrapsychic structures capable of regulating self-esteem and performing self-soothing functions. Consequently, the individual becomes overly dependent on others for satisfaction of the self-object functions.

In self-psychology, as described by Baker and Baker (1987), the therapist serves as a self-object in a therapeutic atmosphere of empathic understanding. The goal is to renew the arrested developmental process by building internal structures that take on the self-object functions. The feeling of 'being empathically understood' enables the client to experience and explore previously unbearable emotions, due to the intensity and/or specific content of the emotions.

The tremendous impact of the empathic moment in TLP can promote self-image development in clients. The presentation of the empathic central issue at the introductory stage of therapy can be construed as an act of *mirroring* that encourages the development of a more positive self-image. Additionally, the overt attention paid to calendric time engages both the client and the therapist in an intensive, active effort to effect change and growth.

Identifying features

Abraham, a 40-year-old native-born Israeli, was married with three children and worked in the educational system.

Presenting complaint

Abraham sought therapy upon the recommendation of his family physician to whom he complained of severe headaches, shortness of breath, and allergies. He reported difficulty in going to work and felt guilty about his limited functioning and inability to support his family sufficiently.

Personal history

Abraham was the oldest of three children born to parents who themselves were distant relatives. His childhood home was characterized by constant, loud quarrels that created a rift in the general atmosphere of secrecy. Abraham was afraid of his father, whom he described as a very sociable, autodidactic professional. His father was always concerned with what the neighbors would say, and raised his children accordingly. Although Abraham described his mother as a sensitive and caring person who was continually humiliated by her husband, he could not specify his feelings toward her. He remembered that when his mother would show pictures of her children, she would point out his younger brother, but ignore Abraham. His family lived in a modest neighborhood, though his parents never viewed themselves as belonging there. Abraham was sent to an expensive school in another neighborhood, but did not feel it was the right place for him. He was not a good student. He was repeatedly told that he was 'capable but did not try hard enough,' an issue with which he struggled throughout his life. Throughout his school career, Abraham's father continuously impressed upon him that teachers are very important people.

From a social perspective, Abraham met with success in his youth movement due to his sociable nature and the relationships he formed with females. He had few male friends, and generally formed relationships with males whom he assessed as presenting no competition for him. He maintained this relationship pattern in adulthood as well. When he was drafted into the army, Abraham served in a technical position. Upon completion of his army service, Abraham married a girlfriend from the youth movement, a woman whom he believed would never pose a threat to him. Although it was not a passionate love, he viewed his marriage as successful. He selected education as a vocation because teaching allowed him 'to be a star.' As he stated, 'How can one be a star, if he isn't tall or handsome, and doesn't know how to sing.' At the time he sought therapy, Abraham was engaged in fierce competition with his superior at work and perceived himself as a terrible teacher with selfish motives. Abraham claimed that despite his efforts to raise his children differently, he often found himself behaving exactly like his father.

After two intake sessions, Abraham was accepted for treatment by the TLP team. Notwithstanding Abraham's intelligence, high motivation for change, and well-focused complaints, there was a considerable lack of clarity surrounding the nature of his object relations. He was diagnosed as possessing narcissistic and dependent personality features. In addition, he was struggling with a phase-of-life problem.

Course of treatment

Treatment consisted of twelve weekly sessions over the course of nearly three months. The treatment stages were similar to the stages theorized by Mann. Following the two intake sessions with another clinician, treatment commenced with a preliminary session with the therapist, followed by the twelve treatment sessions.

In the preliminary session with the therapist, missing details were obtained and the central issue was clarified. Abraham's opening sentence was incorporated into the central issue: 'I have always known what I want and have achieved it. Now I feel detached. I have no goals and no reason to act.' Abraham's statement clearly expressed his state of developmental arrest. A thorough investigation of Abraham's accomplishments enabled the therapist to interpret the conflict in terms of his self-image: 'Your whole life you've deliberated about whether to be the best among the weak, or the lesser among the strong.' This interpretation elicited relevant current material summarized by Abraham as 'I exert all my energy in order to be a star, instead of using it for things themselves.' The therapist detected a budding insight into the debilitating effect of Abraham's narcissistic preoccupation on his ability to invest energy in effective coping.

Regarding his hopes and goals for therapy, Abraham stated: 'I want to fulfill the functions of a father, husband, and son. It seems to me that what I have done until now has only sabotaged that.'

At this stage, the following central issue was presented:

You have always known what you wanted and have achieved it. Nonetheless, you have always been troubled and ashamed because you don't know your self-worth or where you fit into the grand scheme of things.

The central issue highlights Abraham's inner strengths, elucidates the conflict surrounding his self-image, and articulates the chronic pain of shame. It is phrased as an empathic statement, engendering a feeling of being understood. The central issue functions as a mechanism for rectifying the empathic failure of his parents and initiates the process of building self-esteem.

Abraham responded to the central issue with surprise. He had expected something grandiose, 'a bombshell.' Instead, he received a statement that duplicated what he felt. He began to speak about his parents, describing their failure to provide understanding and validation. The therapist interpreted, 'Now you look for validation everywhere, the same way a young child expects to receive validation from his parents.' Abraham began to refer to himself in the third person. He pointed out facts, but had difficulty connecting to his emotions. 'I have no secrets. Everything I experience, I have to tell somebody . . . Abraham is open, as if he is transparent . . . It annoys me that I am transparent. I'm constantly angry at Abraham.'

Toward the conclusion of the second session, he touched upon his feeling of shame: 'The bottom line is that I'm always caught with my pants down.' Once the therapist reflected the sense of shame and named it, Abraham began an account of different situations in which he had felt ashamed. Abraham's difficulty in naming emotions is reminiscent of the mirroring process of development, in which the parent must articulate the child's emotions because the child does not yet possess the language to do so independently.

By the third session, Abraham's strengths had been mobilized and he began to convey a sense of competence. Adhering to the central issue, Abraham reached the conclusion that 'to have worth' was subjective. To his surprise, he realized that people were willing to meet him on his terms when he approached them from his new standpoint. Overall, there was an atmosphere of idealization and overlooking of difficulties. Abraham's extremely positive attitude toward the therapist indicated that the treatment was clearly in the 'honeymoon' phase.

In the fourth session, Abraham related a story about finding himself in a mirror. 'This week I stood in front of the mirror, looked at myself, and smiled. The image reflected in the mirror stayed with me all week.' He added that the therapist's statements led him to the conclusion that just as he respected others by virtue of the fact that they are human beings, then he should respect himself as well. He went on to describe a duality in himself: the Abraham that 'is me,' and 'the Abraham that is watching me.' He said that if he needs to impress someone, it was preferable that he impress 'the Abraham that is watching me.' This is the concept of the *alter ego*. With the therapist's encouragement, Abraham was prepared to declare that he seemed 'just fine.' He commented further on his *alter ego*, 'When I felt I needed support, somebody to rely upon, a friend, it was him. If I have to answer to anyone, it's him.'

The therapist contrasted the burgeoning change to Abraham's previous feelings in front of the mirror, enabling him to focus on his sense of disgust and shame. He recalled an event that occurred when he was four years old. He stood before a mirror and asked, 'Why aren't I handsome?' When he was a child, his mother would tell him he was handsome, but he could not believe her. The therapist used the ugly duckling metaphor to illustrate how a child must identify with the parents in order to feel attractive. The metaphor evoked the question of which parent served as a mirroring self-object.

At this point, Abraham related to the hated father figure whose reflection he saw when he looked in the mirror. Concurrently, an atmosphere of greater ambivalence began to develop, as described by Mann. Toward the end of the session, Abraham began to explore the complexities of his relationship with his father. He felt at once detached, yet very close to his father, because of the similarities in their behavior. He was waiting for his father's death. He expected that when his father died, he would both cry and rejoice. He related to his father as a tremendous weight resting upon his shoulders. Abraham somatized this experience of his father in the form of upper back and neck pain.

In the fifth session, Abraham felt angry, but was unable to verbalize the anger. He reported feeling that he 'was not coping with his father successfully' after the previous session. He expressed feelings of disgust and shame about his parents. He was afraid his father would get so worked up – to the point that he would die. Abraham expressed his ambivalence in feelings of aggression and anger versus fearful subjugation to the authoritative father figure. The therapist interpreted the subjugation as fear of his father's death, something for which Abraham actually hoped.

The sixth session brought an expression of ambivalence toward money. Abraham had decided to go into business and felt like a prostitute. His need for money frightened him. Abraham's description of the difficulty in asking for his parents' help at different stages of his development powerfully expressed the feeling of being disparaged and held in low esteem by his parents. 'It was worse than being alone because at least people feel sorry for an orphan.' In this manner, he emphasized his parents' empathic failure as validating self-objects. The therapist interpreted money as a form of validation of Abraham's worthiness. Nonetheless, it was very difficult for Abraham to endure the powerful feelings toward his parents. The therapist reflected the difficulty and encouraged Abraham to continue reflecting on the issue of how to face his emotions.

In the seventh session, Abraham voiced his ambivalence toward the therapist and her ability to help change his attitude toward his parents. The therapist overcame this first active expression of resistance by acknowledging Abraham's difficulty in asserting himself. He reported that he had contemplated inviting his father to a café, even though it seemed impossible to him, more tortuous than going to hell. The therapist took an empathic stance, reflecting her understanding of the complexity involved in Abraham's tremendous desire to confront his father. Aware of the anxiety level Abraham could tolerate at this point, the therapist suggested a desensitization exercise based upon relaxation and guided imagery techniques. Consequently, Abraham was able to express his emotions towards his father, 'If you never told me that I am okay, how can I believe that I am okay?' The desensitization techniques and specific parameters in which they were employed were of secondary importance, in this case. More significant was the fact that the techniques were utilized as a result of the therapist's empathic understanding of the client's variant needs and experiences of distress at different stages of treatment.

In the eighth session, Abraham reported the occurrence of a meaningful change during the previous session. He had succeeded in confronting his father and explaining his feelings toward him. Abraham felt this was enough for him, adding that if it happened in his imagination it could also occur in reality. With the therapist's encouragement, he spoke about his father and was able to understand his fear of his father. He said that he was less angry with his father and less subservient both toward his father and toward other authority figures than he had been at the beginning of therapy. He likened his childhood relationship with his father to the experience of being on trial. The therapist linked that feeling to Abraham's difficulty in asserting himself.

In the ninth session, Abraham gave an overview of his feelings toward the termination as he experienced them throughout the treatment. He pointed out that he had not received solutions from the therapy. Instead, he had acquired coping skills. He believed the burden he felt would decrease gradually. Abraham said, 'Right now, I'm swimming with a life preserver, but when the therapy ends, I need to swim without it.' His metaphor captured the therapist's role as a self-object. He referred to the therapy sessions as 'an hour of oxygen' and 'the only place where I can feel like a little kid without feeling bad about it.' At this stage, he had difficulty expressing any negative feelings toward the treatment or the therapist.

In the tenth session, Abraham expounded upon his decisions regarding work and income. He saw himself as the owner of a large office with employees, a secretary, and multiple telephone lines. He felt differently about the possibility of earning money. Until now, he only wanted to fail, to prove to his wife that it was hopeless. He took the standpoint of a 'loser': if he did not succeed, it certainly was not his fault. At this juncture, however, he was taking responsibility and considered his business something that truly belonged to him. Abraham accurately noted that he had not spoken about his wife in therapy, despite her centrality to his life. The therapy had focused on his self-image conflict, rather than on his relationships with others.

The eleventh session was held following a previously scheduled holiday taken by the therapist. It began as if it were a follow-up session, bypassing the termination. Abraham summarized his feelings, stating that now he 'walks upright instead of bent over' and his headaches had vanished. He spoke about wanting to hear the sessions again to understand how the therapy works. When asked how he felt about the conclusion of the therapy, he responded by speaking openly and honestly about the emotions he had experienced. However, he related to his current feelings regarding termination in an impersonal and noncommittal manner. He emphasized 'the exercise' in which he simulated a confrontation with his father as one of the most meaningful events in the treatment.

In the twelfth session, the therapist pressed Abraham to relate to the termination more personally. He said, 'If there was a fragment of something personal, it would miss the target . . . I'm reluctant for reasons of modesty to say that there was greatness here . . . Today I feel like the Abraham I would like to be.' He labeled the moment when he heard 'the root of the problem' (i.e., the central issue) as one of the most impressive moments in the treatment. In conclusion, he said that for several days he had considered writing a thank-you letter to the therapist. He actually wrote the letter for one of the follow-up sessions.

First follow-up: one week post-termination

Abraham described his situation after the termination: 'Previously, I was bent. Now, I stand upright.' As a result of the therapy, he felt he possessed many talents as well as the ability and freedom to utilize them for the sake of his development. He had made a significant, but not rash, job change. He had partially moved into a new occupation that was pleasurable, profitable, and allowed him to actualize his ability. He had quit smoking and reported that the presenting symptoms had disappeared.

Based upon his description, it seemed as if Abraham's interpersonal relationships were more balanced and appropriate. The transition from highly charged, 'explosive' relationships to more moderate, restrained relationships was particularly noticeable in Abraham's relationships with male authority figures.

Second follow-up: six months post-termination

Abraham described a complex situation. The transition from one occupation to two was not simple, primarily from an administrative perspective. He was preoccupied with an employer-employee struggle in which he stood firm, yet did not feel exploited or pushed into a corner. He appeared to be coping appropriately with his current task. Abraham reported developments in his role as a parent, attributing the success to his experience in therapy. He did not complain of any symptomatology. The predominant impression was that the achievements of treatment had been preserved, despite the complex reality which Abraham faced.

Third follow-up: one year post-termination

Abraham had resigned from his former teaching position in an appropriate manner, neither instigating a crisis nor losing any rights or benefits. He had begun to work full-time at his new business. He felt it would be difficult to handle the business alone and brought a partner into it. He did not report tensions between himself and his partner. He felt satisfied, although he was aware of existential problems emerging in his new situation. He expressed greater awareness of the deficits in his home life without over-reacting. He expressed some concern that the pathological situation that originally brought him to therapy would return. There was no symptomatological evidence for his concern. He asked the evaluator if he could call the clinic if necessary and was assured he could. Nonetheless, two years after the follow-up session, he had not contacted the clinic.

Discussion

The clinical material presented in this chapter deals with a man stuck at the mid-life stage of settling down. This stage is characterized by intrapsychic conflict that arises subsequent to the consolidation and stabilization of one's career. Settling down in the realms of career and family require narcissistic maturity as childish aspirations are reprocessed. Faced with the reality of the work world, the adult understands that he or she must abandon the grandiose dreams of childhood, replacing them with more realistic aspirations. Failure to settle down leaves the individual feeling inadequate, without a clear professional identity. Due to the failure to transform the childish grandiosity into realizable adult dreams, the narcissistic wound becomes exposed (White, Burke and Havens 1981).

In the case presented above, Abraham had difficulty solidifying his professional identity because his career choice, largely influenced by his father's admiration of teachers, was based upon grandiose childhood dreams of being 'the center of attention.' As a result of his career choice, Abraham felt he did not earn enough money, a feeling that intensified as the needs of his family and adolescent children grew. The arrested adult development, at age 40, was connected to the previously arrested childhood development of his self image, at age 4, when self-image permanence was achieved. From the moment this barrier was lifted, the development of Abraham's self-image increased rapidly and his current conflict dissipated.

The client sought therapy when he reached a developmental stage of adulthood that demanded a higher income. The previously developed defense mechanism of 'being a star' proved insufficient in meeting those demands. There was a clear parallel between the arrested self-image development (and the resulting intrapsychic conflict) in early childhood consequent upon the parental empathic failure and the adult development that enabled Abraham to replace his grandiose childish dreams with realistic ambitions. Thus, he was able to choose a direction that allowed him to earn a sufficient income. In therapy, the empathic central issue facilitated the repair of a previous parental empathic failure.

The time limitation magnified the rapidly diminishing calendric time. Abraham was approaching mid-life, his father was aging and might not be around much longer. At the stage of ambivalence, Abraham felt hopeless, thinking no one could help him overcome the anger toward his parents. Nonetheless, he responded to the therapist's help and validation by confronting his father and expressing his emotions. Thus, Abraham was able to relinquish the infantile fantasy and to begin relating to his father as one adult to another. In his account of the most meaningful moments in treatment, Abraham emphasized these two curative factors. The therapist felt that despite the time limitation, the sense of urgency, and Abraham's willingness to relinquish the childhood fantasy, his great difficulty in achieving change led her to try alternative methods for lifting the obstacles to continued healthy development.

In summary, this clinical description of a man with narcissistic and dependent personality features struggling to advance to the next stage of mid-life development elucidates the developmental elements of time-limited psychotherapy.

Chapter 6

Shame

A source of abandonment, change, and relationship avoidance

Identity

Miriam, a 42-year-old Moroccan-born woman, immigrated to Israel as an infant with her family. Her parents worked on a factory production line in a development town. She was the fifth of nine children and was raised in a simple, hardworking, national religious atmosphere.

The initial contact

Miriam contacted me at the clinic by telephone and introduced herself using her full name. She expressed interest in receiving short-term therapy straight away and asked if I was available to conduct this type of therapy with her. In response to my query, she informed me that her initiative to seek short-term therapy with me came subsequent to reading articles I had published on the topic. She explained: 'Because I'm connected with the mental health services, I took the liberty of approaching you in this unorthodox manner. I hope it's okay with you. I don't have the financial means for private therapy and felt that perhaps I deserve . . .' In response (adhering to my standard reply to short-term therapy inquiries), I agreed to meet with Miriam and assess the degree to which short-term therapy might be helpful to her. When we scheduled the session, I discovered she came from another city. I added that if we found short-term therapy was not appropriate, we would reconsider conducting the treatment in our clinic. She accepted that remark without any hesitation. Her voice was pleasant over the telephone. I suggested we meet on the clinic's regular day for receiving new referrals and requested she complete the standard clinic forms before the session. Though I went through the familiar motions, there was something atypical about this therapy inquiry. At the time, we needed more short-term therapy patients. Yet there was something else about her that led me to accept with such alacrity this nonstandard appeal for help. To this day, I find it difficult to explain my response. (Was it the flattery? Was it the sense of distress? It remains unclear.)

The assessment session

As a result of what was quite possibly a countertransference response, I forgot to record the appointment in the clinic's register. Following a phone call from our puzzled clinic receptionist ('There's a woman here who claims you scheduled a session with her, but I have no record of it'), a well-manicured though unattractive woman of short stature appeared in my doorway. She did not appear feminine, lacked sexuality, and exuded a girlish childlike quality. She slipped into my office and chose to sit in the cornermost armchair. As she gasped for breath, she explained how she had rushed to arrive. In addition to her own rush, she was initially sent to another therapist in the clinic and had difficulty explaining to the receptionist that she had a specific arrangement with me. I got the impression she was very tense or nervous, or perhaps angry that I neglected to organize things before her arrival and had not co-ordinated the appointment with the receptionist. She sat in the armchair, gazing at me in a very scrutinizing manner. Apparently, I displayed a similar gaze and after about two or three minutes, I began to speak.

THERAPIST   As I said on the phone, we'll consider together whether short-term therapy is an appropriate option for you. We'll dedicate one or two sessions to that, depending on the need, and then we'll decide about the therapy. If we consider long-term therapy is a viable option, we won't be able provide it here due to zoning requirements.

MIRIAM   Fair enough. I've already been through private long-term therapy once, which was very helpful. Even so, I don't think I'm interested in long-term therapy right now. I don't want to be in a therapy that will become the center of my world and take over my life.

THERAPIST   What prompted you to seek therapy now?

MIRIAM   My problem concerns relationships with the opposite sex. I'm very worried that time is running out and I'm still alone.

Miriam barely glanced in my direction while she spoke. She spoke extremely quietly; her voice sounded sad and either ashamed or embarrassed.

MIRIAM   I'm very preoccupied with searching for men. I place personal ads and participate in singles' activities, but never successfully.

THERAPIST   What's considered never successfully?

MIRIAM   Men date me once, maybe twice, but never more than that. I've never had a stable and meaningful long-term relationship with a man. I'm embarrassed to admit it, but I've had very few sexual encounters and I never experienced great pleasure from any of them. The men I date never stick around.

THERAPIST   In contrast to the impression I received from our phone conversation, you seem quite shy.

Miriam indicated her non-verbal agreement with my statement. She began telling me about herself in the same sad, quiet, shy tone of voice. She was the fifth of nine children. Her family, of Moroccan descent, immigrated to Israel immediately upon the establishment of the State. They settled in a development town where her father worked in a factory until retirement. Her mother took care of the home and raised the children. Other than Miriam and one of her sisters, all of her siblings were married and worked in good professions. Her parents placed great emphasis upon two things: national religious values and education. Though she grew up in a materially impoverished environment, she was raised on the belief that 'we're different,' 'we're better,' 'there are no criminals in our family.' At the same time, she felt ashamed of her parents, mainly of her mother, especially when she came to school to meet with Miriam's teachers.

MIRIAM   I felt shamed by her appearance, her lack of education. She didn't even understand what it was I excelled at in school. We were more knowledgeable and educated than she was. To this day, my mother still doesn't know how to read and write.

It's shocking. You might say the other parents were better attuned to the mediocrity of their children. In our house, the gap between my parents and us was very difficult for me.

Miriam was an outstanding student and very socially involved with her classmates. She had several friends with whom she had lost contact, even though she was frequently at her parents' home and in the development town where she grew up. She had a car and traveled often. Though she rented a room in Tel-Aviv where she worked and studied, she essentially lived with her parents. After eighth grade, she decided she was unhappy in the development town and wanted to transfer to boarding school. The town was not of a high enough caliber for her and she felt stuck. She transferred to a boarding school on a secular kibbutz, a revolutionary gesture in her family. Her father did not understand how she could do such a thing and her mother was shocked by her decision.

Miriam adjusted well to the kibbutz, though she mentioned feeling ashamed again. She never brought friends home with her. Her adopted parents on the kibbutz were elderly Holocaust survivors. She felt ashamed of them in front of the other children at the school. There were few meetings between her birth parents and her adopted parents, mostly due to her own objections. She became absorbed into the kibbutz, but after about two years she felt like an outcast and felt hurt by the kibbutz children. She decided to return home.

MIRIAM Nobody was happy with my decision to go to the kibbutz. My parents were concerned about the influence of their non-religious daughter on the younger children. I had reservations about returning home after my experimentation with independence.

She attended high school in the neighboring city and excelled in her studies. She decided to serve in the army, though nobody else in her family had served before her. Her decision sent another wave of shock through the family. Nonetheless, she held firmly to her decision and was inducted into the Nachal corps (a special kibbutz army unit) along with some of the youth she knew from the kibbutz. She felt like a misfit. They called her 'the religious girl' even though she was not religiously observant at all.

MIRIAM   I was very offended. My religious stance was a source of conflict within my family for which I paid dearly, and now they called me 'the religious girl.'

THERAPIST   They said you were different from them.

MIRIAM   Yes. That's a whole story in itself – the shame of being different. That's been a central motif throughout my life.

Miriam switched to the regular army service and served successfully in an office administration position. The army offered her a permanent position. Initially, she accepted, but two days prior to her start date, she changed her mind and was released from the army. She moved to an agricultural settlement and took a job working for a prominent family in the settlers' circles.

MIRIAM   I worked as a farmer in their orchards, learning the job on-site. I became very skilled and accomplished in my job. There was something very pioneering and romantic about that period in my life. I didn't have any contact with men and didn't feel the need for romantic relationships. I worked hard and earned a decent living. My employers admired and were impressed by me. They had such personality and a special quality of family life. They were out of this world. They treated me like a member of their family and I admired both of them and the warm cultural and family atmosphere they created. It was a life of Torah, hard work, and basic human decency. I had never experienced anything like it. I could have lived there with them forever, and I wanted to as well.

After a long period of hearing rumors, Miriam discovered for herself that her employer, whom she idealized as a moral and religiously observant man, a father and a leader, was conducting an extramarital affair.

MIRIAM   I was shocked, and no less by the fact that his wife accepted the situation as it was. She didn't do anything, as if it didn't bother her. I was ashamed to set foot in that house. The family that I once felt so content with suddenly seemed different to me. I was ashamed of being associated with them. Shortly after, I left the settlement and returned to my parents' home.

THERAPIST   What did you feel when you left?

MIRIAM   What a question. I left immediately.
THERAPIST   Shame?
MIRIAM   To say the least . . .

She remained at home for several months without doing anything in particular until she began a secretarial job in a large industrial factory. As she had done in the army, Miriam excelled in her work. When they offered to promote her to a senior position, 'I felt frightened. Paperwork, filing, and typing – no thank you. I wanted to work with people. Something alive.'

To her family's surprise, Miriam enrolled to study early childhood education. She was a very successful student. Nobody in her class knew anything about her background, until she completed her studies. Then her classmates discovered she had received an academic scholarship from the municipality of her development town and had committed to teaching there after graduation. Once again, the feeling of shame returned.

Miriam worked in the development town for two years. She enjoyed it, but no more than that. She struggled with the authority of a more senior teacher. Furthermore, she wanted to do something hands-on and practical. She enrolled in another course, this time in a very practical paramedical field. She was an excellent student and began working in her field at a hospital in the center of Israel. She worked for several years until she grew envious of her colleagues working in a more prestigious field and felt she wanted to join them. She grappled with this dilemma, until a conflict arose in the workplace which served as a trigger for another change of career about one year prior to therapy.

It is important to note Miriam's high level of achievement throughout all of her career endeavors, which was consistently accompanied by the sudden decision that she was unable to continue in that profession and must switch directions. I asked about her intimate relationships with men.

MIRIAM   I've never had a fully intimate relationship with a man. I've had some male friends and one man with whom I had a sexual relationship. There's nothing to tell – it was a case of mutual exploitation. He thought he was taking advantage of me by just sleeping with me. What he didn't know was that he was more or less the only one, and that's not such exploitation.

Additional exploration of this relationship revealed her feelings of shame. At the conclusion of the session, Miriam stood in the doorway and said, 'You'll probably tell me I'm not suited to short-term therapy.'

Though I did not respond to her comment, I already had the central issue almost entirely composed.

Treatment session one

Miriam arrived at the session looking less tense. She sat quietly and waited for me to begin.

THERAPIST   Do you remember the end of the previous session?

MIRIAM   The end, I remember the whole session. How is it possible in one hour to speak about all of the most important things in my life?

THERAPIST   What was the most central thing for you?

MIRIAM   Mainly all of those changes. It's not normal the way I switch professions and locales so often.

THERAPIST   Do you have any idea why you do that?

MIRIAM   I don't know. I must be expressing something in my behavior. It means something but right now I don't know what.

THERAPIST   Anything else?

[*Silence.*]

THERAPIST   How did you feel during the last session?

MIRIAM   Pretty uncomfortable. But when I think about how much I told you, it can't be that I didn't feel comfortable.

THERAPIST   You spoke more than once about a feeling of shame.

MIRIAM   Even now, as you say that, I'm blushing. Yes, embarrassment, shame, about who I am, what I am. I'm actually a success who is a failure. Do you understand what I mean?

THERAPIST   In fact, our entire agreement is based on that duality.

MIRIAM   [*Gave me a puzzled look.*]

THERAPIST   You want short-term therapy. It will have an ending and that ending will be very close to the beginning. Without short-term therapy, there won't be therapy at all. We spoke about that possibility as well, right?

MIRIAM   You mean in either case, I'll adjust to you for a little while and then you'll leave me.

THERAPIST   No, it means that after a brief therapy we'll say goodbye, or so I hope. I hope you won't run off before then.

MIRIAM   If I decide I want short-term therapy.

THERAPIST   That's right, but you wanted short-term therapy didn't you?

MIRIAM   I wanted that too.

THERAPIST   What else did you want?

MIRIAM   I want to speak with someone who cares about me, someone who will take a genuine interest in me. And I have a lot to talk about. It's not easy living with myself in this world.

THERAPIST   And if not, then you'll exchange me too. You'll abandon the therapy as well.

MIRIAM   Yes.

At this point, I presented the central issue, which was really not very simple.

> You are a woman of many skills, which you actualize with unbridled success. At the same time, you've spent your life feeling ashamed, and that prevents you from forming relationships and leaves you feeling worthless and rejected. To counteract that difficult feeling, you protect yourself by abandoning or switching.

Miriam responded by asking me to repeat the central issue one more time. I repeated it word for word.

MIRIAM   I think the point is more the pride and aggression I feel whenever I'm pushed into feeling small, pitiful, and inferior. That feeling of pride pushes me out, and then I switch people or jobs.

THERAPIST   Yes, but what causes you to feel small, pitiful, and inferior?

MIRIAM   The shame. You know, I remember how once I was sick and the teacher came to visit me. I must have been in fourth or fifth grade. My sister was sick too and she was roaming around the house naked. You know, I didn't dare speak to the teacher at all. I was so ashamed that she saw the wretched state of our house, my naked sister, and my primitive mother. I just got into bed and said I was too sick to speak with her. I think she understood me. She understood how ashamed I felt.

THERAPIST   You're telling me what you expect from me.

MIRIAM   Look, it's no secret what people want from a therapist. He should listen, understand, and be there for me.

THERAPIST   I shouldn't make you feel ashamed so you won't need to flee from here.

We worked out the therapeutic contract, though there were some issues regarding the contract. She wanted to complete therapy before the school year began, so we agreed upon an eleven-session therapy. Although it was somewhat of a deviation from Mann's classic model, it was certainly an acceptable deviation if circumstances required it. We scheduled exact dates for the sessions and clarified the procedures for absences, cancellations, etc.

MIRIAM   You're very rigid about the time issue.

THERAPIST   The issue of time is important to me.

Session two

Miriam looked much brighter, less made-up, and more casually dressed. She felt euphoric.

MIRIAM   Everything looks beautiful . . . I hadn't noticed how nice the room was . . . I read about brief therapy again. I don't feel stressed about the time issue at all. I'm completely content with your decision . . . I succeeded in maneuvering you, or perhaps getting you interested in my case. A friend told me that you don't accept just any therapy case.

THERAPIST   How does that make you feel?

MIRIAM   That I'm very special, interesting, and I know how to maneuver and work things out.

THERAPIST   I think you're telling me these things, praising me, to prevent us from reaching a situation in which you feel you have to run away from me.

MIRIAM   What kind of situation might that be?

THERAPIST   You tell me.

MIRIAM   Look, if I get angry with you, it won't be good.

[I looked at her with an expression of confusion.]

MIRIAM   Right, no good. Once I get angry, which doesn't happen often, then I become so . . . I don't know what, I'm so . . .

THERAPIST   Ashamed?

MIRIAM   I'm so ashamed that I have to leave. I want to lean my head on someone's shoulder, to be loved, but I won't take chances. Unless it's completely clear that I'm safe, I'll leave.

THERAPIST   You're hinting at shame felt from the rejection of intimacy. Shame is also an emotion linked to sexuality.

MIRIAM   I don't understand what you mean.

THERAPIST   In the last session, you spoke about feeling ashamed in front of your teacher when she saw your nude sister running around the house.

MIRIAM   Yeah . . . well . . . I can't talk about that. I'm too embarrassed.

THERAPIST   By what?

MIRIAM   It's hard for me to discuss with you. It's not the same as leaning my head on your shoulder.

THERAPIST   You're already leaning your head on my shoulder, so to speak.

Miriam spoke hesitatingly, but at length, about the shame of seeing herself naked in front of a mirror. She disliked her body and was angry at being so thin. She felt defective because her other sisters were very good-looking. 'Mainly the sister I told you about when she was younger, she's really sexy.'

During the session, there was a non-threatening sense of intimacy.

Session three

Miriam told me about a blind date, which she condemned to failure before it even began. She described in detail the humiliating experience of arranging blind dates.

MIRIAM   You have to describe yourself like a piece of meat. It's so humiliating. And the man does the same thing. So, what I usually do is I check out the scene a little ahead of time and try to envision how it will be. I have all sorts of silly signals that I use to determine whether or not it will be a success, though it always turns out not to be.

THERAPIST   When faced with the humiliation you feel, you protect yourself by predicting failure. It becomes a self-fulfilling prophecy.

MIRIAM   After these dates, I always feel horribly lonely. It's a terrible loneliness. I go home, knowing he won't call again. I'm certain of it. But they never say anything. Most don't even bother to call and make some sort of apology, like 'I don't have time,' or something along those lines. They just vanish.

THERAPIST But you know that will happen ahead of time. Isn't it just what you planned for or expected?

MIRIAM Yes, but it doesn't help. I really want a relationship, and I don't have one. I'm not attractive enough. I'm not good enough. I know that. Okay, that's nothing new. Maybe it is for you. You look like the type who's got it all going for him. Tall, smart, talented. You've probably never been alone for a minute. I'm talking such nonsense.

THERAPIST Nonsense?

MIRIAM Don't tell me, I'm projecting on to you . . .

THERAPIST I don't need to tell you. You said it yourself.

MIRIAM I had fantasies about you. Is it okay to not discuss them?

THERAPIST I think you're starting to feel ashamed and in order to escape that feeling you wonder aloud, 'Am I allowed to not discuss my fantasies?'

MIRIAM I imagined how you were falling in love with me, how with you it could work out because you understand me. The interesting thing is I'm not so embarrassed to discuss this with you. Well, that's no news flash. It's all nonsense anyway.

THERAPIST It's not necessarily nonsense. True, they are fantasies, but they are capable of stimulating very powerful feelings of shame and discomfort. But that's not how you feel, at least not at the moment.

MIRIAM That's true.

Session four

Miriam arrived approximately ten minutes late. In an aggressive tone she commented that surely I had something to say about her late arrival.

THERAPIST What?

MIRIAM That I don't want therapy. Resistance – that kind of nonsense.
[*I waited silently and observed her aggressive movements. She played with the handle of the chair, moved around slightly, tensely.*]

THERAPIST   Is there some sort of difficulty here today?

MIRIAM   Difficulty?

[*Silence.*]

MIRIAM   [*in a restrained manner*] I don't know if I did the right thing by coming today. I think I'm going to spoil the good thing I have going here.

THERAPIST   What do you mean?

MIRIAM   Last time, I left here feeling happy and content. How wonderful, what an amazing therapist, and before I knew it I started hating you more and more. Why are you stimulating so many things in me? Why should I feel anything toward you at all? I told you I wasn't looking for a therapy that would become the center of my life. I don't want all of my thoughts to revolve around my therapist. Here I am, like an idiot, immediately telling you what I'm thinking, and telling you how I think you are falling in love with me. I was so mortified that I didn't want to come back today.

THERAPIST   You're describing something familiar.

MIRIAM   Familiar?

THERAPIST   Yes, familiar.

MIRIAM   I don't know what you mean.

THERAPIST   Think a little bit.

MIRIAM   I don't know.

[*She thought silently and grew increasingly agitated.*]

THERAPIST   Do you remember the central issue?

MIRIAM   Yeah . . . so . . . shame which prevents me from forming relationships. So what?

THERAPIST   Shame, which prevents you from forming relationships, and against which you protect yourself by leaving or switching. Or, in this case, either you don't show up or you come late.

MIRIAM   You really caught me red-handed. I knew I wouldn't get away with being late.

THERAPIST   I don't think you need to get away with anything. That's not the issue at all. I think the issue is the shame you feel here, in front of me. It's the feeling of inferiority and the consequent desire not to be here. That's the issue.

MIRIAM   What can I tell you. You caught me red-handed.

THERAPIST   No, we encountered the central problem. That's simply how it works here.

MIRIAM   So, what does that do for me? Okay . . .

[*This led into an entire discussion about her ambivalence toward therapy and toward me.*]

MIRIAM   I don't want emotional involvement, but I am involved. It clenches me tighter and tighter . . .

Session five

Miriam arrived, radiant with joy. 'I have a boyfriend . . .'

The blind date had called. She spoke about him at length. He understood her. She felt wary, although she was becoming more and more attached to him.

MIRIAM   It can't be because of therapy. Well, maybe it's because of therapy. We also have a sexual relationship. The truth is I'm pretty surprised by how open I was to the whole thing. In fact, I feel desire and really turned on. I've never felt that before. What could possibly be the connection between those feelings and therapy? We never even spoke about this topic and there isn't much to tell. I've barely had relations.

Reminding her of the shame issue from the central issue, I interpreted: 'The fact that you can experience shame without the need to escape or switch provides relief.' Miriam smiled with relief.

Session six

Miriam's relationship with her boyfriend had become complicated. He turned out to be quite complex, perhaps disturbed, and afraid of her.

MIRIAM   I feel him starting to avoid intimacy, which makes me angry. If I'm not right for him, he should just say so. If he wants to leave me, he shouldn't be afraid to tell me. I can take it. I don't think I'll fall apart. I can't stand when people aren't straightforward with their feelings, when they're not direct.

THERAPIST   It's very frustrating. The relationship has just begun to form, it seems good, yet there's already the threat of abandonment and separation. And the threat isn't coming from you . . .

MIRIAM   Frustration isn't the word. It's awful. I'm allowed to take off, switch, leave, but for somebody else to do that to me? If that's what's in store for me, then he should just tell me directly. 'It's over,' 'I've had enough,' 'I'm not interested in you,' or whatever it is he's thinking. Just tell me. He shouldn't keep me guessing and leave me feeling like he's evading the issue, avoiding it, or those types of things.

THERAPIST You seem hurt by two things: One is you sense he wants to leave you and the other is he hasn't told you.

MIRIAM The second is the main one – him not being honest. What's he ashamed of? [*She laughs.*] He should come to shame therapy. You'd know what to say to him.

THERAPIST Your cynicism is a way of expressing your anger toward me.

MIRIAM Toward you? You psychologists are always so certain people are angry with you. You have a problem with that.

THERAPIST I feel that right now you're going around and around as if you're joking, when actually it's incredibly painful.

[*The atmosphere changes. Miriam remains silent and withdraws into herself.*]

THERAPIST What are you thinking about?

MIRIAM Nothing. Just thinking.

THERAPIST There's more to it than just thinking. You've already said what you think of people who abandon you without saying anything to you about it. The same thing is happening here.

MIRIAM I don't understand what you're talking about.

THERAPIST It's hard and you're feeling that difficulty now.

MIRIAM What difficulty?

THERAPIST You're speaking about separating from your boyfriend, and what's more, about the frustration of him not discussing it with you, and a similar thing is happening here. We're approaching the end of therapy, but we haven't spoken about it. You feel it and you're angry with me for not bringing it up directly. When I do bring it up, you disregard it.

MIRIAM I hadn't thought about that at all. How many sessions do we have left?

THERAPIST How many?

MIRIAM Another ten, nine? Something like that.

THERAPIST Another five.

MIRIAM That's not very many.

Session seven

MIRIAM [*angrily*] My boyfriend left me. I knew he would. He wasn't serious. He was turned on at the beginning but as soon as I responded, he got scared and bolted. Men are such heroes. Even more scared than I am. I'm telling you.

THERAPIST   I hear you telling me.

MIRIAM   You're starting with that again. It has nothing to do with you. It really doesn't. I finally had a boyfriend. What am I saying, a boyfriend. He wasn't really my boyfriend. Just a few cheap thrills and he was off and running.

THERAPIST   Now you need to nullify him altogether. You can't run away because he already has, so you downsize him, nullify him. Your response seems to substitute for feeling pain or grief.

MIRIAM   What's there to grieve for? He came and went. It's infuriating, but it's no cause for grief. You know what, I'm lucky it happened now. I wasn't particularly attached to him. It was very brief.

THERAPIST   So is the therapy.

MIRIAM   You never relent. Well, you know what we're supposed to talk about in therapy.

THERAPIST   And you know what you feel in therapy.

MIRIAM   [after a long silence] Look, it's been a while since I discussed the topic that came up at the beginning of therapy. You probably don't remember. What am I saying? After all, you remember everything. So you must remember I spoke about my fantasies that you're falling in love with me. Well, I still have them and I still really enjoy them. Also, I saw you somewhere and I felt very excited. The whole idea of not wanting to feel anything toward you because I wanted a sterile therapy, advice on how to handle the time that's slipping away from me – that's all falling apart. No matter how much I don't want it to happen, it happens anyway.

THERAPIST   Why do you not want it to happen so badly?

MIRIAM   Why should it, what will I get out of it? Before we know it, we'll have to separate and you already know that's my weak spot. It's no problem for me just to leave. But to separate and say goodbye – absolutely not.

THERAPIST   What's the difficulty?

MIRIAM   What's the difficulty? Come on . . . all of the emotions stirred up by good byes, they're altogether inexpressible. It's shameful.

[Miriam burst into silent tears, which she tried to smother with her handkerchief.]

Session eight

Miriam did not show up. Two days later, she phoned and said she completely forgot about the session. She wanted to speak on the phone if I had time. I suggested we speak in the next session.

Session nine

Miriam began by commenting that only four sessions remained, which seemed very little. I responded that only three sessions remained, which was even less. She tried to argue with me, until she eventually remembered. I returned to the issue of the missed session.

MIRIAM   I told you I forgot. Do psychologists acknowledge forgetting or is everything intentional?

THERAPIST   I don't think you forgot. Rather, you had a need, perhaps an unconscious need, not to come to the session, to escape it.

MIRIAM   I already see where you're heading. I was ashamed of something, therefore . . .?

[*Silence, followed by a long monologue about the relationship Miriam had developed with me.*]

MIRIAM   Actually, in the beginning I was certain I wouldn't want a long relationship because I didn't think you'd be interested in treating me for a long time. I think I requested short-term therapy because I was afraid of an extended relationship. Although, at the moment my feelings have changed and I think it would have been worthwhile to continue in therapy. We didn't know it would succeed. And if it's really been successful, which I think it has, why not continue? There is a problem, though. My car is starting to give me trouble. It's making all sorts of noises. I'm pretty scared by the noises. I've had the car for nine months and even though I hesitated when I bought it, it's been just fine. But now it's really problematic. It's complicated because besides the technical and practical issue of switching cars, there's also the emotional element. I've become attached to it. I always laughed at those men whose cars are like their lovers. Now I see I'm in an identical situation. It's really difficult for me. Besides that, it's aggravating that I can't afford to fix it. It will probably be a long, serious repair job.

And it's disappointing also. Granted, it wasn't a new car, but after only nine months?

THERAPIST You're speaking about your car, but what you've said can also be applied to me. It's only been nine sessions and it's aggravating that we have to say goodbye. 'I didn't intend to get close but look what happened to me anyway.' You referred to your car as something beloved, and also useful, from which you must part, and it's sad, and it's aggravating, and it's disappointing. Yet, at the same time, it doesn't leave you feeling inferior or rejected.

Session ten

Miriam looked very serious and somewhat tense.

MIRIAM What do you think I accomplished in therapy? We should summarize because next week we say goodbye.

THERAPIST And how do you feel toward that event?

MIRIAM It's too bad, too bad for me. I've had it good here with you. I feel safe and understood. I'm really not ashamed, even though I have more than a few things not to be proud of. I moved a while ago. I didn't tell you. You can't imagine what an accomplishment it was for me. Usually by the time I make any realistic change, buy or sell something, meet someone, travel somewhere, I've already talked about it so much. Because I do so few things I can be proud of, I think when something finally happens, I make a huge deal out of it. But I didn't have any need to talk about moving, even though it was complicated.

THERAPIST What was complicated about moving?

MIRIAM I lived with a woman who constantly humiliated me. She was pretty, attractive, and lucky with guys. She works with me. She's nothing special job-wise, but socially, she's a star. When she suggested we live together I couldn't have been happier. If she wanted me to live with her, it was something. But I quickly realized she's a monster. She had something to say about everything. Mainly about how I look, how I dress, that I smell bad, and so on and so forth. At first, I just took it all even though I was deeply offended by her. It didn't occur to me that I could leave, that it was simply a bad situation and I could leave. A month ago, I summarized for myself what we had discussed in therapy, what was taking place here. I thought about the focal point. It was right. I feel ashamed and I don't form relationships easily. And I run away and escape because I don't want to feel rejected or abandoned. That realization hurts. I thought about my flat mate and realized I'm not ashamed. I just can't stand her because she's a horrible human being. She's pretty and sexy, but that's it. She's rotten, rotten, rotten. So why should I tolerate her? I didn't move flats because I was afraid of abandonment but because I really deserve a good place to live. So, I searched for a flat, found one, and moved.

THERAPIST You said it was difficult for you to tell me about moving flats.

MIRIAM Yeah, because I was afraid you'd immediately say I feel rejected by her, but that isn't true.

THERAPIST It really isn't true. And what's most interesting is despite your fear, you truly have a need to share this with me at the last minute.

MIRIAM Well, it's so you can see there are results. If the therapy continued for a year, I think there would be even more things.

THERAPIST You're trying to tempt me into extending the therapy.

MIRIAM Right.

THERAPIST What brings you to that?

MIRIAM It's a temptation that isn't shameful. The temptation is easier to handle than the fantasies about falling in love with you.

THERAPIST You fantasized *I* was falling in love with *you*.

MIRIAM I fantasized both . . .

THERAPIST And now you don't feel ashamed to tell me about them.

Session eleven – the final session

Miriam arrived a few minutes early and sat in the waiting room. She looked very sad as she entered my office. I looked at her and no longer recognized the lean almost identity-less woman who had slipped into my office for our first therapy session. There was a brief silence and I felt there was no point in speaking because it would all end today anyway. On the other hand, I identified the feeling that it might have been a good idea to continue the therapy. Miriam was absorbed in herself.

THERAPIST Today is our last session.

MIRIAM I know.

THERAPIST What do you feel?

MIRIAM   I feel sad. I'm stupid. If I hadn't suggested short-term therapy, would you have suggested long-term therapy?

THERAPIST   Do you feel you spoiled it for yourself?

MIRIAM   Maybe.

THERAPIST   If you recall, we spoke about the fact that therapy could only be short-term, and nothing else, because of the zoning issue.

MIRIAM   That's not the point. I know those are the rules, but right now I feel sad about saying goodbye. I have no idea how to separate from someone who cares about me. How do you feel?

THERAPIST   I have mixed feelings. I enjoyed working with you and I'm sorry it has to end, but I also have the sense of fulfilling a mission, which pleases me. It doesn't console me, but I can imagine that another situation, without that satisfaction, would be more difficult.

MIRIAM   If nothing had been accomplished, parting might not be sad.

THERAPIST   Not necessarily.

MIRIAM   I brought you a gift. [*She took out a large basket and a miniature plant.*]

THERAPIST   It's very tiny and cute.

MIRIAM   He was ashamed to grow.

[*There was a lengthy silence until five minutes before the end of the session.*]

THERAPIST   We have another five minutes until we say goodbye. [*Another sorrowful silence.*]

MIRIAM   I want to ask you something. If I wanted to give you a kiss, would you consent?

THERAPIST   If you're not ashamed to give one, I'll accept it.

MIRIAM   That wasn't the answer I expected.

THERAPIST   What did you think I'd say?

MIRIAM   [*imitating my deep voice*] What do you think?

[*I rose from my armchair, as did she. She approached me and very hesitatingly clung to me with a kiss. She left the room, then returned.*]

MIRIAM   I'm incredibly grateful to you for this therapy. It wasn't as brief as I thought.

First follow-up: six months post-treatment

I invited Miriam to the session and she responded happily. She described a complex situation. In one respect, no change had occurred in her life. Other than completing her studies and beginning an internship, her life continued as usual. At the same time, she had been pondering the meaning of the fact that she had never changed the address on her identity card. She had done little about it, but was contemplating changing it. Even though it was inconvenient, she felt she must make this decision and officially 'leave home.' Her affective state had improved. She was no longer tense and did not feel worthless or inferior. She primarily described her feeling that despite all of her abilities and talents it was possible her life had flown by with little meaning. She would work and develop but never know love. She felt the supervision of her clinical counseling internship was helpful and felt she was coping with personality-related questions throughout the supervision. When I asked about her feeling of low self-esteem she shifted to speaking about sadness: 'Not depression. I don't feel depressed and I don't think I am depressed. Sometimes I'm very sad about what has happened to me. I don't feel inferior. I mainly feel sorry for what has happened and for what hasn't happened, then I wonder what I can do to alter the situation.'

In response to my question, she replied, 'I haven't thought about going back to therapy because I'm managing alright. I understand what's happening to me and at the moment I feel capable of coping alone with the things that come along. Sadness isn't a disease.'

Second follow-up: one year post-treatment

Miriam opened the session immediately by announcing she had a great deal to tell. She had met a physically disabled man who was her age and suffered from a degenerative disease, which was currently in an inactive stage. He was considerably disabled physically, yet very active and creative both spiritually and emotionally. She felt attached to him. She did not idealize the situation nor did she describe him in especially vibrant colors. On the other hand, she felt and described heartwarming feelings of intimacy, love, and caring toward her and the stimulation of her mutual feelings toward him. I asked about the sadness she expressed in the previous follow-up session. Miriam said she still felt sad, but not because of loneliness this time, rather because of what it seemed would never occur in the future. She was disturbed by the fact that she would most likely not be able to have children, and she spoke about this fact heavily and sorrowfully. Though not 100 per cent certain, she thought she preferred being close to someone, even if he was not the ideal man, over continuing her search and winding up empty-handed. She described the fury she felt when a friend questioned her, 'He's a charming man, but why are you settling for so little?' Miriam responded angrily: 'What you call "so little" is that he loves me, and there's nothing little about that.' He described how her partner did not pressure her but did remind her that they both know the time they had together was limited.

I reminded Miriam of the statement she made during our first session: 'Time is running out.' She felt choked up and cried, 'It's running out for all of us, but I'm not alone. Perhaps.'

Though I was unable to locate Miriam one year later for another follow-up session, I gathered the information that she had left the development town.

Discussion

Miriam's presenting problem is one typically experienced by many women over the age of 40 who have not found a mate. Even more difficult for these women, they carry around a feeling of having failed in their ability for a spousal relationship. The internal and external pressure exerted upon these women is enormous. During the first assessment hour, in what sounded like a direct quote from Mann (1973), Miriam said, 'I feel that time is running out,' and, thus, was kind enough to describe her perception of calendar time.

This treatment presented an interesting theoretical and technical challenge for me when I faced the selection of the central issue. As seen in Miriam's assessment hours, it was not especially difficult to locate and select a central issue. At the same time, a problem arose related to the defensive pattern Miriam had adopted over the course of her life, namely the tendency to distance, run away from, and avoid difficult emotional situations. One of the defining characteristics of TLP is the bypassing of the patient's defensive patterns, based upon the understanding that the process of treating defenses requires a long time. (Already in 1963, Malan designated defenses and their treatment as one of the factors for assessing dynamic psychotherapy.) The a priori central issue designated for Miriam did not address her avoidance-based defenses. During the third session, the clarification and the attempt to validate the central issue components prior to its presentation created a situation in which Miriam responded to the therapist's question by asserting her viewpoint that the multitude of exchanges and changes throughout her life (i.e., her defensive response) were the most identifying phenomena in her life. When the TLP therapist attempts to find the most central element for any given patient, it is acceptable and worthwhile to incorporate things considered important by the patient, even if they deviate from the theory behind the original formulation of the treatment. In order to accelerate the development of a rapid therapeutic alliance, and to strengthen it, the central issue ought to include material, topics, verbal expressions, and central themes from within the inner world of the patient, in his or her language, according to the quality of his or her experience.

Miriam's therapy was first and foremost a significant corrective experience for her. As frequently occurs in TLP, the dominant affect in the life of the patient arises in an experiential form in the transference immediately upon commencement of the treatment. Indeed, the shame, selected as the affect which characterized, and was incorporated into, the central issue, appeared immediately at the beginning of the therapeutic relationship. This occurred against the backdrop of the contrast between the decisiveness with which Miriam dealt with all issues and the shame and near avoidance she experienced in things connected to personal relationships. The circumscribed nature of TLP coupled with the explicit guideline of attentiveness to the affective dimension from the outset elicited a merger of the decisiveness and the shame within Miriam, and raised them as an integrated experience already during the first and second assessment hours. The 'good fortune,' if it can be called that, or the professional guideline as formulated in Mann's (1973) therapy model, was that I picked up on this internal contradiction, its components, and the specific affective dimension it generated within me. The willingness to work with this contradiction rapidly engendered the immediate formation of a good therapeutic alliance, despite the embarrassing mishap that occurred at the beginning of the therapy and threatened to create a crisis immediately at the start of therapy.

There were two additional factors in the success of Miriam's treatment. One was her personality features: in terms of the selection criteria for patients suited to TLP, Miriam possessed strong motivation for change, a superior ability for introspection, high symbolic ability, intelligence, and despite the many emotional deficits, she possessed internal traits that could gain external expression relatively easily. Miriam was an ideal candidate for any dynamic psychotherapy, including TLP.

Miriam's previous experience in extensive therapy contributed to her readiness and ability to reap great benefit from TLP. We cannot view previous therapy as a condition for the success of TLP, but on the other hand, it is neither right, nor fair, to ignore the influence of prior therapy. Any therapy, primarily therapy experienced by the patient as a positive experience, adds to and develops the patient's ability for growth and development.

In the follow-up sessions we learned about an additional development in Miriam's emotional life. That development was not the mere fact of finding a mate, but her internal decision to make a choice grounded in the profound understanding that indecision had led her nowhere for the last forty years. What might appear to be a compromise is actually an outgrowth of her ability to decide and select, but this time she decided neither impulsively nor in the service of her defenses, but for the sake of fulfilling her deepest desire – a meaningful and non-shameful relationship. Some would claim that the selection of an ill and disabled man was a defensive choice of another variety: an anti-phobic choice. The quality of Miriam's description of her considerations and the motives behind her decisions at least convinced the therapist that her decision was not an anti-phobic one, but rather a recognition that time is indeed running out, and if she did not reach a decision, she would remain alone. Thus, Miriam relinquished the myth of perfection and the perfect choice, and nevertheless selected a mate who provided her with a satisfying emotional life.

The brief therapy enabled Miriam to experience an intensive, partial, and satisfying relationship. Theoretically, one might hypothesize that the partial, time-limited experience, built upon intensive transference emotions ultimately experienced as satisfying and non-shaming, released Miriam from the feeling that all imperfections are defective, shameful, and should be avoided. She utilized this feeling to rescue herself from the cycle of loneliness, and although there was a price to pay, she did not relinquish the gratification of her emotional needs.

Chapter 7

Depression

Coping with separation and loss

As experts in issues of separation and loss, Mann (1973, 1981, 1991) and Mann and Goldman (1982) viewed life as an endless series of separations and losses that elicit the most painful human responses. According to Mann, one cannot face separation without experiencing the painful emotions embedded within one's psyche, especially when time-limitations play such a prominent role.

Arlow (1984, 1986) and Hartocollis (1975) discussed the issue of psychotherapeutic time. Like Mann, Arlow distinguished between two ways that the client experiences time. He linked the development of calendar, or 'objective' time to the acquisition of object permanence that creates a sense of self-continuity. Arlow likened the individuation process to the process of building a concept of time. Hartocollis emphasized the relationship between time and emotion, suggesting that the experience of time derives from its emotional context.

Identifying features

Julia, a single Christian, Arab woman in her forties, was self-referred for treatment.

Presenting complaints

Julia complained of an ongoing depression for two years, since separating from her Jewish boyfriend. She suffered from anhedonia, sleep disturbances, depressed appetite (although there was no significant weight loss), frequent crying spells, restlessness, impatience and irritability toward others, low self-esteem, and suicidal ideation. Despite the abundance of reported symptoms, Julia managed to maintain her premorbid level of functioning.

Personal history

Julia was the fourth daughter in a family of eight children. As a child, she felt shunned by her mother whom Julia believed loved her less than her siblings. In contrast, she described her father as a loving and protective man who shielded her from her demanding and discontented mother. Julia's mother died four years prior to treatment. Throughout her life, Julia strove to achieve exemplary behavior at home, in school, and, eventually, at work. She still regretted the loss of previous marriage opportunities that never came to fruition for various reasons.

Fifteen years prior to treatment, Julia became involved romantically with a married, Jewish man. Although their relationship was never fully consummated, three years later they eliminated its limited physical aspect. A deep and sincere friendship developed that became the most important relationship in Julia's life. After thirteen years of daily contact, the man's wife died and he began distancing himself from Julia. She claimed the relationship deteriorated more each day and wanted help in returning to 'the way we were.'

After two detailed intake sessions,[1] Julia was accepted for Mann's method of time-limited therapy based on several factors: she sought therapy in the wake of a painful separation and loss and presented a well-focused problem; she displayed appropriate levels of intelligence and motivation, as well as an ability to connect current difficulties to past events; finally, Julia formed an immediate connection with the interviewer and demonstrated the ability to express emotion. Julia's limited psychological mindedness, however, raised doubts regarding her suitability for time-limited therapy. She tended to polarize her emotions and to blame her misery and other occurrences in life on bad luck (see Arieti and Bemporad 1978).

1 The therapist did not conduct the intake sessions. Instead they were conducted by an evaluator from the time-limited therapy team, as was customary for short-term referrals. Therefore, the therapist held thirteen sessions with Julia rather than the twelve sessions recommended by James Mann.

Course of treatment

Thirteen sessions were held on a weekly basis for three months. In the first session, Julia and the therapist became acquainted with one another as the therapist gathered details that were missing from the intake interviews. An outstanding feature of both the intake interviews and the first session was Julia's tendency toward pleasing others. Furthermore, she described herself as feeling unloved and unwanted by her mother and her former lover.

The central issue was based upon clinical material gathered in the assessment interviews:

> You are a talented and capable woman who has always tried to behave like 'a good little girl.' Nonetheless, you have always felt, and continue to feel, undesirable.

This central issue integrated the time element with Julia's feelings toward herself, acknowledging her strengths and abilities while highlighting the continuous pain of feeling undesirable. The therapist strictly adhered to the theme as the treatment unfolded into the three distinct stages outlined by Mann.

Mann's first stage, 'the honeymoon,' was characterized by the establishment of a therapeutic alliance and the rapid development of a positive transference. Julia's frequent crying spells throughout the first four sessions created an emotionally charged atmosphere. She responded strongly to the presentation of the central theme by detailing her experience as an object of rejection and injustice, victimized by her mother. She considered herself the victim of colleagues, other family members, and her former lover as well.

Julia felt tremendous relief at the opportunity to divulge the secret of her relationship with a Jewish man. She designated the willingness to listen as an indication of the therapist's ability to help her. When she lacked an appropriate Hebrew expression, Julia expressed difficult emotions in Arabic. The therapist's understanding of Arabic increased Julia's confidence in her and drew her closer to the therapist.

Julia expressed despondency through the belief that there was nothing left for her and that she had no chance of marrying at her age. 'At least there was hope when I was young. If something didn't work out, I could tell myself there would always be another chance.' She wished that she were dead and claimed she would commit suicide if it were not for the *fadicha* (shame) it would bring upon her family.

The therapist linked the mourning for lost opportunities to Julia's chronic emotional pain. Through emotional exploration, the therapist likened the pain of being rejected by her mother to the current anguish of being cut off by her lover. Julia's grief over her lover's detachment magnified the perpetual sense that she was undesirable. Despite their newness and strangeness, Julia responded to the emotional insights offered by the therapist. She described her attitude toward her lover, 'I loved him. I loved him like a father, a mother, even an entire family. He was my most cherished love. That was how much I loved him and believed in him. I told him my problems. I told him everything.'

While her former lover behaved as if there was never anything between them, Julia spent two years hoping that if she maintained contact with him, their previous relationship would be restored. With the therapist's encouragement, Julia managed, albeit with great difficulty, to express her fear of confronting him. She was afraid of finding out that the relationship was really over: 'I don't want to lose him.'

At this stage of treatment, there was little interpretation of the transference. Instead, the focus was on using the central issue to explore the emotional thread linking Julia's past experiences to her present reality. Those connections elicited many childhood memories, recalled in vivid detail. At this stage, there was no change in Julia's symptomatology, including the intense and frequent crying spells during sessions.

The middle stage (sessions five through nine) was characterized by rudimentary expressions of ambivalence, verbally and behaviorally. Nothing magical had occurred and Julia's initial optimism began to dwindle. She observed that the treatment was approaching its midpoint; its imminent conclusion was in sight. At this point, Julia began to grasp the impossibility of returning to times past, both in life and in therapy. This realization evoked the wish 'that God would strike me down, so that nobody could say anything about it.'

Julia addressed her feeling that nothing had changed. 'I want you (the therapist) to know it's not that I don't believe in you, God forbid.' The therapist interpreted Julia's remark, 'You want to see how and where I can help you.' Julia responded by listing all the people that had disappointed her, emphasizing her mother and her former lover, tallying all that she had lost. The therapist continued, 'Now you feel I can't help you either.' Julia answered through her tears, 'You won't be like the others because you'll be able to listen to me.'

The therapist's emotional response reflected Julia's disappointment and ambivalence. In supervision, the therapist described how she internalized the heavy and existential nature of Julia's depression. This elicited a parallel process of doubt and ambivalence, in which the therapist questioned the utility of short-term therapy in treating a depression of such magnitude.

Sparks began to fly when the therapist connected Julia's 'good little girl' behavior and expectation of reciprocity ('if I'm good, then others will be good to me') to the perpetual feeling that she was undesirable to others. Julia used the central issue to understand that her father's insistence on maintaining the *status quo* in their relationship and his disregard for her current fragile state caused her to feel unaccepted. Furthermore, Julia tried to clarify her former lover's detachment, wondering if there was ever anything genuine between them. 'He doesn't seem to value what we had together; that's what kills me.'

Julia felt conflicted about her involvement with a married man and thought she deserved punishment. The therapist questioned whether Julia attributed the demise of their relationship subsequent to the loss of his wife to the fact that he was Jewish and she was Arabic. Julia responded that they always knew neither one would cross the bridge. She returned to feeling that she could not part from him, describing the depth of their relationship as eternal. She recalled his proclamation that, 'We'll grow old together. Our relationship will always stay the same.' Julia tried to resuscitate the relationship by bringing him olives as she did every year, yet she felt, 'It's as if he doesn't want anything from me.'

The therapist interpreted Julia's behavior in terms of the focal issue: 'You're playing the role of the "good little girl" whose attempts to win closeness through pleasing the others are repeatedly rejected.' Julia responded by relating a story about her mother, whose heart condition prevented her from eating the olives she so much enjoyed. Whenever Julia rinsed the olives to wash away the salt, her mother became angry. Julia thought her mother should have been grateful for her assistance in watching her diet and elongating her life. Julia found it difficult to comprehend the multifaceted nature of the issue. Sometimes, her mother preferred not to be faced with her medical condition, but Julia's stringent dedication did not allow room for her mother's wishes. Julia had trouble seeing facets of herself that threatened the perception of herself as 'the good girl.'

The therapy continued with greater clarification of Julia's internalized image of her mother as she mourned her loss. Julia discovered a warm, strong woman who worked hard to keep her family united. She also recognized that her mother depended on her more than on her sisters. Notwithstanding these realizations, Julia still felt insecure. 'The problem is she died and I don't know if she loved me or not.'

Julia spoke bitterly about her mother's request that Julia remain nearby during her final days. 'Maybe she was worried that my siblings would tire of sitting in that chair all night.' Julia rehashed the rejection by her mother; however, this time she was ready to see their relationship from a new perspective. The therapist suggested that a person on her deathbed would choose somebody close to her to stay by her side. Julia was touched and responded by sharing moving memories of intimate moments shared with her mother prior to her death.

The uncontrolled crying prevalent in prior sessions ceased in the eighth session, with the exception of a few isolated incidents. Occasionally, the therapist asked Julia to express her feelings toward the image of her former lover. Julia reported that she decided to confront him directly with her feelings for the first time: 'You treated me like a toy. You played with me whenever you wanted to and then discarded me when you were done.' He explained to her that his wife's death was very hard on him and he didn't see how her complaints could compare to his devastation. Julia understood that he was consumed by his grief and was dealing with things not connected to her. She respected his mourning and said, 'I'm afraid this is really the end.' At this stage, she began to exhibit signs of increased enjoyment of life and her self-esteem was improving.

In the final stage of therapy, Julia's harsh feelings toward herself were reawakened. She refused to be abandoned by the therapist as she had been abandoned by her mother and her lover. As she worked through the separation, Julia described herself as floating through life with her lover, feeling oblivious to the passage of time. Yet, when the relationship ended, she discovered her chances for marriage were diminished. She was faced with the reality of being childless, having no one to support her in old age. She thought perhaps she was being punished for her sins, however the ability to discuss these difficult feelings enabled her to view herself more completely. She no longer saw herself exclusively in 'good little girl' terms, perceiving herself as a woman with adult desires. She acknowledged her perfectionist tendencies and identified her internal anger and criticism as more than merely a response provoked by others.

Change occurred in Julia's daily life as well. Her father was less demanding and more understanding. Upon his wife's suggestion, her brother spoke with her more often and promised to look after her. Her self-confidence was enhanced by a tempting job offer; she felt accepted in her office and appreciated the praise she received. The presenting symptomatology disappeared and no suicidal ideation was evident. Within the therapy itself, there were flickers of humor and light-heartedness. Julia attributed the apparent recovery in self-image to the initiative she took with her former lover and within her family and to her increased assertiveness at work.

At this stage, the therapist helped Julia see the similarity between her feelings toward the separations from her mother and lover and her feelings toward the upcoming separation from the therapist. Julia felt she could not cope without the therapist and asked if she could return in the future. Likewise, the therapist experienced the difficulties of separation, but felt Julia had benefitted from the therapy and could successfully part from the therapist. At the same time, Julia did not want to be deserted by her lover and continued to link her self-esteem to him: 'I know that if he went back to the way he was before, everything would change, as if I were nothing without him.' Nonetheless, there was a steadily increasing awareness and acceptance of the end of their previous relationship. This awareness was aided by Julia's initiative in their arranging to meet each other, and the consequent lowering of her expectations.

The therapist interpreted Julia's feelings toward the rapidly approaching termination of therapy as a renewal of the question, 'Does mother love me or not?' Julia responded, 'I believe my mother would have loved me,' and added that the therapist had not disappointed her. Nonetheless, 'It hurts to end it. Where else does anybody listen to you like this?' It appeared the internalization of the therapist as a positive object enabled a trilateral separation – from her mother, her lover, and the therapist.

In a follow-up session held six months after the termination of treatment, Julia reported normal functioning and improvements in her mood, although there still remained an element of melancholy. Although the relationship with her lover remained static, she was not excessively preoccupied by thoughts of him. The improvements in Julia's mood and self-esteem remained stable through an additional follow-up session held one year after the termination of therapy.

Discussion

The intensive treatment described above rendered a significant change in a woman unfamiliar with the psychological approach presented by the therapist (see Gorkin 1986). The structural features of the treatment, particularly the fixed time restraint and the central theme, significantly influenced the course of the treatment. The existential feeling that time was slipping away as she approached middle-age was paralleled by Julia's experience in therapy, where the allotted time waned with each session (see Arieti and Bemporad 1978). She successfully utilized the opportunity to work through the separation process while she mourned previously lost opportunities. Furthermore, the similarity between the life events occurring outside of therapy and the processes that unfolded within therapy amplified the effectiveness of Julia's treatment.

Calendric time prevailed over *infantile time* in regard to the inner conflict over how time is experienced. At the same time, Julia's progress in the individuation process bolstered her ability for successful separation. The connection of the central issue to Julia's struggles with unprocessed separations and feelings of rejection expedited the development of the therapeutic alliance and increased the influence of the therapeutic interventions.

The empathic and interpretative therapeutic environment engendered a corrective experience in which Julia felt accepted by the therapist. The central issue, based on Julia's enduring self-concept, was used to dismantle the pain of deeply ingrained emotions and increase her self-esteem. The central issue guided the therapist's interpretations, helping her to elucidate the influence of past events on Julia's current experience and feelings of being undesirable. The juxtaposition of the pain of feeling undesirable opposite the pattern of 'good little girl' behavior revealed in the transference yielded insight into the nature of Julia's relationships with significant others. This insight enabled her to engage in interpersonal relationships from a position of greater maturity and independence.

An additional element of the central issue that led to the success of the treatment derived from Julia's personality structure. The central issue did not specify conflicts with 'significant others,' which, according to Mann, would immediately activate the client's defenses. Julia was raised on strict adherence to the value of 'honor thy parents.' Mann's technique, therefore, bypassed any resistance and put her in direct contact with her most immediate pain. Julia quickly overcame her cultural barriers and independently initiated the analysis of her conflicts with significant others.

Although she sought help for a specific problem, Julia dealt with several separations in therapy. In addition to coping with the separation from her lover, she underwent a renewed and more successful separation from her mother. Julia was able to process her grief and feelings of rejection while incorporating new aspects into the internalized image of her mother. These separations, as well as the separation from the therapist, were achieved through the exploration of Julia's negative feelings toward herself.

Mann called his therapeutic method 'a separation processing laboratory.' The theme of termination and separation that is aroused in the initial stages speeds up the therapeutic process, similar to the final stages of long-term dynamic psychotherapy. In Julia's case, separation was the underlying motif throughout all stages of the therapy. The integration of the central theme into the separation process enabled Julia to break down the negative self-perceptions that formed the crux of her depression.

Chapter 8

Overcoming helplessness

The integration of letter writing into time-limited psychotherapy

One of the four basic universal conflicts outlined by Mann (1973, Mann and Goldman 1982) is the conflict surrounding unprocessed bereavement. In these cases, the strength of time-limited psychotherapy (TLP) lies in the creation of a context for processing separation issues that integrates the task of coping with a new situation involving loss (of the therapist) with the feeling that time is running out. The treatment presented in this chapter was initially headed in another direction. As the termination and time issues became the more salient features, however, the focal point was refined, and the impact of the treatment increased substantially.

Identifying features and presenting complaint

Isaac was a 34-year-old single man who worked in a building supply store and lived alone. He presented with feelings of confusion and helplessness regarding his identity and his future.

Personal history

A native-born Israeli, Isaac was the sixth of seven children. He described his home as filled with warmth and caring. His father worked for a construction company and was often away from home on business, while his mother ran the household. He characterized his mother as nurturing, but also emotional and over-protective. Isaac attributed his mother's pampering of him to the large age gap between the sister born before him and his younger sister.

At the age of 14, Isaac was sent to a nearby boarding school, an event he recalls as one of the most difficult in his life. He had trouble adjusting to the fact that he was 'ousted' from his home and sent to a strange place amidst unfamiliar conditions. He longed to return home, especially because he was shy and did not form new friendships easily. He persevered, and completed his studies at the boarding school with a partial matriculation certificate.

At the age of 18, Isaac was drafted into the army and chose to serve in the Machal framework, on a kibbutz. He fitted in well on the kibbutz, and even developed a deep emotional relationship with a young woman he met there. Throughout the relationship, Isaac constantly 'tested' his girlfriend and after a few months, the relationship ended as a result of one of the many tests.

After completing his army service, Isaac began a university preparatory course. He nostalgically recalled that period as 'the golden era of my life,' a period in which he worked, studied, and was well-liked by his peers. He became involved romantically with a domineering woman, with whom he lived for nearly two years. He was very attracted to her self-confidence and decisiveness. Upon completion of the preparatory course, Isaac was not accepted to study Economics, his first-choice field. Instead, he completed a bachelor's degree in Sociology.

The relationship with his girlfriend began to head downhill and they decided to go their separate ways during an extended holiday in the United States. Two months into their trip, his girlfriend returned to Israel, but Isaac remained in the US. Shortly thereafter, however, he was notified that his father had died suddenly, and he returned to Israel immediately. Isaac moved back in with his girlfriend and found it very difficult to separate from her. Approximately two months before beginning therapy, he had ended the relationship and moved out.

Isaac was accepted for TLP. Although twelve sessions were scheduled, he 'forgot' the tenth session. Therefore, the treatment consisted of only eleven sessions.

Course of treatment

In contrast to Mann's theoretical construct, the initial stage of treatment was not characterized by a 'honeymoon' phase. Rather, the early sessions were full of sorrow and confusion. Isaac focused primarily on his recently ended relationship and difficulties in separating from his family, especially his mother. The sessions also centered on Isaac's commitment difficulties and fears of not living up to his commitments and proving himself a disappointment. The therapist had difficulty formulating the following central issue, which was not presented to Isaac until the third session:

> Despite your achievements, whenever you are faced with a separation from the past in which you must reach a decision involving issues of independence and commitment, in addition to meeting others' expectations, you fear failure, feel trapped and helpless, and flee.

The central issue expressed the chronic pain of feeling that he never did things as well as he should. Even when Isaac succeeded, he found little value in his success. The presentation of the central issue elicited an emotional response from Isaac. He began to explore the difficulties with his family and his romantic relationships in terms of the central issue. He spoke about recurrent themes in his romantic relationships, which the therapist interpreted along the lines of the central issue. Isaac repeatedly became involved in dependent relationships with dominant women who pursued him. He responded to their pursuits and consistently became the passive partner in the relationship. Although Isaac found the relationships satisfying at their onset, problems inevitably arose.

Isaac described the problems in his recent two-year relationship. He and the therapist pinpointed the beginning of the troubles to immediately after Isaac and his girlfriend decided to marry, when he felt his girlfriend became more demanding. The therapist wondered whether Isaac was reminded of any other demanding figures in his life with whom he had problems. Isaac linked the problems with his girlfriend to his relationship with his mother. The therapist's interpretation compared Isaac's relationships with parental figures to other significant relationships in his life. Isaac took the interpretation further, focusing upon his difficulties in coping with separation from various significant figures. He painfully spoke about his separation difficulties and about his feelings of low self-worth subsequent to a separation.

At this stage, rather than offer an interpretation, the therapist asked Isaac to re-read the central issue and look for parallels in recent life events. As a result, one of Isaac's greatest fears was revealed. He feared that a permanent relationship with a woman (such as marriage) would force him to relinquish his family ties. The issue of the dependent relationship with his mother came up again. This time, however, Isaac responded with greater force and awareness of the dependence-independence conflict: his mother tried to pull him back into 'the nest' while he tried to avoid being pulled back, yet felt horribly guilty. This realization elucidated an additional fact that ultimately shifted the focus of the treatment.

Isaac's mother had suffered from physical ailments throughout the years, whereas his father remained always the strong, healthy parent. As mentioned above, his father had died very suddenly while Isaac was traveling overseas. When he spoke of his father, he expressed tremendous sadness. Despite the therapist's feeling that the selected focus was appropriate, he felt Isaac growing distant toward the conclusion of the third session. Isaac was restrained and had great difficulty expressing his feelings, as if he were on the verge of an emotional breakthrough. The therapist searched for a passage into these feelings, observing that the instances of emotional arousal occurred only when Isaac spoke about his father. The therapist concluded that he must relate to Isaac's separation from his father, otherwise the therapy would not progress. Therefore, the therapist suggested Isaac write his father a goodbye letter.

Van der Hart (1983, 1987) and Bergman and Witzum (1987) have described the technique of using separation rituals and letter writing in therapy, especially in cases of loss and bereavement. There are two different techniques. In one, the client writes an ongoing letter. In the second, the client writes a single letter to a significant figure who cannot be contacted directly, such as a deceased person. The letter-writing process serves as a separation ritual.

In Isaac's case, the intention was to write a single letter in which he would tell his father what had happened to him and separate from him. The request aroused strong resistance on Isaac's part. He insisted that the idea could not be implemented because the pain was too great to put into writing. Furthermore, his father was already gone and there was no point in writing to him. The therapist asked Isaac not to reject the idea outright but to contemplate the possibility of writing the letter.

The treatment trudged along until the sixth session. Isaac arrived very late to the session, appearing exhausted and completely worn out. With great fervor, he told the therapist that he had barely slept the previous night. In a flurry of emotion, he had written a letter to his father. While writing the letter, he felt tremendous anxiety that perhaps his mother would pass away as well. As he wrote the letter, he recalled many things he had been unable to remember since he had returned to Israel upon notification of his father's death. The newly recalled memories revolved around that horrible day. Throughout the journey from the airport to his parent's home he held back his tears because he had been told that he needed to be strong and balanced for his mother who had completely broken down. All his energy was invested in maintaining his composure in front of his mother. Only afterward, he went outside and burst into tears in seclusion. Since that day he had not allowed himself to cry, until he wrote the letter to his father. The emotional breakthrough enabled Isaac to recall many forgotten events and experiences.

Although he finally experienced the pain and despair he had avoided for so long, Isaac felt extremely relieved to have completed the letter and handed it over to the therapist. In the letter, Isaac told his father of the pain he was experiencing and expressed how much he missed him. He complained of the foreshortened time. He wished he could go backward and spend more time with his parents, bringing them joy by inviting them to his university graduation ceremony. The letter revealed that Isaac related to his father and to the issue of time in a childlike manner.

As the letter continued, Isaac yearned for the last day he spent with his father before his trip overseas, the last memory of his father. He described the mixed emotions he experienced after receiving the sad news of his father's death and the empty space that was created by the loss. He expressed confusion, shock, and anger. Isaac explained that his father left behind a broken family, especially his mother who was going through an acute crisis from which she was unable to recover. His mother's behavior caused Isaac to feel guilty. He could not meet her expectations that he support her and move back home after his father's death. Isaac apologized to his father, but declared himself incapable of fulfilling this function. In the letter he asked his father to legitimize the desire to be released from his mother's dependence upon him. Isaac felt torn between his family duty and the need for self-actualization and independence. As a result, he was left 'neither here nor there; drifting between worlds.' He felt helpless, under constant duress.

For the first time, Isaac remarked upon an unexpected phone conversation he'd had with his father, ten hours before his sudden death. It seemed Isaac's father had some sort of premonition. Even though his father had never called him before, this time he did. The conversation lasted about twenty minutes and Isaac mentioned it several times throughout the letter. The letter concluded with a description of the phone call that turned out to be a farewell call, however, Isaac 'just didn't know it' at the time.

The letter raised again the central issue themes. Isaac requested his father's permission to leave home and become independent. Empirical studies have demonstrated that when a separation conflict is not specified in the central issue, separation always serves as a secondary focus that arises as the treatment enters its final stage and the termination is imminent. The descriptive, emotional, and cathartic components of Isaac's letter each contained contrasting time constructs. Like a child, Isaac hoped his father would live forever. At the same time, the letter contained the mature, albeit disappointing, realization that the time with his father was limited and had ended. Isaac's letter exemplified the encounter of the two time concepts. Because the termination date is predetermined, the TLP process represents realistic calendric time. According to Mann, the curative power of TLP relies heavily on the parallel process. In this case, the letter-writing technique facilitated both direct and indirect processing of Isaac's separation from his father. In the following session, Isaac read the letter in a heartfelt manner. In the third stage of treatment, however, the letter was not discussed. The therapist interpreted Isaac's final telephone conversation with his father as a goodbye present.

The letter represented a turning point in the therapy. It was followed by a series of changes in Isaac's life. Having 'revived' his capacity for emotional expression, Isaac permitted himself to express negative emotions and to become more assertive. For the first time, he was able to feel empathy toward his mother. To his surprise, the newfound empathy enabled him to refuse her without feeling guilty. Furthermore, Isaac understood the extent to which his father's death had shattered the entire family. In particular, one of his brothers reacted especially strongly, developing a clinical depression. Isaac supported his brother by visiting him and encouraging him. Isaac took on a leadership role in the family. He asserted himself with his mother, establishing boundaries in their relationship without feeling guilty. For example, he delegated the responsibility of being the sibling representative in visiting his mother, a role that he despised, to one of his brothers.

In the second stage of treatment (sessions seven through nine), Isaac and the therapist revisited the central issue, refining it in light of the letter. Isaac complained of the difficulty in meeting others' expectations of him, particularly his mother's expectations. He focused on the struggle between his desire for self-actualization and the disappointment he felt when he failed. He felt a change had begun, and now he was capable of greater self-actualization. Shortly thereafter, he found a new romantic interest whom he actively pursued. Once the therapist interpreted the difference between his new relationship and previous ones, Isaac 'noticed' that this time the basic structure of the relationship differed from his usual pattern. Even when the relationship did not proceed as he had hoped, he did not respond by feeling disappointed and rejected. Instead, he kept looking and found another romantic interest. Again, he took the initiative, feeling less sensitive to the risk that she might reject him or that he would disappoint her.

Despite the problems involved and the internal resistance interpreted by the therapist as separation difficulty, Isaac went to his parents' home during the holiday season. He finally explained to his mother that although she was very dear to him, he had a life of his own. He took the opportunity to visit his father's grave site for the first time since his death. This was an extremely difficult experience; his tears expressed the pain he felt. Isaac did not attend the tenth session, explaining that he 'couldn't wake up in the morning.'

The final two sessions dealt with the imminent termination and separation from therapy. During that period, Isaac celebrated his first birthday since losing his father. It was a very sad day of soul-searching. Everything seemed so different to him and he felt time was flying by too quickly. Isaac was angry at the unfairness and the therapist's insensitivity in terminating the treatment just when he was beginning to progress more rapidly. He expected the therapist to grant him special consideration and extend the duration of the therapy in light of all that he had been through.

The therapist acknowledged Isaac's anger and the injustice of the arbitrary time limit, leading Isaac to discuss the ongoing separation from his father. He described the experience of attending the synagogue where his father used to pray during the holiday season. Although it was very difficult for him to attend the synagogue knowing his father would never pray there again, Isaac forced himself to go. He complained again of confusion and a feeling of emptiness. In therapy, he expressed signs of anger at the therapist who insisted on terminating the treatment as scheduled. The therapist interpreted the anger, sadness, and emptiness in terms of the impending separation.

The final session focused primarily on Isaac's fears of losing the therapist and being on his own again. The therapist expressed his confidence in Isaac's ability to successfully continue the work they had begun. Isaac reported that he dreamed of his father less often. He was beginning to feel that he missed his father more and was less angry at him. The therapist attributed the change to the anger and resentment Isaac expressed in therapy toward the therapist and toward the termination.

In summary, Isaac was a young man struggling with the conflict of dependence versus independence, particularly in the realm of separating from his parents. The first stage of therapy uncovered issues surrounding the unprocessed bereavement over the sudden loss of his father. Although it initially seemed to be a parameter superimposed upon the treatment, the letter-writing technique facilitated Isaac's separation from his father, which ultimately sharpened the therapeutic focus and elicited an emotional catharsis. The TLP separation process bound by predetermined time constraints paralleled Isaac's return to childish time in relation to his father. The result was a highly effective and meaningful treatment process.

First follow-up: post-waiting period and pre-treatment

Isaac's general state was poor. He felt tense, irritable, and confused. He had broken up with his girlfriend because he could no longer bear being in a 'relationless' relationship. Even though he felt very lonely in the relationship, he feared the break-up itself. He could not tolerate being alone. Nonetheless, he reported no urge to work the situation out with his girlfriend, nor was he immediately drawn toward picking up other women or becoming involved in casual relationships. He had registered for a Masters in Administrative Management at university and worked in a job related to the family business. Although Isaac did not enjoy his job, he felt secure in it. He kept in touch with his friends, but did not see them often. The intense relationship with his mother remained static and Isaac felt unable to alter his behavior. He felt obligated to take care of her, even though the obligation troubled him. He was not sure what he expected or wanted from his relationship with her.

Second follow-up: one week post-termination

In Isaac's words, 'I've changed tremendously.' In regard to the presenting symptomatology, he both appeared and reported that he felt much calmer and no longer confused. His daily functioning had improved. 'I've gotten over my father's death a bit. Today, I see things from a different angle. I understand better what happened to me. In therapy, I separated from my father.' Isaac was involved in a generally stable romantic relationship, in which he and his partner occasionally discussed the possibility of marriage. He had made no occupational changes and still felt dissatisfied working in the family business. Nonetheless, he did not dare alter the situation. Unfortunately, the Master's program to which he had applied was closed for the following year. Therefore, Isaac had no plans to continue his education. His relationship with his mother had become more balanced and he felt released from the burden of obligation. He saw her less often, yet maintained frequent telephone contact with her. Isaac attributed his transition from one life stage to the next to the increased self-understanding he achieved in therapy.

Third follow-up: six months post-termination

Isaac was pleased to announce his impending marriage. Although he felt overwhelmed by existential problems, he felt able to cope with them. He was troubled by concerns regarding the quality of the relationship with his bride-to-be. He felt she doted on him more than he doted on her. He did not think it was entirely acceptable if he did not feel completely dedicated to her. The matter troubled him only to a certain extent, however, because he viewed the situation as the way to avoid future pain. Despite his dissatisfaction, Isaac had not changed jobs, wavering between the ease and security of working among family and his desire for independence. He reported the development of satisfying new friendships. The relationship with his mother remained reasonable and he was happy to report his mother's acceptance of his fiancée.

Fourth follow-up: one year post-termination

Isaac's wedding took place a few months prior to the follow-up session. He felt happy and content in his marriage. He was preoccupied with purchasing an apartment, a mortgage, and debts. He appeared to handle the new challenges effectively. He decided to leave the family business and had already informed his family that he intended to open his own business. He felt qualified to start a business, but lacked the funding. Isaac regretfully reported that continuing his education was not on the horizon. He believed he could not realize his desire to study, especially as he sank more deeply into home and family commitments. On a practical level, he seemed to have come to terms with the thought of not pursuing further education as he had previously planned. Isaac felt happy when he thought about the children he would eventually have, yet he worried about the additional financial burden. His relationship with his mother appeared balanced; he was able to relate to her without overdoing it or holding back too much. Periodically, he thought about therapy, remembering it as a pleasant source of support, contemplation, and understanding. 'Sometimes, I really miss it.'

Discussion

The experience of helplessness in separateness and separation can be a paralyzing one. Isaac experienced this paralysis in the difficult combination of separating from his girlfriend who went abroad and the proximity of the loss of his father. The sudden circumstances of his father's death and their final telephone conversation dramatically increased the sense of helplessness linked to separation and death.

For years, Isaac carried around the feeling that he could not separate, that he was incapable of separation. The sense of helplessness and the consequent paralysis when coping with separation is an overwhelming, incapacitating feeling. It lay at the base of Isaac's sadness and of his search for a path in life that led him to seek therapy.

He was a young man who possessed a reasonable amount of psychological mindedness. He was neither overly absorbed nor preoccupied with understanding himself and his motives, yet he did show an ability for symbolization and abstract thought regarding himself. He was self-aware, in touch with his emotions, and capable of maintaining a long-term interpersonal relationship, as ascertained from his life story and reflected in the development of a relationship with the therapist. He functioned reasonably well. His motivation for change was strong and he sought therapy out of a desire to change things within himself. Isaac was a patient who did not exhibit any contraindications to TLP.

The culture in which he was raised heavily emphasizes doing rather than being, and as such, Isaac felt more connected to the concrete dimensions of doing. In therapy, the therapist, who formulated a central issue concerned with separation as an act of independence, rapidly encountered the impact of the grief over his father's death. This tragic event would have lead to a measure of independence but for the difficulty Isaac experienced in coping with the event and its implications. In extensive therapy, there would have been room for exploration and processing of the influence of the transference emotions that Isaac developed toward the therapist, a figure who possessed markedly authoritative and charismatic traits. The fact that Isaac began to withdraw emotionally from the therapist subsequent to his positive response to the central issue indicates the unmistakable transference element within their relationship. The therapist opted to handle Isaac's state of disconnection and distancing from him by taking action. Though it may have appeared paradoxical, this action in essence demonstrated an unambiguous and empathic perception of Isaac's abilities and tendencies. The therapist picked up on the fact that Isaac would do well to work in therapy by means of active coping with a defined task. He proposed letter writing, a technical parameter well aimed at Isaac's feeling of helplessness. The therapeutic messages contained within the instruction to write a letter were that there is a way out, there is a direction. Isaac fully comprehended this instruction and responded to it. Along with the emotional contents contained within the goodbye letter to his father, Isaac encountered his ability for doing, his ability to cope.

In his book on psychotherapy rituals, Van der Hart (1983) emphasized the important nonverbal, mediating role of various rituals, among them letter writing. Bergman and Witztum (1987) and Witztum and Roman (2000) highlighted the curative cathartic effects in psychotherapy of writing letters to significant figures. Letter writing provides a catalyst for therapeutic processes. Indeed, from that point on, Isaac's therapy was conducted in accordance with the classic TLP formula, the processing of contents related to the central issue accompanied by powerful emotional strength. The feelings linked to separation, anger, fear, and grievance, were transferred to the therapist in an intensive experience, against the backdrop of Isaac's unwillingness to accept the time limitation of the treatment. These emotions were processed through holding, acceptance, and empathy on the part of the therapist, concurrent with a clear stand on the time framework. This was an unequivocal declaration of the therapist's faith in Isaac's ability to cope with this separation, leading Isaac along a secure path toward independence.

Isaac's treatment was conducted within the framework of the research project described in Chapter 11 of this book. He belonged to the waiting list group and, consequently, had to wait three months between the assessment process and the start of therapy. At the end of the waiting period, Isaac underwent a second assessment process, during which his state had visibly slightly worsened as a result of waiting. He had tried to function in new directions, though unsuccessfully. This fact had significance on its own. We learn quite blatantly that the passage of time does nothing. Despite Isaac's desire for change, despite the motivation for change initiated through his request for therapy and the implementation of the assessment process, which can in effect boost the beginning of change, certain types of changes apparently cannot take place without therapy.

The struggles subsequent to the termination of therapy indicated a continuation of the grounding of the achievements attained during therapy. In addition to the absence of symptoms, the meaningful experiences accumulated during therapy continued to impact upon Isaac after completion. We observed the bolstering of the developmental path toward independence in various areas: the establishment of an appropriately distant relationship with his mother, leaving the family business, meeting a woman who eventually became his wife, with whom he had a positive feeling of partnership. The opportunity to witness Isaac's continuing development subsequent to the termination of therapy strengthened the sense that therapy was an intensive, yet limited, intervention in the course of the development of Isaac's life that enabled him to remove an obstacle and continue along his developmental path.

Chapter 9

Low self-esteem

Working through separation processes in both patient and therapist

When reality dictates the necessity for highly focused short-term psychotherapies, coping with the time constraints and the intensified separation process is often no less complicated or distressing for the therapist than these elements of the treatment are for the client. The following case study utilizes the interpretation of a dream to illustrate the emotional experience of a therapist who was simultaneously drawn toward conducting a new therapy method (TLP) and challenged by some of the treatment's defining components and limitations.

Identifying features

Anat, a 51-year-old woman of Persian origin, was the mother of three sons, aged 14, 25, and 26. She was separated from her husband and worked as a high-school teacher.

Presenting complaints

Anat sought therapy on her own initiative one year after her estranged husband filed for divorce. She presented with complaints of internal tension, anxiety, reduced concentration, depressed mood, and sleep difficulties, in addition to feelings of hopelessness and insecurity. A psychiatrist present at the first intake session offered Anat medication to alleviate her distress, which she declined. She requested psychotherapy instead.

Personal history

The youngest of three children, Anat was 5 years old when her family immigrated to Israel. For reasons unclear to her, upon the family's arrival in Israel, she was placed with a foster family for several months. She recalled this traumatic separation from her family as her earliest memory.

Anat's mother barely spoke Hebrew and suffered tremendous difficulty in acclimatizing to her new environment. Anat described her mother as preoccupied with her numerous somatic complaints. As a result, Anat took on the parental role in the mother-daughter dyad. Her mother died fifteen years prior to Anat's therapy. Anat's father, formerly a merchant in Persia, worked in Israel as a bank clerk. He spoke Hebrew and was the dominant figure in the family. He treasured his wife, and had difficulty adjusting to life without her. He passed away five years after Anat's mother. Throughout treatment, Anat frequently lamented the loss of her parents.

Anat remembered her childhood as happy and filled with friends. She recalled, 'They told me I was a pretty girl.' She was a good student, well liked by teachers and peers. When her elementary school principal transferred to an agricultural high school with boarding, he encouraged Anat's educational advancement by offering her admission to the school. She completed her high-school studies with distinction. Although she described the experience as 'nice,' Anat also recalled feeling very homesick. She visited her parents once a month, like clockwork. After high school, Anat served in the army as a soldier-teacher. When she completed her service she attended a pedagogical seminary and married Moshe. Throughout the treatment, she alternated between referring to him by name and referring to him as 'my husband.'

During their twenty years of marriage, Anat's love for Moshe had grown strong. He came from a family of financially stable proprietors who were of European descent. Moshe's family owned a business in the food industry and he held a university degree in political science. He worked for the Foreign Ministry and often brought home overseas guests whom Anat hosted. She worked as a teacher, helped with her in-laws' business, and took care of the children. She complied with Moshe's often exaggerated sexual demands, traveled with him overseas for work, and moved to a new house for his comfort. Despite Anat's tireless efforts to accommodate his needs, Moshe's attitude toward her was cold and sometimes aggressive, even physically abusive.

Ten years prior to therapy (after twenty years of marriage), Moshe left Anat and moved to another city with his mistress whom he had met two years before through work. Anat described Moshe's mistress as a sensual woman. She was ten years older than Moshe (fifteen years older than Anat) and was married with adult children.

Because she was unable to handle their separation and the drastic change, Anat refused to grant Moshe a divorce. According to her, he had left suddenly and there had been no contact between them since. Nonetheless, she still wore her wedding band. Anat remained at home with their three children, who at the time were 4, 15, and 16 years old. Their two elder sons harbored much resentment toward Moshe, whom they remembered as detached and aggressive. They refused to see their father because he was unwilling to see them outside of his new companion's presence. Therefore, Moshe only maintained contact with their youngest son.

For the ten years since she and Moshe had separated, Anat supported herself and her children without alimony or child support. She worked two jobs and tutored privately in order to maintain a reasonable standard of living for her children. In addition, she took care of her mother-in-law, who lived nearby. One year prior to therapy, Anat's mother-in-law died and Moshe pressed charges for divorce and the division of their shared property.

In addition to the historical chronicles she provided in the three intake sessions, Anat also described great pain and suffering. Her desire to please others led her to feel simultaneously taken advantage of, yet guilty. Furthermore, she was aware that she experienced difficulty in expressing negative emotions. Anat hoped the therapy would help her acquire tools for coping with her current situation, which she considered 'a complete disaster.'

Course of treatment

The intake sessions indicated that Anat was an intelligent woman who possessed ego strengths and functioned well at work and at home. Nonetheless, she needed constant outside assurance of her self-worth. As a result of her low self-esteem, Anat was constantly in motion. She was so involved with 'doing' that she never let herself just 'be' for a moment. The intake sessions were packed with tears and emotion. She painfully voiced her belief that if she had behaved differently 'none of this would have happened.'

The therapeutic alliance and positive transference developed rapidly. The therapist noticed that Anat avoided using the term 'to separate.' The therapist sensed Anat's reluctance to relate to the prospect of eventual separation, as if it were a concept that would not be relevant to them. Thus, the therapist noted the importance of confronting Anat with the notion of separation within the therapeutic context. In addition, Anat did not wear a watch. She wanted to remain oblivious to the time limitations, consequently never having to face the inevitable separation. (Mann's concept of infantile time includes ignoring the reality-based meaning of time. The most basic form of this is ignoring the quantitative aspect of time.)

At the conclusion of the assessment process, there was some doubt whether TLP was the treatment of choice for Anat. Despite the ten years of physical separation, Anat had not cut the emotional ties to her estranged husband. Therefore, it was unclear whether she would benefit from a treatment that hinges on the processing of separation anxiety. TLP was positively indicated by Anat's strong motivation for change, her level of intelligence, a history of meaningful relationships, her ability to quickly establish a connection with the intake interviewer, and her capacity for emotional expression.

Anat and the therapist scheduled twelve weekly treatment sessions. By determining the termination date at the outset, they laid the structural foundation for the entire treatment. The following central issue was presented in the fourth session (the first of the twelve treatment sessions):

> You're always doing something. Even though you've torn yourself to shreds for everyone else, you've never acknowledged your efforts. You've tied up so much of your energy in trying to gain esteem from others that you wind up feeling sad and alone.

Anat listened intently to the central issue, concentrating on comprehending its full meaning. The presentation of the central issue communicated the therapist's sincere empathy with Anat's chronic pain, enabling Anat to experience intimate contact with an understanding 'other.' At the conclusion of the session, Anat remarked that for the first time she had not cried during the session. She also reported sleep improvements and an overall improved state of well-being. Anat's positive feedback and optimism continued throughout the first four treatment sessions, signaling that she was in the 'honeymoon phase' of therapy.

Anat began the second treatment session with an attempt to better understand the central issue. She behaved like an obedient student striving to complete an assignment successfully. The emphasis quickly shifted to her fears concerning a court hearing scheduled for the following week. She was afraid of feeling paralyzed, virtually non-existent, when she faced Moshe. Anat tearfully re-experienced the degradation of her mother-in-law's belief that Moshe could have done better than Anat. Throughout the therapy, Anat described an endless trail of attempts to win the esteem of Moshe and his family.

As the session continued, Anat referred to her separation difficulties, but avoided using the word separation. When the therapist remarked on the avoidance, Anat concurred with the therapist's observation, illustrating the point with several examples. Since Moshe left, the only change Anat had made in the bedroom was sleeping on 'his' side of the bed. Even his work clothes were still hanging in her bedroom closet. Anat bred birds in her house. She revealed a habit she had of repeatedly checking on them. Returning to the central issue, the therapist interpreted Anat's fear that they would die if she did not check them constantly. She behaved as if she could maintain control and prevent loss by being permanently engaged in activity, such as tearing herself apart for the birds.

Anat concluded the session by recounting a recent dream. In the dream, she bumped into Moshe in the courthouse. Suddenly, everything fell into place and they made peace with each other as a result of the encounter. Anat accepted the therapist's interpretation: 'You still hope you won't have to separate from Moshe.'

By the fourth session, Anat appeared more relaxed. She reported a general improvement in her emotional state. She was sleeping more peacefully, in contrast to years spent feeling exhausted by her dreams. One of the most vivid dreams occurred the year before Moshe moved out (eleven years prior to treatment!). In the dream, Moshe informed her of his decision to leave. She was terrified by both the dream and the manifestation of the dream in reality. Anat had felt Moshe's withdrawal and fortified her efforts. She put all her energy into housework, the children, and her in-laws' business, but to no avail. She still endured the chronic pain of not gaining the appreciation for which she yearned.

The therapist relied upon the central issue to interpret Anat's behavior as an effort to gain the self-esteem she lacked by investing herself in others. Gradually, Anat began to internalize the therapist's message and started dedicating more of her energy to herself. Anat showed rudimentary signs of cutting her emotional ties to Moshe. The therapist associated Anat's burgeoning capacity for separation with the impending separation between herself and the therapist.

Anat responded by providing an 'overview' of the 'honeymoon phase' of their relationship. Even though she cried often, Anat felt the therapy provided a tremendous feeling of relief. She was learning to express herself and to take care of herself for the first time in her life. Additionally, she reported improved relations with her children. At this juncture, the therapist presented the flip side of the central issue: the combination of investing energy in herself and feeling more content in her relationships with others produced greater satisfaction.

Anat validated the interpretation by further exploring her attempts to avoid fully separating from Moshe. By giving of herself, she tried to recruit help from Moshe's family in realizing her hope for the relationship to work out. As usual, her efforts went unrewarded. Anat started reframing her perception of the situation. She realized Moshe did not leave because she had not been good enough or did not do enough for him. Instead, his departure was motivated by his need for an older, more mature woman. Adopting a supportive stance, the therapist showed Anat that she could separate from Moshe by attributing to him the responsibility for his actions. She could separate even further by taking responsibility for elevating her own sense of self-esteem.

Unlike the previous sessions to which she always arrived fifteen minutes early, Anat arrived late to the fifth session. The therapist understood the late arrival as an expression of Anat's need for control and fear of becoming dependent upon the therapy. For several consecutive nights, Anat had been awakened by dreams that left her feeling frightened and shaken. On the basis of the two most vividly remembered dreams, she tried to understand the dreams' deeper meaning. In the first dream, she saw Moshe with a large, open wound on his leg. Anat cleaned up the oozing blood and bandaged the wound. 'The other woman' stood nearby, just watching. Anat was still the one who nursed Moshe's wounds, even though he had left her. In the second dream, Moshe's sister was injured. Similar to the first dream, Anat nursed her sister-in-law's wounds.

Anat and the therapist interpreted the dreams on several levels. First, they examined the element of projective identification in the dreams: Anat's wish for Moshe and his sister to nurse her raw emotional wounds. An alternative understanding of the dream focused upon its overt meaning: in essence, the central issue. That is, the objects in Anat's environment who demanded she nurture them in order for her to feel valuable. This interpretation unlocked memories of Anat's overzealous dedication to Moshe's parents, providing for their most basic needs when they were very ill. As the session progressed, Anat was able to analyze her behavior patterns and the consequent pain. She re-experienced the feeling of inferiority engendered by the self-deprecating comparison she often made between her Persian, working-class family and Moshe's European, well-established family. This time however, she understood that she tried to cope with the feeling of inferiority through servitude to his family.

In anticipation of an upcoming court session, Anat claimed to feel more self-confident and less overwhelmed by her fears. Although she was still emotionally attached to Moshe, she was able to address her separation anxiety. It was particularly difficult for Anat, however, to acknowledge any emotional projection of that separation anxiety on to the imminent therapy termination. The therapist raised the issue by linking Anat's general feelings toward separation to her ultimate separation from the therapist. Anat admitted it would be difficult, commenting on the empty space that would be left inside: 'the time is short, but must suffice . . .'

Anat expressed the ambivalence typically seen in the middle stage of TLP semantically, emotionally, and behaviorally. The idyllic feeling of the initial stage diminished as it dawned upon her that the treatment had passed its middle point and was rapidly approaching its conclusion. The return of the presenting symptomatology provided one indication of Anat's ambivalence.

Anat further expressed her ambivalence when she phoned to reschedule the next session by telephone, after a time conflict arose between the session and a work seminar. She felt very disappointed by the therapist's refusal to change the session. Nonetheless, Anat decided to miss the seminar and attended her therapy session instead. In the session, she first focused on the positive aspect of being forced to make a decision. She construed her decision as evidence of her ability to choose independently, without being concerned with pleasing her boss and consequently missing her therapy session. Conversely, the enforced choice between therapy and the seminar prompted Anat's comment upon the rigidity and arbitrary nature of institutional judgments (e.g. Moshe or the legal system). She voiced her resentment at being stripped of control, 'It really tears me up inside.' Noting Anat's despondence, the therapist suggested that even though Anat was pleased with the outcome of her decision, she still experienced the therapist's adherence to the preset time schedule as arbitrary and rigid.

In the following session, Anat still appeared tense and melancholy. At first, she avoided displaying overt disappointment with the therapist by speaking about the rigidity of others. As the session continued, however, the therapist intervened and encouraged Anat to voice her anger. She burst into tears and cried, 'This really isn't working for me. Everything's turning bad again. I'm tense and worried, and I don't know where this is heading and what the final solution will be . . .'

The therapist encouraged Anat to clarify the essence of 'the final solution,' as she understood it. Anat explained her desire to maintain the status quo, but Moshe would not allow it. Instead, he filed for divorce. Each court session forced Anat to face the legal ramifications, emphasizing the finality of the separation from Moshe. With the therapist's help, Anat discovered that she equated the separation from Moshe, 'the final solution,' with death. Anat began to express her anger toward Moshe and toward her guilt-ridden belief that he left her because she was not good enough for him. The therapist emphasized the similarity between Anat's feeling toward Moshe and her feeling toward the therapist when she refused to reschedule the previous session.

The uncovering of Anat's ambivalence and the consequent burst of anger created a heavy, almost oppressive atmosphere. The eighth therapy session was marked by a break in the crying that had typified the previous sessions. Appearing troubled, Anat described a conflict with her eldest son. Her son had brought up the hardships he experienced when his father moved out, causing Anat to feel guilty and blame herself. The therapist 'explained' Anat's feelings by returning to the central issue, transforming Anat's downtrodden facial expression into a stupefied smile of relief.

At this point, the therapist reiterated Anat's lack of attention to the impending therapy termination. In response, Anat revealed that she had checked her daily planner, so she knew how many sessions remained. She was afraid of how she would handle the empty space that would be left inside. She recalled several significant separations in her life. She described a strong need to say goodbye to her mother after her wedding. Anat kissed her mother and hugged her tightly so she could feel her warmth. She also recalled holding her mother close for half an hour after she died, refusing to let her go. She immediately followed up a description of her father's death with a description of Moshe's dramatic departure from their home. He threw away his wedding ring and left the country.

Toward the end of the session, Anat approached the issue of separation from another angle. Her work supervisor suggested she continue higher level studies and attend a seminar. Anat perceived these studies as a means of nurturing herself, in an attempt to feel worthy. She hoped her own educational advancement would help her cope better with the separation from Moshe.

The separation issue weighed heavily on both Anat and the therapist. In her supervision sessions, the therapist was herself struggling with the pain of separation and the guilt of abandonment, elicited by the imminent separation from Anat.

Anat commenced the ninth session with a description of her emotional and financial struggles. She expressed her fear of not providing sufficiently for her children. She knew that giving to them affirmed her existence to herself (as stated in the central issue). She went on to describe several movies about battered women she had recently seen. She identified with those women because she considered herself emotionally abused. She immediately qualified her statement by limiting it to the past, stating that today she felt and behaved differently. She was in a different emotional place than she had been prior to therapy.

Finally, she spoke about the pressure of the time limit and the feeling of not managing to accomplish everything she wanted and needed. She was very conscious of the waning time left in therapy, feeling unsure how she would get by without it. She felt very alone and lamented the inner emptiness. The therapist's interpretation reiterated the central issue: 'It's the same old story. Now matter how much you do, you wind up alone . . .'

In the tenth session, Anat was anxious about the upcoming division of property between her and Moshe, scheduled for that week. She couldn't bear the thought of selling her house and splitting the money with Moshe. When Anat referred to the arbitrary nature of the court's decisions, the therapist wondered aloud if Anat also felt the termination of their relationship was arbitrary. Anat replied, 'No, you aren't tearing it out of my hands.' The therapist connected the tearing imagery to the ritual tearing of garments by Jewish mourners. Anat confessed her reluctance to count how many therapy sessions remained in her daily planner. She added that the weekly sessions provided nourishment that sustained her for the rest of the week.

The eleventh session was held after the dreaded court hearing. Anat felt crushed by the judge's ruling that she and Moshe must sell the house and split the money between them. She was furious with Moshe and bitterly disappointed by the cruelty revealed in his desire to tear her out of her home (again, the use of the tearing motif in the context of loss and mourning). The therapist interpreted Anat's angry feelings in terms of her imminent separation from the therapist. Anat rejected the interpretation, insisting that the therapy helped her and she did not see any reason to be angry. When asked how many sessions remained, Anat said she did not remember, perhaps four. She had written the termination date in her daily planner, but did not want to look at it. She was shocked when the therapist informed her that only one session remained. A silence fell over the room. Once Anat regained her composure, she conducted a quasi-summary of the treatment.

Anat's apparent difficulty in facing the impending separation magnified the therapist's own fears and uncertainties regarding the termination. She seriously doubted her ability to abandon Anat just when she was being forced out of her house. The therapist discussed her ambivalence toward the termination with her supervision group. That night she dreamed the following dream: it revolved around an arranged marriage and was set in a large room. A respected Jerusalem rabbi was drawing up a marriage contract between the therapist and an unknown man dressed in the traditional black garb of ultra-orthodox Jews. The therapist and the groom sat next to the rabbi at a wide table, even though they did not know each other. While the rabbi wrote up the agreement, he told the therapist what a worthwhile match it was and how good the groom would be for her. The rabbi persuaded her with his pleasant demeanor and soothing smile. When he completed the marriage contract, he wished her good luck. The therapist looked around, trying to gauge others' responses to the match. The guests present in the room joined in the rabbi's blessings, voicing support and encouragement. Some of the therapist's close friends joyfully expressed optimistic hopes for the marriage.

The therapist observed a sadness in her prospective groom, as he stood next to the rabbi. He appeared introverted, disconnected from the joy of the occasion. The therapist wondered what kind of relationship could be forged with such a melancholy and hesitant groom. Despite the rabbi's blessing and the guests' happiness, the groom remained forlorn and reluctant. The figures in the dream resembled caricatures, reminiscent of a Jewish wedding scene depicted in a picture hanging in the therapist's house.

In supervision, the rabbi was interpreted as the facilitator of the supervision group who had persuaded the therapist to try TLP. The remaining members of the supervision group were the wedding guests and the downtrodden, hesitant groom was Anat. The therapist was unsure whether the source of Anat's melancholy was the therapy itself or its termination. The bride in the dream represented the ambivalent therapist who had been carried away by the encouragement she received from the facilitator and the other members of the supervision group. The therapist had invested herself in the therapy. She was pleased with her show of ability, but was ready to end the emotionally taxing exercise. Furthermore, she was satisfied with the treatment's outcome. She felt Anat had achieved a significant degree of autonomy as the treatment neared its conclusion. Nonetheless, the therapist was moved by Anat's sadness. In addition, she found it difficult to separate from a client who responded so well to her interventions. Regardless of the treatment's clinical success, both members of the therapeutic dyad approached the final session with trepidation.

Anat began the final session with an admission of how hard it was for her. She looked sad as she described her uncertainty that morning over whether to take a bus, allotting herself time for contemplation, or to drive. She ended up missing the bus and came in her car. The therapist interpreted the dilemma in terms of taking responsibility, 'driving' her own life versus letting someone else direct her. The therapist validated the inner strength Anat had used to take responsibility for herself that morning. Although it was difficult, Anat described her efforts to find a way around the judge's ruling that she must sell her house.

Next, Anat commented on the changes in her self-image. In the past, she had put Moshe on a pedestal, leaving herself feeling inferior to him. Now, however, she considered herself his equal and stood up to him. She described the achievements that earned her a certificate of recognition at work. She finally recognized herself as valuable. In a brief overview, Anat recalled her first visit to the clinic and her refusal to take the medication offered by the psychiatrist. She reflected upon the therapeutic alliance and expressed gratitude for the therapist's help. Anat parted from the therapist with a tearful kiss goodbye.

Follow-up session

Approximately five months post-termination, the therapist called Anat to schedule a follow-up session. Pleasantly surprised by the phone call, Anat was certain the therapist had known she was in the midst of negotiating the final division of property with Moshe and feeling very tense. In the session, Anat's assumption was interpreted as a wish always to be understood and accepted by the therapist. Anat accomplished important emotional work in the session. She finally confronted and accepted her separation from Moshe, despite the ten years of stalwart efforts aimed at avoiding taking the final step. Nonetheless, anticipation of signing the final settlement wrought severe anxiety in Anat. In terms of the difficulty in terminating therapy, the therapist acquiesced to her own emotional demands and decided to schedule two additional sessions with Anat.

In the second additional session, Anat was preoccupied with the financial and organizational endeavors necessary to fulfill her end of the divorce settlement. In order to remain in her house, she had agreed to pay Moshe a significant sum. Anat's reorganization of her life was very impressive. The therapist interpreted the changes as an addendum to the central issue: 'You're tearing yourself apart again, but this time for your own sake.' In this session, Anat also reflected upon her children's successes, crediting her contribution to their accomplishments. She was able to accept and be grateful for her children's help with the emotional and material hardships caused by the divorce settlement. Finally, Anat expressed her hopes for a new romantic relationship in the future.

Discussion

After ten years of refusing to accept the estrangement from her husband, the active, intensively focused treatment described above generated significant improvement in Anat's self-image. This case exemplifies the influence of TLP's structural characteristics on the treatment's curative ability.

The empathic central issue enabled Anat to seize the opportunity to go through the mourning process necessary to separate from her estranged husband. The similarity between her experiences in therapy and outside of therapy intensified the treatment's efficacy. The inner time conflict was resolved when the perception of realistic calendric time overcame Anat's infantile perception of time. Furthermore, with the change in her self-image, Anat was able to mobilize her strengths more effectively. As a result, she underwent a process that culminated in a successful separation.

The presentation of the central issue directly addressed Anat's diminished self-esteem and the painful experience of loneliness. As a result, the development of the therapeutic alliance, and the positive transference, were accelerated. Because Anat experienced her as an empathic object, the therapist quickly became a meaningful figure in Anat's life. The central issue was used to break apart painful emotions, bringing a feeling of relief and a rapid improvement in self-esteem. The central issue guided the therapist's interpretations throughout the entire treatment process. By examining previous life events through the perspective of the central issue, the interpretations aimed to facilitate a re-experiencing of the phenomenon of 'tearing herself apart' for others in hopes of receiving the approval she did not give herself. Concurrently, the therapist fostered Anat's growing ability to take care of herself, helping her to prepare emotionally, and logistically, for the final separation from her husband. Anat's improved functioning indicated progress in her development of a sense of autonomy and in the elevation of her self-esteem.

Anat sought help in coping with the specific difficulty of separating from her husband. In therapy, however, she coped with several separations (from her husband, his family, and the therapist) as she simultaneously sifted through and confronted her negative self-perceptions. James Mann (1973) labeled TLP 'a separation processing laboratory.' The issues of termination and separation arise in the initial stages of treatment, causing an acceleration of the separation process, similar to the concluding stage of long-term dynamic psychotherapy. In Anat's case, her separation difficulties formed the crux of the central issue and were present at every stage of therapy. The depressive presenting symptomatology was significantly reduced by consistent reliance upon the central issue in processing Anat's negativity toward herself.

This case study contains several additional curative factors. The first was the fit between the client and the selected therapy method. One of the crucial elements in the success of short-term therapy is the selection of clients that can benefit from the particular therapy method (Crits-Christoph and Barber 1991; Messer and Warren 1995; Sharar 1995; Shefler 1988). Positive indicators for short-term dynamic psychotherapy success include high motivation for change, the ability to remain focused, consolidated ego strengths, and the ability for interpersonal attachment.

The second curative factor in the therapy was the therapist, despite her lack of previous TLP experience. After an intensive training period, she was highly motivated to try the new therapy method. Furthermore, her close adherence to the theoretical model contributed to the positive treatment outcome.

The third curative factor was the mutuality that created an intense emotional atmosphere. The client's hopes for greater emotional health and the empathic therapist's readiness to help achieve that goal were synthesized into a therapeutic dyad that transformed an intensely painful process into a profoundly supportive emotional experience.

Mann emphasized clients' tendencies to deny the separation process, especially as they approach the termination date. By preventing avoidance of the separation issue, the therapist provides an outlet for expression of the client's negative emotions toward both the therapist and other significant figures. Mann (1973, 1991) also emphasized therapist resistance to the separation process. A therapist coping with unresolved separation issues can magnify the level of angst and guilt produced by the treatment's termination. Active coping with these feelings without elongating the therapy enables the client to internalize the therapist as a positive figure. Substitution of the therapist for the ambivalent object enables the client to cultivate an improved outlook upon his or her self-image. In TLP, both client and therapist must continually cope with issues of separation, death, and the finite nature of human life.

In this case study, the therapist's dream served as an expression of her resistance to separating from the client. In-depth processing of the dream in a supportive setting enabled the therapist to address her own separation anxiety and identify countertransference reactions. As a result, the therapy terminated successfully.

Chapter 10

Borderline personality disorder with dependent features

Description of an unsuccessful therapy

Identifying details

Hannah was a 28-year-old, unmarried, high-school mathematics teacher. She was the fifth of six children, born into a Sephardic family of eastern descent.

First assessment session

During her initial interview at the clinic, Hannah complained of difficulty in forming relationships with men, primarily the lack of meaningful, long-term relationships. Consequently, she felt bad, though she could not specify the feeling. She also worked excessively, repeatedly taking upon herself almost twice as much as she could accomplish under normal circumstances. She felt worn out and could not understand why she took so much upon herself. Hannah had a manicured appearance, a beautiful face, a well-maintained and shapely figure, and an impressively refined and attractive style of dress.

The indistinct bad feeling began approximately two weeks prior to Hannah's initial arrival at the clinic. Her anxiety manifested in an overall anxious affect with somatic expressions, weakness, lack of concentration, and the tendency to cry about practically anything.

These feelings were triggered by an argument with Uri, a man whom she dated for an extended period of several years, but without any commitment on his part. While on a trip together, Uri said some harsh things to her, by which she felt very hurt. He told her he did not understand why she took so much upon herself. As soon as he tried to get closer or make a commitment to her, she pulled back from him. She was afraid of giving him control over her. 'Anybody who brings me flowers – I know he has no chance with me.' She easily attracted male interest and began many relationships. Her relationship problems began when she was in high school. Her relationships with women were superficial and often fell apart as a result of her distrust. She felt betrayed by her female friends and experienced them as disloyal. Hannah went on to describe her father.

HANNAH   He was a simple man from a good, educated family. He considered knowledge and learning very important. He was an impressive man. On the one hand, he spoke nicely, while on the other hand, he was violent and unpredictable. He passed away a year and a half ago. He was a difficult man, addicted to alcohol, and aggressive and violent at home. My parents got divorced seven years ago. I really hated him them. I didn't speak to him for several years. Just before he passed away, my mother agreed to let him come back home and she took care of him until he died. As a teenager, I loved him; I was attracted to him. He had a magnetic quality. Along with the attraction, I felt hatred because he would beat me. I sustained many beatings as a child and as an adolescent. In the army, I was an office clerk, then, after a while, I took an officers' training course. I served in an administrative position and was very successful.

INTERVIEWER   Tell me about your relationships, particularly those with the opposite sex.

HANNAH   When men pursue me, I feel repulsed. As long as a guy is indifferent, I stay calm. When he starts pursuing me, I go out of my mind. I feel stressed and nauseous, until he keeps his distance, and then I'm okay. I feel horrible when I'm being pursued. I used to think it was natural to feel attracted to anyone who didn't chase after me and put off by anyone who did. Now, after discussing it with my mother and my sisters, I understand that it isn't normal.

INTERVIEWER   You mean, as soon as a man starts pursuing you, it arouses your suspicions.

HANNAH   Not suspicion, but repulsion. Repulsion. I mostly feel physically repelled. I'm afraid of physical contact.

INTERVIEWER   Have you had intercourse in the past?

HANNAH   Yes, but I have problems with it. It was okay with one guy, but usually I don't like it. I can't open up, and it hurts.

INTERVIEWER   Do you see any connection between what we've spoken about so far and what you just told me?

HANNAH   No.

INTERVIEWER   I see. And do you feel any difficulty here with me?

HANNAH   You're trying to understand me.

INTERVIEWER   And in order to understand you, I'm attempting to get closer to you. Does that generate any familiar feelings?

HANNAH   No, it's different here. I don't think so. You're a professional. You're not turned on or attracted to me. That can't be. I should have come here a long time ago, when the problems with my father were so terrible. Maybe it's too late now. I've had a friend named Uri for four years already. I don't want to talk about him. He's different. I don't have to worry with him, because he doesn't try to get intimate with me. We went on a trip together, and after what he said to me, I came for therapy. I should have gone into therapy five years ago. I was dating a guy, and my girlfriend tried to hit on him. I was really hurt. I didn't have the money for therapy, so I asked my mother, and my father. They didn't have anything, and my father wouldn't consent to giving me money. I have identity problems. I've shed many a tear over the feeling of not knowing where to put myself.

From her personal history

HANNAH   I grew up in a poor family. My mother and father didn't get along; my father was drunk and violent. He was also handsome, macho, and elegant. He belittled my mother and cheated on her, while she worked hard to support the household. I was his favorite child. I was named after his mother. My father nurtured me until I was 14, and then he became terribly detached from me. I don't know why. My siblings got married while my mother, my younger sister, and I remained at home alone with my father, unprotected. When I was 15, he beat me to a pulp because I asked him not to dirty the house with his cigarettes after I cleaned. He was a charismatic man; everyone loved him at work.

INTERVIEWER   A confusing man: charismatic and impressive, yet violent at the same time.

HANNAH   That's true. He always had people around him. He served in a security position. They didn't know he was violent.

He cultivated his education, his learning, but at the same time he was violent. He came from an intelligent family. My mother and her family were really stupid people who didn't understand anything. Yet with all of my father's extremism, I used to sit on his lap until the age of 14.

The problems with boys began when I was 14 years old. I wasn't interested in them. I wasn't ready for a relationship. I looked terrible, covered with acne. I started menstruating on time. There weren't any problems, as far as I could tell. I was happy to get it, and I was ready for it. My mother had prepared me.

Second assessment session

[*The session begins in silence.*]

INTERVIEWER   Have you thought about anything in regards to last time?

HANNAH   No, but it was interesting.

[*Another silence.*]

INTERVIEWER   What was interesting?

HANNAH   What we spoke about.

[*Silence again.*]

INTERVIEWER   Shall we pick up where we left off the last session?

HANNAH   Yeah, sure. I've never left home. I'm very – too attached to my mother. Then my father got sick, and in light of the distressing circumstances, they got remarried. I really didn't want them to remarry, but when they did, it was very pleasant. There was immense tranquility in their second marriage, until six months before he died, when he became completely dependent and deteriorated considerably. He couldn't even perform the most basic functions. He was totally helpless, an absolute rag.

During the transition to high school, I had to take exams, and I performed extremely well. Immediately after the beginning of the school year, I began having severe problems. They transferred me to a different class, a lower one, and I managed to stand out again. It was terribly difficult for me. Then the Yom Kippur War broke out. My father became depressed and started drinking and I stopped going to school. Everything became difficult. That was when I decided to become a teacher, to prove to myself and to the world that I could. I decided I would become a teacher at the same high school I had attended as an adolescent. And that's what came to pass. I became a math teacher at the exclusive school where I hadn't been accepted socially as a child, where I was looked down upon. I made a decision, and I saw it through.

I had a few very good girlfriends, and one with whom I had an amazing relationship. I had a relationship with a gorgeous American guy, who pulled up next to me in his American car one day. He said he was 25, and I was in twelfth grade. He was actually 31 years old. Strange, and absolutely crazy.

My father humiliated me, spat on me. Even now, I can barely speak about it without crying. He hurt me so badly, humiliated me. Once, I yelled at him so hard that he said he wanted me to take a tissue test, to prove that maybe I wasn't his daughter. He couldn't stand my rebelliousness, that I dared to tell him to shut up and things of that sort. When they finally got divorced, it was a huge relief for me. The house became quieter, and my headaches disappeared. I took the matriculation exams and was drafted into the army. I made friends with quiet, easygoing girls, but I always missed home and went back whenever I could. In the army, there were incidents of sexual harassment: a guy my age, an older officer, one of the officers' drivers. They tried to come on to me. They didn't attack me, but they got close in an uncomfortable, and perhaps even dangerous, way. I met one guy who became my boyfriend. He told me I wasn't pretty, but I was very attractive. Afterward, I met a gorgeous guy from an élite unit. But I didn't love him. I don't know exactly what happened, but I wasn't attracted to him. When he traveled abroad as a military emissary, I didn't miss him. Why won't you be the psychologist for my therapy?

INTERVIEWER   Are you growing attached to me?

HANNAH   Yes, I'm getting used to you. I feel comfortable talking with you.

INTERVIEWER   Getting used to me?

HANNAH   Not just that. I also feel comfortable. I don't know if that means I'm getting used to you. I don't know what getting used to someone is like. I want to have relationships with people, but I'm afraid, and I withdraw. It's been like that with so many guys. One was a commander in an élite unit. The next one became a very successful academic. In other words, they were very serious people, as you can see, and they were also very physically attractive. I think the issue is the repulsion in the attraction. The fact is, when I want somebody really badly, I feel equally turned off by him. It's a trap.

INTERVIEWER   And in therapy?

HANNAH   What's that got to do with it? Therapy is different. It's not the same thing. I had a similar story with a guy I was attracted to, but instead I kept trying to hit on his friend, even though his friend was taken and not interested in me. I'm not even certain I was interested in either of them.

INTERVIEWER   Perhaps you wanted to ensure you wouldn't form a relationship with either of them.

HANNAH   I don't understand, but it could be. I have a brother, truly the black sheep of the family. He's a carbon copy of my father. He has the potential to succeed, but he sabotages every possible potential success. He's disruptive and destructive in everything: relationships, the family, everything. After my father died, it was amazing to see how alike they were. At some point, my mother invited him to live at home, because he had no place else to go. He abandoned his home, although he didn't actually get divorced. Just like our father. Who needs another one of those? Get rid of one and along comes another.

Third assessment session (first session with the therapist)

HANNAH   What were the results of the assessment? What did you think of me?

THERAPIST   You want an exact answer.

HANNAH   My brother and mother traveled abroad together. I'm pleased about it, but also jealous. [*She retells the therapist about the unfinished saga with her father.*]

THERAPIST   You managed to make transitions from lower to higher levels, but your brother takes you back there. He provokes you, extracts unpleasant things from you, things you don't want to remember or realize are part of you.

HANNAH   I want to make them disappear, forget them, distance them. I've been trying for years, and he reawakens them just like that, immediately. He stirs up and revives the problems I had with my father. The resemblance is intolerable.

THERAPIST   As well as the renewed need to protect your mother. The very strong bond to your mother weighs heavily upon you.

[*Hannah describes another brother who is the diametric opposite of her father. She feels torn between the two of them.*]

HANNAH   I'm not sure how similar I am to my father. I don't think I am, but my strong drives and impulsiveness might be precisely reminiscent of my father.

THERAPIST   How much did you fear your father? That he would do something bad to you physically, sexually, or beat you?

HANNAH   I wasn't really afraid of him. My mother frightened us terribly, saying our father had a knife and one night he might stab us. When he died, we were ashamed and didn't tell anyone he died of severe liver failure as a result of alcoholism. We said he had cancer. My mother was illiterate; she wasn't smart or intelligent. She was a very limited woman. When they argued he was ugly, aggressive, and violent, yet impressive, strong, and bright. She was really pathetic. She would shout but not say anything, scream without having any effect. She doesn't know how to read or write. I tried to teach her, but it didn't work. I have a very impressive sister, the opposite of our mother. She has a serious job, a magnificent house, and a wonderful family. Her life is perfect. And I have a younger sister who's horribly jealous of me. I can't do anything without her interfering. I suppose she grew up without absorbing any sense of discipline. She's a very disturbed girl.

THERAPIST   Everything seems quite extreme in your family.

Therapy session one

HANNAH   You're very nice. I'm in a difficult position. I'm looking for an apartment, though it might not be worth my while to leave home. [*She hints at difficulties with dependence and separation.*] I have everything I want there. [*She denies the hell of living with her brother.*] The principal of my school called me in for a discussion and started telling me about his relationship problems. He used to be a man who supported me, but now he's overwhelmed with his own problems, and I feel like my support is being pulled right out from under me. He's preoccupied with himself and not available to me. I have problems of my own. And I'm terrified by his romantic propositions [*like her father, brother, etc.*].

The therapist suggested the central issue:

Despite the difficulties you experienced in childhood and throughout your life, you've succeeded in attaining impressive achievements. Nevertheless, you have always carried a feeling of humiliation, which prevents you from forming a truly intimate relationship with a man. Along the way, you've fought for your place between two worlds, between the world in which you grew up and to which you don't want to belong, and the other world in which you try to assimilate yet never fully succeed. You are torn between the two worlds. And you are always hiding something.

Hannah listened and concentrated, absorbed in thought. She asked a clarifying question, then sat silently.

THERAPIST   What do you think?
HANNAH   It seems to me what you said must be true. So it seems.
THERAPIST   That will be our focus in therapy. It's quite a bit of food for thought. The therapy will last for twelve sessions, including today's session.
[*They schedule an exact date for the final session. Afterwards, silence falls over the room.*]
THERAPIST   What are you thinking about?
HANNAH   I met somebody while I was traveling abroad. He wanders around with his baggage, and doesn't know where to put it down. His name is Robert. He's incredibly sexy and good-looking.
THERAPIST   Perhaps you also don't know where to place the baggage of life.

Hannah recalled a lover who was particularly humiliating and controlling. He was able to take her wherever he wanted. Whatever he wanted, he got from her. If he called in the middle of the night after not seeing her for a year, she would run right to him.

THERAPIST   Did he transport you between the worlds?
HANNAH   Maybe. I don't know.

(Notice that the therapist did not adhere to the selected central issue, nor did she relate to the questions regarding separation raised in this hour.)

Session two

HANNAH   I was given an apartment; it belongs to my friend's mother. My brother came over, and I'm afraid he's going to stick it to me later on. First he behaves nicely, and then he becomes cruel.

The relationship with Robert, the guy from abroad, is developing. I feel repelled and attracted. He keeps a journal, and he told me I've filled the pages of it.

THERAPIST   Are you asking if you hold a central place with me as well?

HANNAH   No, this is therapy. It's different. Robert is very hesitant about his relationship to me. He's like me: wants me but doesn't want me, attracted and repelled. He still feels hurt by a woman who abandoned him (like me). And I don't want to be the girlfriend of somebody trying to heal himself at my expense.

[*Hannah describes herself as feeling suspicious of him and repelled by him.*]

THERAPIST   He transports you between the two worlds. He doesn't really take you seriously. It's unclear what he wants, whether he wants a one-night stand, a quickie, or a deep relationship?

HANNAH   You know, I've never gone through the process of developing a deep, slowly maturing relationship. It's always been a sudden thing. Love at first sight, so there's no process, just a passionate beginning and immediate disappointment. Maybe it's because I don't have an ounce of patience.

THERAPIST   It's not a matter of patience, but of emotion. You often speak without emotion. When you speak about difficult things, it seems as if you are above them. You don't really touch them, and they don't really touch you. [*The therapist does not relate to the selected central issue, perhaps because it was not focused enough. In effect, she offers a new central issue.*]

HANNAH   I don't understand what you're talking about.

THERAPIST   You hover like a butterfly, torn between two worlds. You invest a great deal in concealing the parts of yourself that you don't like. Maybe that's part of not being fully here.

HANNAH   I'm not completely open when I speak with you, but I did come here on my own initiative. I want to be helped and to help myself.

THERAPIST   How did what I said affect you? Were you hurt by my words?

[*They both ignore the difficult interaction that had transpired between them.*]

HANNAH   I don't know what I feel. It's unclear. I'm confused.

The therapist confronts her: what is happening to you now? What do you feel? (She did not attend to the emergence of the central issue at this point.) Hannah felt ashamed, embarrassed, and stupid. She did not have any emotional understanding of the situation and, consequently, closed up.

HANNAH   I came here to work on myself.

THERAPIST   Which you are capable of doing. You can work on yourself and move forward with what is happening to you.

The therapist made this statement, rather than relating to what had occurred between them in the therapy hour. She did not facilitate a connection between Hannah's feeling of vulnerability and her hopes for change, nor the more complex emotional processes involved in Hannah's overwhelming hate-attraction dynamic. The split between good and bad was liable to overtake the therapist, as well as Hannah's perception of the therapist.

THERAPIST   You give the impression that it's dangerous to invest in yourself. You invested in your father and he disappointed you. You are convinced others will do the same. [*She remains unfocused, and certainly nowhere in the vicinity of the central issue.*]

The two worlds between which Hannah shifted back and forth corresponded with the two contrasting aspects of her father: his charismatic, philosophical, intelligent side versus his drunk, dangerous, violent side – the impulsive and inconsiderate side.

HANNAH   My father confused me. He saw me as a girl-woman, as both attractive and as an object for violence. I didn't know if I was good or bad in his eyes. As a girl, I felt unwanted. I didn't feel like I counted among the other children, or at home. Because I was serious, a very good student, I was treated with a sort of respect, even by the children. When I matured and became sexually attractive, it burst forth and confused me. My body is very confusing.

The therapist attempted to link the two elements – the physical impulses and the intellectual-moral element. She gave Hannah the sense that it was possible to integrate these two elements (and thus abandoned the central issue, yet again).

Session three

HANNAH   I was upset after the last session and I looked for somebody to talk to. I wanted us to talk every day. You really soothed me. Robert, my boyfriend from abroad, also soothes me. What'll happen when he leaves me in another three months?

When Hannah spoke about relationships with men who had abandoned her, the therapist reiterated the focus on two worlds, consequently ignoring the direct and obvious emergence of the separation question. Then, she persistently delved into a central issue that apparently did not interest Hannah or contain any meaning for her. This situation engendered tremendous pain. Hannah cried as she spoke about Uri, her lover, and the relationship with him which never reached fruition. At this point, the therapist did raise the issue of their separation in therapy, and Hannah responded strongly with an intensification of her crying, providing additional evidence that this was the relevant pain-filled area.

Session four

Hannah said 'After I left here, I wanted to end the relationship with Robert. I didn't want him any longer. I can't determine whether he wants me or not. (The therapist did not interpret Hannah's inability to determine whether the therapist wanted *her* or not.) The therapist (erroneously) connected Hannah's statement to the two worlds. Reducing the central issue to two worlds and the movement between them prevented any consideration of the emotion linked to that movement. Apparently, the therapist felt the central issue was not stimulating the desired therapeutic momentum and suggested an alternative central issue:

> Your many successes are accompanied by a feeling of humiliation and lack of trust that you are truly loved.

Hannah responded enthusiastically to the new central issue and asked if it was true in regards to all people, or just regarding the opposite sex? She then spoke about girlfriends with whom she had a basic trust problem.

THERAPIST Perhaps here with me, you also have difficulty trusting that I'll give you the best? [*Another inaccurate reference to the central issue.*]

HANNAH How much can 12 sessions really help? [*Another reference to the general question of separation, particularly in the context of therapy.*]

THERAPIST Maybe in that I can help you overcome the feeling of humiliation.
[*Hannah switched topics to a discussion of her sexual relationship with Robert.*]

HANNAH When I sleep with him, I feel not only physical pain, but emotional pain as well.

THERAPIST You miss him. Perhaps you also miss the humiliation of the relationship you had with him?

HANNAH No, no, I just can't believe anybody loves me. Not him, not my father, not anyone.

THERAPIST [*repeating a combined version of the two central issues.*] You've succeeded in many things: on the plane of leaving home and serving in the army, then in your studies. As a teacher, I understand that you accomplish things and perform well in everything you do, socially as well. Yet, you constantly feel you deserve humiliation, along with a lack of trust that anybody can truly love you. Men can't love you; they only humiliate you.

HANNAH I've shed a lot of tears over that constant feeling, the feeling of instability. My life has never been stable, or sheltered.

This is the first time those words have ever left my mouth. I don't belong to either of the two worlds, not the distressed, impoverished world and not the organized, established world. [*Hannah in effect, returns to the first central issue.*]

THERAPIST You don't belong to your mother or to your father.

HANNAH I belong to my mother very much. I can't abandon her. It hurts me to leave her. And my father hasn't been with me since adolescence.

THERAPIST Are you angry with him? [*Another diversion from the new central issue, in which the central emotions are humiliation and distrust, not anger.*]

HANNAH Yes, sometimes. I also miss him. But he never let me out.

THERAPIST Are you angry at his lack of trust in you?

HANNAH I'm angry about the atmosphere he created at home. We all feared him.

THERAPIST You had to walk on tiptoes, so he wouldn't be angered or annoyed.

HANNAH Yes, very much so. I don't know . . . even today, I tiptoe around men, as if . . . I try to understand what happens to me, but unsuccessfully. Robert said to me, 'It's impossible to touch you. You're unreachable.'

THERAPIST I told you the same thing a few sessions ago.

HANNAH I feel blocked. I behave as if I'm forming a relationship, but I'm really not.

THERAPIST You're anxious about reaching your most difficult emotions, your deepest emotions.

HANNAH I don't understand myself at all. I feel blocked. I never know what I'm really feeling.

THERAPIST During childhood, your emotions were played with to the extent that today you are actually incapable of knowing what you feel, and your feelings change all the time.

HANNAH I don't feel I love Robert. I very much want the relationship, but I don't love him. I'm certain he feels more for me than I do for him. He feels . . . [*Hannah cries*]. I've wanted to cry all day long but I couldn't. I felt empty. Now I'm going home.

THERAPIST To your mother or to your apartment?

HANNAH To my apartment.

THERAPIST Moving on to something of your own is a significant achievement.

Session five

HANNAH I met a new guy, very impressive. He asked for my phone number, and I gave it to him. He called and immediately asked if I liked him. I started feeling terribly afraid. He was so self-involved. I didn't interest him at all. Robert didn't call the whole week either. When he did call, he didn't sound genuinely interested in me. I moved to my mother's apartment. Robert's starting to hassle me. He says all sorts of things to me: 'You're only interested in yourself. Right now, you're a threat to me. You demand for me to be with you only.' That doesn't work for me. I'm not prepared to let him dictate when I can and can't see him. The new guy only cares about how good-looking he is. He said to me, 'What would you do if we went to a party and other women were interested in me? Would you mind, or would it be okay?' I don't like that at all. I was afraid he would be violent. I immediately felt uneasy with him.

THERAPIST The anxieties rise to the surface immediately, like with your father.

HANNAH It's always been that way for me. I feel suffocated when men pursue me.

THERAPIST Who made you feel that way? Who gave you the suffocated feeling?

HANNAH My father. When I was little, my father made me feel like I wasn't pretty or attractive, like I had to study all the time, otherwise, he wouldn't want me.

THERAPIST Just like the things he said to your mother and the way he behaved with her. He was attached to her, but not close. He didn't love her or respect her. He humiliated her.

HANNAH In my dreams, Robert resembles my father, and he [Robert] says to me, 'I'm sick of all your analyses. All day long all you do is analyze and talk.' We came back from a trip together today. I dropped him off at his house. He didn't want to come to my house. He said it was better this way and he wanted to sleep. It bothered me that he made excuses, and I won't accept him dictating what our relationship will be. I won't let anyone control me . . .

THERAPIST You want to take part in decisions regarding yourself.

HANNAH Right, but I don't see anything like that developing for me. Men are always incredibly enthusiastic about me, but they never remain enthusiastic. I don't excite them. I don't develop. It just isn't it.

THERAPIST We're back to your basic feeling that nobody will really love you, and you convey something of the sort from the beginning. If something good happens, you'll abandon it.

HANNAH That definitely happened to me with Robert. I conveyed my sexual anxieties to him. I also told him up front. He has problems, too. He told me sex exhausts him. How can emotions just drop off all at once? Vanish? That's what happened yesterday with him. Do you believe the feelings can come back, too?

THERAPIST If his anxiety is high, he should control some of it. After all, he wants you. Even when people love each other, some things are difficult. His anxiety might activate your controlling behaviors. His leaving you doesn't necessarily mean he doesn't like you or you aren't worthy in his eyes. [*The therapist focuses on Robert rather than on Hannah.*]

HANNAH He told me getting involved in relationships with women who control him is becoming a pattern for him. He feels I want all of him.

THERAPIST It's partially something within him reacting to you, from within his inner world. [*Again focusing on Robert, not Hannah.*]

HANNAH I dreamed I scheduled a date with Robert and sat with him in a café. My friend Ruthie was there. They sat together. I went somewhere, and said I'd be back. They were supposed to wait for me. When I went out, I saw Uri, my lover. He said we would be together, and he would come to my apartment. I go back inside, and instead of Robert, Uri the lover is sitting there. And an old woman told me Robert found his love with Ruthie. The Robert figure was replaced by Uri.

THERAPIST What was your feeling during the dream?

HANNAH That was a week when I really thought Robert wanted Ruthie more than me. When a man wants me, I'm certain he wants somebody else, that it isn't me he wants. It's horrible. I'm so disturbed. It's because of my father. Once, I went to buy a few books, but I came home with only one book. I was probably about 14 years old. And he said, 'Why can't you do exactly what you're told.' And then he said to my sister, 'I'll kill her. You'll see, she and her mother will be here dead.' I was so terrified, and it happened because once I exploded at him, and

said I was ashamed of him and I didn't want him to be my
father. And he said, 'You're not my daughter.' He was drunk,
but I was terrified.

THERAPIST   Because he revoked his special attitude toward you?

HANNAH   Yes, something like that.

THERAPIST   As if he expelled you from the Garden of Eden?

HANNAH   He always loved to make an impression. He wanted to
impress others. I'm telling you, it's a good thing he died. I say
that at home also, and everyone is shocked by it. He heavily
damaged all of us, myself included. Even when he was alive,
we prayed he would die. He was like the Satan of the house.
He beat my mother and me. When I was 14, he strangled me.
He nearly killed me. It was horrible. My brother was right
there, but he couldn't help me. He was scared to death of my
father, absolutely helpless. My friend was supposed to come
over, and I was wearing shorts. I had marks all over my legs
from the beatings.

The therapist tried to clarify whether there had been any attempt at
sexual contact between her father and Hannah. She fervently
denied any such contact, and emphasized her father's violent side.
The therapist emphasized the possibility that perhaps her father's
violent outbursts were a type of sublimation of his sexual desires
toward her. The violence might have occurred in order to prevent
expression of his sexual impulses.

Session six

HANNAH   I can't leave Robert. My thoughts about him are beyond
all proportion.

THERAPIST   How does that connect to the focus of the therapy?

HANNAH   I don't know.

THERAPIST   You're successful in many things. Nonetheless, you
constantly feel humiliated, and a lack of trust that you are truly
loved.

HANNAH   I don't know what that has to do with Robert.

THERAPIST   It has to do with your entire life, and Robert too. You
don't believe people truly love you. Here too, you don't feel
comfortable when it seems like you haven't met my expectations. You're not a good girl. You've disappointed me.

Hannah went back to discussing the previous session. She was very upset when she thought about what the therapist said to her: that her father tried to fool around with her sexually. Robert is trying to avoid her. Even though he tells her he loves her, and says maybe he'll even buy her the apartment she lives in, he still goes and visits a female friend in another city, and doesn't call after promising he will. At the same time, she feels repulsive, unattractive, and hairy. She is jealous of women who look good and don't need to shave their legs. Her father was hairy, and always wore short pants. He emphasized his sexuality. It seems frightening to her. She thinks she can only form good relationships with children.

Session seven

Hannah said, 'I don't have anything to talk about today. Everything's calm. I'm not at all interested today in what we spoke about last time.' The therapist tried to stimulate further exploration of this topic, but Hannah insisted there was no chance. 'Everything is subdued today.'

At some point, Hannah recalled: 'During the officers' training course, all of the girls received something from their parents at graduation. I was the only one who didn't receive anything. I felt different, left out. In order to avoid getting hurt, I shut down. I felt nothing, not even disappointment. It's still the same today. It's best not to feel anything.'

THERAPIST   It's difficult to live with such humiliation. It's hard to be the daughter of parents like those, a mother who is like a rag and a father that doesn't pay any attention to your mother. There's no way you can compare yourself to the successful children, the children living the good life.

HANNAH   It was hard for me to come to therapy today, but I thought I needed something. In fact, maybe I should have a long-term therapy, so if I feel I need it, I'll be able to come. Today, I just didn't feel like it.

Hannah remained silent for about 20 minutes, until the end of the session. She wanted to go home.

The therapist related to the question regarding termination of the therapy, saying it was the seventh session and asking if Hannah had anything to say about that. The therapist asked what came to mind, but Hannah ignored the question, and did not respond.

Session eight

Hannah arrived half an hour early and told the therapist she had wanted to push the session up to two days earlier. She did not look well and said she felt bad. The therapist asked if her feeling was connected to the reminder regarding termination of the therapy, brought up during the last session. Hannah told the therapist she had broken up with Robert.

THERAPIST   Perhaps the break-up with Robert is connected to what's happening here, separations on the horizon?

HANNAH   It's difficult, because right now I'm not in a good emotional state. It's important for me to know I have somewhere to turn. I understand the relationship with Robert disrupted my therapy. Even though I miss things about Robert, I ignored the fact that life is difficult for me, and I wasn't available to work on that in therapy. I haven't brought up important things in therapy.

The therapist repeated the central issue and the feeling that Hannah did not believe someone could truly love her.

HANNAH   I really expect the therapy to last longer than twelve sessions. Think it over again. It's terribly difficult for me to envision how it will be. The last few days were calmer. My mother helped me, even though she isn't smart and doesn't understand. Even so, she was able to listen to me, to be with me, and that was very important for me.

THERAPIST   What kind of mother am I for you here? After all, I'll soon be abandoning you altogether.

HANNAH   Everybody abandons me. I'm used to it. No guy who I wanted has ever stuck around. Why are only unreliable men attracted to me? You know, I once thought if I ever had a son, I would name him after my father. Despite everything, he raised me positively. At home, I loved him more than any of my brothers or sisters loved him. I missed him after he died. Even when I say it's a good thing he died because the abuse stopped, I still miss him. [*She cries.*] I was very worried he would wind up in hell, because of my anger toward him. I don't know how to prevent it. I missed him terribly. But it's complicated, because I barely saw him over the last few years. I visited him maybe once a year. Once, I visited him in the hospital, and he was already really sick with his liver disease. He insulted me in a loud voice, in front of everyone. I've always been afraid of saying and being what I want, and now my mother is the same way. Starting first thing in the morning, my mother pressures me to come see her. I must visit her every day. She doesn't let me live my own life. She takes advantage of the fact that I come to her when I have trouble with Robert. It confuses me, and I don't know what my true desires are. I don't know for myself, but I let everyone influence my desires, influence me. And then it turns out I don't know what I want for myself.

THERAPIST   Which repeats itself in the relationship with Robert. There is no full intimacy, only intimacy with a limited guarantee.

HANNAH   Yes, Robert isn't using me. He doesn't want me for what I can do for him, but he wants me according to his needs. I trust him.

THERAPIST   You trust him to break-up with you if he's not interested in a relationship, not simply to throw you away like other men have before him.

HANNAH   Yes. It's so confusing. You know, the relationship with my father was also very ambivalent.

THERAPIST   What did you love about your father?

HANNAH   It's hard to say. He was an educated man, an intelligent man. He had potential. Not that he ever realized it, but he still had it. My brother is the same way, and so am I, but I haven't realized my potential. Nothing has come of me. That's all. [*She sobs.*]

THERAPIST   Is it difficult experiencing those feelings about yourself from up close?

HANNAH   Very difficult. I feel frightened when they get so close.

THERAPIST   When I get close as well?

HANNAH   Yes, very. I'm afraid of you penetrating me. When we spoke about the relationship with my father, I was frightened. Very frightened. When I read a book about incest, I felt very frightened.

THERAPIST   By the sexual feelings between father and daughter?

HANNAH   Yes. When the principal at school tried getting closer to me, I felt utterly repulsed.

THERAPIST   Your desire as a young girl to be close to your father, when the boundary between body and emotion remains unclear.

HANNAH   My sister said to me, 'You had such developed breasts, and you still sat on Daddy's lap.' I also went to the pool with him, and I had a tiny little bikini.

Session nine

HANNAH   I've had a rough week, but not the roughest. It could have been worse. I left here and cried a lot. I felt so sorry for myself.

THERAPIST   About what?

HANNAH   About my unhappy life. I don't have any meaningful framework in my life. Here I am, living in an apartment, yet so frequently at my mother's house. We're revolving around the central issue in therapy, and I feel as if nobody loves me. I was riding the bus, and an elderly man sat down next to me. He told me I looked sad. I told him it was because of the book I was reading, a book about betrayal. He told me his wife had cheated on him throughout his entire life. He said to me, 'Leave him. He doesn't deserve you. Put on make-up, you'll see how pretty and attractive you are. Find yourself someone worthy of you.' I didn't take him seriously.
[*Silence.*]

HANNAH   I was in the hospital emergency room, because I didn't feel well before my period. I had an uncomfortable irritation. The doctor's examination was very painful, and she yelled at me to go see a psychiatrist. I felt confused because I was angry with Robert for abandoning me and for disrupting my therapy. Every time I felt difficulty in therapy, I acted as if everything was fine with him, but it was 'as if.' He wasn't the one. Now, he's no longer around, and therapy hasn't helped me as much as I wanted, as much as I need it to help me. I need much more of you. Get closer to me.

THERAPIST   Do you regret what didn't take place between us?

HANNAH   Yes. I can't say exactly. Maybe I wanted you actually to hug me, not just virtually. A hug of friendship, so you could project your love on to me. So you could tell me I'm not as horrible as I feel.

THERAPIST It's precisely our focal point. You've always succeeded in the things you've done. Yet, you don't believe someone will truly love you, and constantly feel a sense of humiliation. Here, from the beginning of therapy, it was clear it would come to an end. Here as well, you can't believe I could love you.

HANNAH At the beginning, I thought what are twelve sessions? What difference does it make how many sessions there are? But now, I can't even contemplate the end. I need you too much. It's easier for me when I know I'm coming to see you.

THERAPIST Nevertheless, it angers you to know that after twelve sessions, I'll be abandoning you. How can you really trust someone who would say goodbye when you're in such a difficult state.

HANNAH I can't leave this therapy yet. It sustains me. It puts me in touch with myself. The astrologer told me I should write children's books. That suits me.

THERAPIST Like reliving your childhood? Being in the world of children, according to your own design?

HANNAH Yes, it's easier there. I find this process of developing a relationship difficult. I usually get involved quickly and immediately. There is no process. Here, with you, I've gone through the process of building a relationship. With guys, it always happens too quickly. It's all about the external, the sexual, the sensual, the animal. Like with my father. On the surface, there's something clear and explicit that men see and respond to. Then, afterwards, they abandon it, and nothing's left. That's what happened with Robert. The strong, sexual, lustful attraction ended, and it was all over for him. I suppose, subconsciously, I'm attracted to lust and brutality, like my father's. But how can I detect it in advance?

THERAPIST Attraction to something unattainable, an attraction to your father who is adored and enabling, yet humiliating. The positive elements in his personality instilled in you the entire aspect of education and taking an interest. Your father played an important role in those things. He knew how to speak and tell stories, but he was also brutal and sexual.

HANNAH That's what's left of him – the brutality, the humiliation. He didn't give me a home.

THERAPIST   He gave you everything and more, including elements that were less impressive, but contained meaning for you.

HANNAH   [*getting upset*] Maybe my father was mentally ill, paranoid. Maybe I'm just like him? I'm suspicious of everyone. I don't trust anybody, it doesn't matter whether they're a boyfriend or a female friend. I was raised not to speak. Nobody listened to me. Nobody at school knows what I'm going through either.

THERAPIST   Yet, here you are, speaking to me and telling me how hard it is on you, and then I abandon you.

HANNAH   It's going to destroy me, it'll crush me. I'm already up in the air. I can't reach myself. I left home, but not really. I'm neither here nor there. My mother helps me. She says I'll get set up and marry a wealthy man, because I'm pretty. And I get annoyed with her. I know I have strengths.

THERAPIST   Like we said in the focal point, you have the strengths to succeed, and you've successfully achieved things in your life.

HANNAH   But I'm completely shattered.

THERAPIST   How is it you're not angry with me for abandoning you?

HANNAH   I'm not angry with you, only with men. I think the more significant men in my life couldn't reach me because I was out of touch with myself. Completely out of touch.

THERAPIST   How can somebody else love you if all of your wounds and scars prevent you from loving yourself? The difficulty in separating from me is crucial for you. All these years, you've tried to ignore the difficulty in your separations from men, from your father, from every meaningful thing you had. It's very important for you to feel the inherent pain of separation now, and to put it into words.

Session ten

HANNAH   I've thought about my relationships with guys. As sexy as I am, and as often as I'm told, I don't feel sexy. I feel disgusting.

THERAPIST   You respond to the feeling of humiliation.

HANNAH   I'm worthless. And I don't say anything, because I don't believe I have anything. I'm empty, lacking any internal content. And then I turn to guys who are attracted to my sexuality, so to speak, and I'm attracted to theirs. Then words are unnecessary. The sexuality takes over and leaves me feeling that the real thing I could have had with them hasn't happened.

THERAPIST   You use them to prove to yourself time and again this is what you deserve, a man can only be interested in humiliating or taking advantage of you, and satisfying his desires. This is the way you can allow men to notice and pay attention to you.

HANNAH   That's true. My parents only related to our outer shells, not to what we really were. But what can I do? I like gorgeous guys. Isn't that normal? They're not concerned with me. They don't give me what I really need, but what they need from me.

THERAPIST   Here too, the therapy doesn't take into consideration how much you need it. Instead, there's a limit.

HANNAH   Who should I speak to about that? It's not right. I won't let the therapy end. It can make me worse. Lately, I've been recording the sessions, writing down what I feel. It's what sustains me. Sometimes, I take a shot of whisky, out of desperation. So now what? Should I become an alcoholic?

THERAPIST   It's very difficult to accept that as much as therapy has given you, it also must end.

HANNAH   I can't. Do you understand me? I can't get along without it.

THERAPIST   Things that are important to you are not always endless.

HANNAH   As far as I'm concerned, this therapy cannot end. It's as if I've only begun. It's my support.

THERAPIST   You've always felt like a reflection of a mud puddle, which is changing now. The puddle is unaware of its contents (if you can say that). It contains water, minerals, vegetation, many forms of life, but it draws its existence from everything reflected in it. It contains mud and decay, but it has other things as well. It's filled with contradictions and an abundance of life, not just destruction. Every intimate interaction stimulates and evokes the dirty, contaminated facet as well, but not exclusively. For some reason, you're certain the dirt and contamination are the only visible things within you. You're not in touch with the beautiful elements of yourself: the children, your writing, your studies.

HANNAH   I feel suffocated, and I can't feel what you are saying. I'm erratic, like my father. I'm afraid I'll go crazy like he did, afraid I won't know what to do with myself.

THERAPIST   You're allowing yourself to express the deep negative emotions toward yourself. You're uncertain where it will lead, but it's very important. For the first time, you've let yourself remove the external masks, allowed yourself to feel what lies beneath. Hell is painful and frightening, as is the fear of never being loved. The fear surrounding the conclusion of the therapy is not especially soothing at the moment.

HANNAH   I can't think about the therapy ending. It's too terrible for me.

THERAPIST   The situation is different here. You have the opportunity to learn and understand what you're experiencing. It's a repetition of other previous experiences.

HANNAH   I don't understand. I feel difficulty right here, not the difficulty from some other time. Right now I have to cope with this difficulty. I'm afraid of being alone in my apartment. I'm afraid of being sucked back into my mother's house. You must understand that. If not you, then who else?

THERAPIST   You want therapy, or me that is, to prevent you from experiencing any more fear or pain, to enable you to experience only good things.

HANNAH   I want to have an easier time with myself. I don't want to be afraid.

Session eleven

HANNAH   I need therapy like I need air to breathe. If I had gone for therapy after the break-up from my second boyfriend, I wouldn't be such a mess. But my father wouldn't consent to therapy. [*She feels sorry for herself again.*] When I think about my life, I think I always look successful, pretty, and attractive from the outside. I'd be willing to give it up to just feel good about myself.

THERAPIST   What's emerging here is your difficulty with expressing emotions about yourself.

HANNAH   I loved my father. I didn't like showing how much I loved him, because everyone else at home was angry with him and hated him.

THERAPIST   It's hard knowing that the man you loved and adored so much was also so disappointing and everyone, including you sometimes, saw him as dirty, repulsive, disgusting, and abrasive.

HANNAH   I felt proud walking down the street with him. He looked good and knew everything. I felt proud inside.

THERAPIST   Your father hasn't died for you. He's still alive. You haven't separated from him.

HANNAH   Right now, he doesn't exist for me. He really doesn't. I go for walks with my mother. It makes it easier on me, and on her.

THERAPIST   Is being close to your mother like hating your father?

HANNAH   Yes, to a certain extent. But what will happen after therapy is over? Today, I thought perhaps it'll be better when all the probing ends. What do you think? I can't stand for it to end, just like that. Look, when you go to a doctor for treatment, he says you have a disease, he gives you medicine, and then you return for another follow-up, and another treatment. When does it end? When the disease is gone. Shouldn't it work the same way here?

THERAPIST   It's different here.

HANNAH   Today, I thought I might feel better if I didn't probe so much.

THERAPIST   Therapy gives you tools for coping and continuing to work on yourself in the future.

HANNAH   I can't even consider being without therapy. How much does private therapy cost?

THERAPIST   Look, here at the clinic, we think you should give yourself some time. See how things work out, and we'll see along with you.

HANNAH   It seems more difficult now than when I began therapy. Something has happened to me. I don't know what, and I don't know how. I'm confused.

THERAPIST   True, many things appear confusing right now. You've gone a long way in a short time. Our therapy focused on exactly what took place in your life at this time. You're successful at work. You're completing a very successful year. On the other hand, your relationships with men lead you to feelings of humiliation, disappointment, and pain.

Session twelve (the final session)

HANNAH   I had a rough time after the last session. I felt very emotional after the attempt to get closer to the image of my father. At the university, one particular woman has been hanging around me lately. I don't know how to explain it. I keep seeing her over and over again. At some point, I suddenly saw Robert approaching her, and they were walking hand in hand. I'm better looking than her, much worthier. I have no doubt about that. I felt happy about the ability to see myself as worthy.

THERAPIST Can you part with the pathetic image of the unsuccessful person who always misses the mark, and allow another part of you, another part of the puddle, to take over and have an effect?

HANNAH I think something has changed inside of me. Yesterday, I saw a good-looking guy in the store. I felt very attracted to him. We began talking, and he was ready to take me to his car so we could party, and I stopped myself, easily. I said, 'This isn't what I want from myself.' And I didn't regret it. A similar thing happened on the road. At a traffic light, somebody asked me what I would do with him. He was really cute, charming, and stunningly beautiful. Without thinking twice, I said to him, 'With you, nothing.' I enjoyed watching the face of that 'sexy success' fall. I need to continue nurturing the inner part of myself, my personality, so I won't hide it in a relationship. Although, it's still very hard for me, because I still feel insecure.

THERAPIST You need to let go of the part of yourself that prevents you from believing you deserve what's good, from believing somebody can love you just as you are.

HANNAH I don't know what effect I have on others. I have a lot of energy inside. I need to find something to work on, to invest myself in something creative. My mother will help me, I hope. I need something that attracts me and keeps me fully occupied. Therapy has helped me to understand what's what, both in regards to myself and to others.

THERAPIST What do you mean?

HANNAH Such as, regarding Robert's girlfriend – I can see I'm better than she is. That's a new discovery. I'm almost certain I won't go back to my ex-boyfriend. I have no reason to go back to somebody who took advantage of me. What do you think happened to me in therapy?

THERAPIST You allow your thoughts to have more control over your impulsive side. You are also more connected to your emotional side. As a child, you fled from anything related to emotion, because your emotions were very painful. Today, you can cope better. You've worked very hard, but it's a never-ending process. It's impossible to say everything works out easily, but now you have more tools to stop and think. You also believe in yourself more. You believe you have value and that you're a whole person. You have the sense of an image in which you are an entire world unto yourself on the one hand, while on the other hand, you're the puddle.

HANNAH   And if it doesn't work? What if I don't find the way?

THERAPIST   Then there are additional pathways for obtaining help. You can always return to the clinic.

HANNAH   It took me so long to open up and feel I was working hard, and now the therapy is over, just like that.

Approximately two months later, prior to the conclusion of the first follow-up period, Hannah contacted the clinic and requested to speak with her therapist urgently. She reported herself as having more or less managed to get along for four weeks. She felt okay, and whenever she longed for the therapist or felt any other emotion toward her, she tried to soothe herself by telling herself it would pass. Simultaneously, she began noticing two phenomena of concern. The first was extreme sexual promiscuity, a fervent awakening of sexual desire, along with almost uncontrollable seductive behavior and attraction to men. Second, her functioning at work had declined. At first, she felt a sense of freedom, as if she had been released from something, which she enjoyed. After a while, she began worrying, and feeling ashamed and extremely distressed by her out of control behavior. This condition was accompanied by panic and an extreme anxiety syndrome, manifested in crying, shakiness, and decreased concentration. She returned to the clinic in an acute state of anxiety.

The therapist saw Hannah within an hour of her arrival to the clinic. She felt extremely guilty about what had transpired in the therapy and in the termination, and accepted her back into therapy, which lasted for another three years.

Discussion

Based upon its outcome, Hannah's therapy is an example of TLP gone awry. One to two months subsequent to the termination of therapy, Hannah felt worse than when she initially sought therapy, and was functioning on a level that endangered her very existence.

She had become entangled in sexual escapades and massively damaged her work at school. To what can we attribute the lack of success in this therapy?

Three clear reasons can be identified for the failure of this therapy:

- Hannah was not a suitable candidate for TLP.
- The therapist had difficulty maintaining the focus of the therapy.
- The separation was not processed.

Patient selection

Hannah was a young woman with a fundamental disturbance in the core of her personality organization. Her functioning was characterized by large gaps. Whereas she achieved reasonably well at work, she exhibited deficits in the interpersonal arena and functioned on a deteriorated level. These deficits manifested themselves in the quality of the interpersonal relationships she formed. She was incapable of forming fully intimate relationships as defined by Sifneos (1972), relationships characterized by mutual exchange of give and take. She perceived all relationships as one-sided, consequently damaging her ability to enjoy any emotional connection. The reasons for her relational difficulties appeared to stem from the extremely problematic relationship that developed with an unstable father figure, a figure toward whom she developed severe ambivalence during her early years. She lived her adult life under the shadow of this ambivalence, without having resolved Oedipal or pre-Oedipal problems. The massive use of primitive defense mechanisms in her personality, such as splitting, idealization, and denial, was a contraindication and should have served as a warning against her suitability as a TLP candidate.

Apparently, the evaluators erred in respect to Hannah on two dimensions. The first was the misleading nature of her striking appearance. It was difficult to recognize deep-rooted self-image difficulties in such an attractive and well-groomed woman. The second dimension was her high functioning (unstable though it was) in her work at school. One final dimension overlooked in her assessment interview was the dependent element of her personality, which caused her to experience a rapid feeling of attachment to the therapist, followed by tremendous separation difficulties which ultimately sent her back into therapy.

The diagnosis of borderline personality with dependent features was essentially a contraindication of Hannah's suitability for TLP. However, for the reasons outlined above, this diagnosis was apparently not obvious enough to the evaluators, nor to the therapist, at the beginning of the therapy. Mann (1973) and Mann and Goldman (1982) clearly state that people with borderline personality organizations are not suited to TLP. This claim is supported by extensive research related to TLP patient selection and to the relationship between patients suited to brief psychotherapy and positive outcome as a result of this type of therapy (Hoglend 1993a, 1993b, 1996). The presence of borderline personality disorder, as diagnosed on axis II of the DSM-IV, and the existence of enduring interpersonal problems in the pre-therapy personality, serve as predictors of poor results for brief psychotherapy. Another group of researchers focused on the quality of object relations in the patient and its relationship to positive brief therapy outcome (Piper et al. 1991a; Piper et al. 1991b; Piper et al. 1995). The main findings were that quality of object relations was a good predictive measure of outcome, manifested in symptomatic changes and alterations in functioning. The clinical descriptions of Hannah clearly indicate deteriorated object relations, even though they were not measured quantitatively using the measurement scales utilized by Piper et al. in their research.

Difficulties in the therapist's focus

Following the assessment sessions, the therapist identified a central issue and presented it to Hannah. It is repeated here:

> Despite the difficulties you experienced in childhood and throughout your life, you've succeeded in attaining impressive achievements. Nevertheless, you have always carried a feeling of humiliation, which prevents you from forming a truly intimate relationship with a man. Along the way, you've fought for your place between two worlds, between the world in which you grew up and to which you don't want to belong, and the other world in which you try to assimilate yet never fully succeed. You are torn between the two worlds. And you are always hiding something.

Besides its length and awkwardness, the central issue was not focused enough. It described Hannah's lifetime strengths and the experience of failure in her relationships with men. From here, the therapist shifted to the struggle of living between two worlds. This struggle differed from Hannah's relationship failures. It was an undefined conflict, leading to a scattering of the patient's emotions, as seen in the following therapy hours. Furthermore, the therapist stated Hannah was hiding something, though she did not specify what Hannah was hiding. Also, the central issue lacked any reference to the essential element of Hannah's feelings toward herself. Although the therapist certainly recognized Hannah's serious self-image difficulties, she neither explicitly nor implicitly included this point in the central issue, thus damaging the coherence of the central issue as a central and healing interpretation.

The therapist sensed the central issue was ineffective in the therapy process, and she suggested an alternative central issue in the fourth therapy session:

> Your many successes are accompanied by a feeling of humiliation and lack of trust that you are truly loved.

This time, the correction erred toward the opposite extreme. The new central issue contained only emotion and strengths, and lacked the integration the central issue is intended to provide. It can be hypothesized that the fluctuations of this highly competent TLP therapist between these two poles stemmed from disorientation, as a result of the splits in Hannah's personality. The difficulty experienced by the therapist was a direct by-product of the basic personality structure of the patient. In addition to its debilitating effect on her ability to propose a well-formulated central issue, Hannah's personality also led the therapist to avoid or overlook the central issue on many occasions when there was an opportunity to utilize it.

In TLP, the main function of the therapist is twofold: first, the therapist must formulate and present the central issue, and second, the therapist must maintain and adhere to the central issue throughout the treatment. In my estimation, the therapist had difficulty performing the second task, as stated, due to the splitting and diffusing effects of Hannah's personality. The therapist also had difficulty adhering to the second central issue and centering her interpretations upon it, and she occasionally even fell back into

interpreting based upon the first central issue. As such, her identification and collusion with Hannah's diffusive tendencies severely
reduced her ability to help Hannah by means of TLP. These
processes are dealt with extensively by Wiseman et al. (1993) and
Tishby, Shefler, and Sargel-Zvieli (in press) and are described and
discussed at length in Chapter 11, which focuses on research in
TLP.

With convincing clinical evidence, the therapist exemplified the
claim of Barber et al. (1996) that adherence to the therapeutic
model, or therapy manual, is the key determinant of a therapy's
success and positive therapy outcome.

Avoidance of coping with separation in therapy

We appointed two primary functions to the TLP therapist. The first
function entails the selection of the central issue and its maintenance throughout the therapy. The second function of the TLP
therapist involves directly relating to the questions of separation
and time, even if the therapist must initiate these questions on
occasion. Mann (1973, 1991) claims the therapist's empathic handling of the pains of separation is one of the central curative factors
in the treatment. The ability of the therapist to evoke and contain
the problematic and painful emotions of the patient surrounding
the separation from the therapist provides the most direct path
toward better coping with future separations.

The therapist was rapidly confronted with Hannah's separation
difficulties, consequent on both Hannah's dependent personality
features and the severe distress that characterized her development. Throughout her adult life, Hannah had been bruised by
traumatic separations, the main separation being the death of her
father; whereas, throughout her earlier years, she sustained emotional damage from injuries relating to attachment and intimacy.
Hannah's striking difficulties in these areas distanced the therapist
from direct and confrontational coping with the separation issues,
which arose immediately, as soon as therapy began. The reader
may take issue with many points in the first six therapy sessions,
and ask how it might have been possible to create more dynamic
links between the separation difficulties in the transference and
Hannah's current, and past, reality. It seems Hannah's extreme
vulnerability, coupled with the therapist's resistance to brief

therapy, biased the therapist toward adopting a more supportive stance whenever Hannah required her to relate to their imminent separation. This led to massive acting out of the separation processes, avoidance of discussing any negative emotion crucial to these processes, and, ultimately, negation of the separation by Hannah's return to extended therapy, following the development of a potentially dangerous situation which could not be ignored, either ethically or clinically.

This case demonstrates how inappropriate patient selection, difficulty in maintaining the focus, and avoidance of separation issues apparently led to the unsuccessful outcome of TLP. I believe the inappropriate selection of this particular patient for TLP was responsible for the inappropriate actions taken by the therapist throughout the therapy and for its poor outcome. I raise these final claims not as definitive conclusions, but as hypotheses to be examined empirically in similar cases in the future.

Chapter 11

Research in time-limited psychotherapy

In the introduction to his first book on time-limited dynamic psychotherapy Mann wrote:

> I have made no effort to support my clinical observations with numbers or statistics. The exposition of my treatment model is sufficiently clear and precise to allow for its testing by others in many psychiatric clinics. If it stimulates others to do it and to compose research designs to verify its validity, then my efforts in treating and in writing will have been sufficiently rewarded.
>
> (1973: xii)

The academic challenge made by Mann was approached in a few clinical settings in the USA, Norway, Canada and Israel. This chapter provides a detailed and up-to-date review of the research work on time-limited psychotherapy.

Empirical studies of any kind of psychotherapy, including time-limited psychotherapy, fall into two major divisions, outcome research and process research. Outcome research addresses the questions of (1) whether psychotherapy has any effects at all, (2) which forms of therapy can be proven effective and for whom, and (3) how stable are the outcomes over time? Process research focuses on the issue of *how* change occurs, undertaking the empirical investigation of the therapeutic processes experienced by both clients and clinicians throughout the course of treatment. The two types of research are not entirely distinct and separate categories, rather they are intertwined. Empirical examination of treatment outcomes generates many questions pertaining to therapeutic processes. In turn, the inquiry into therapeutic process is meaningless unless it is accompanied by information regarding the outcome of the therapy under investigation.

I OUTCOME STUDIES

Two preliminary uncontrolled outcome studies took fundamental first steps in bridging the gap between 'unscientific' clinical observations and empirical support of time-limited psychotherapy's effectiveness based upon systematic measurement.

In Norway, Hoglend (1988) compared the effectiveness of TLP in the treatments of four 'well-adjusted' patients and four 'less well-adjusted' patients. The less well-adjusted patients suffered from serious pre-Oedipal pathology and were characterized by unstable interpersonal relationships, weaker social support systems, less coherent self-images, greater denial of dependency needs, and depression experienced as emptiness or anger. The outcome measures assessed the changes in symptomatology and dynamic structure and included a standard mental health measure. Although the less well-adjusted patients made modest gains, the results of a two-year follow-up showed considerably greater gains among the well-adjusted patients as compared to the less well-adjusted patients. In his discussion of the supposed processes that led to the outcome disparity, Hoglend suggests that the fixed termination date brought separation issues to the forefront for the well-adjusted patients, allowing the therapy to unfold into the three distinct phases delineated by Mann (see p. 64) and the therapeutic work of each phase to be accomplished. In contrast, the less well-adjusted patients tended to engage rapidly in a power struggle and to have greater difficulty coping with the activation of their emotional needs, the recognition of interpersonal adaptive failures, and the pain of separation.

The preliminary data gathered in another uncontrolled trial with a two-year follow-up (Witztum et al. 1989) provided the groundwork for a larger, controlled outcome study in the same mental health center (see section on the Jerusalem Time-Limited Psychotherapy Project, p. 217). Six patients were treated with somewhat modified forms of TLP: in two cases the termination date was set during the final phase of treatment and the fixed time limit of another case was eighteen sessions rather than twelve. One patient was blind, another suffered from post-traumatic stress disorder, and a third presented hysterical personality traits. Thus, half of the patients were atypical instances of TLP cases. The outcome measures evaluated symptomatology, proband complaints, and goal attainment (assessed by independent judges), and focused primarily on self-esteem and social functioning. The results demonstrated significant improvements on measures of goal attainment and proband complaints that were maintained, and even tended to increase, during the two-year follow-up period.

Although the aforementioned studies reported positive results for TLP, the lack of a controlled design renders their findings scientifically less substantial. Notwithstanding the methodological flaws, these studies comprise the earliest ground-breaking attempts at systematic observation of TLP.

One of the best designed investigations to-date was a comparative outcome study conducted in Edmonton, Canada (Piper et al. 1984) of four forms of psychoanalytically oriented therapy, categorized according to therapy type (group vs. individual) and duration (six months vs. twenty-four months). One hundred and six patients were assigned to the four groups: short-term individual, long-term individual, short-term group, and long-term group. Randomization was only possible in terms of therapy type, whereas duration assignment was determined by whether the proband sought treatment in the earlier or later stages of the study. Each therapist treated one set of patients with each of the forms of treatment, thus intervening therapist factors were controlled. There was no control group in this study. Two-thirds of the patients received DSM-II diagnoses of neurosis and just under one-third of the patients received a diagnosis of personality disorder.

The wide variety of outcome measures that assessed interpersonal functioning, symptomatology, and personal target objectives were drawn from three sources: the proband, the therapist, and an independent assessor. Analyses of the seventy-nine patients who remained in the study for the full duration suggested that neither therapy type nor duration were independently correlated with treatment outcome. The significant factor was the particular combination of therapy type and duration. Long-term group therapy demonstrated the strongest correlation with positive outcome, while short-term individual therapy was a close second. Short-term individual therapy proved more effective than long-term individual therapy. The outcomes either remained stable, or even showed a tendency toward improvement, throughout the six-month follow-up interval.

In another comparative design, Brockman et al. (1987) compared the outcomes of eighteen patients treated with Mann's TLP to the outcomes of thirty patients treated with a twelve-session 'cognitive-analytic' therapy (CAT). In contrast to the brief interventions, the patients presented with relatively long histories of emotional difficulty. Despite the lack of a no-treatment comparison group, the researchers contended that the brevity of treatment, the long histories, and the specificity of the therapies enabled them to attribute emotional change to the treatments under study. This point, however, is debatable. Additionally, none of the therapists had experience with short-term therapy nor did they receive formal training or regular supervision. An attempt was made to control for therapist differences by assigning each therapist to treat patients in both treatment type groups.

The combination of universal and individual outcome measures used was based primarily on proband self-report. The universal measures included three standard symptom questionnaires; individual measures focused on cognitive changes in attitudes toward self and interpersonal relationships. Pre- and post-therapy interviews as well as a therapy experience questionnaire were used to measure the patients' assessments of effectiveness of their treatments. Follow-up evaluations, conducted by post, were held at inconsistent intervals ranging from eight months to twenty-two months for reasons not specified by the authors.

Both forms of brief therapy demonstrated similar efficacy in reducing presenting symptomatology in cases of equivalent severity. The CAT method, however, demonstrated greater change on measures of underlying assumptions regarding self and relationships. The changes in symptomatology and assumptions were maintained throughout the follow-up period. Though interesting, the outcome differences are somewhat less informative when sample-matching difficulties and potential supervisor bias are taken into account. The randomization procedure created a CAT group with more severe symptomatology than the TLP group, thus the groups were not matched in terms of severity. Furthermore, the supervision of both types of therapy by the originator of the CAT approach may have introduced a degree of bias into the intergroup comparisons. The results regarding treatment efficacy would have been strengthened by the inclusion of a control group as well as independent raters of outcome.

Outcome research can also be useful in identifying populations for whom a particular therapy method is most effective. In an exploratory attempt in the USA to define patient characteristics that predict success in brief dynamic psychotherapy, Hovne (1984) examined the relationship between assessment measures and outcome in seven patients treated with TLP and one proband treated with an alternative brief psychotherapy. The mean number of therapy sessions for each proband was eighteen, indicating that Mann's TLP model was approximated, but not strictly followed. The presenting problems consisted mainly of interpersonal difficulties and intrapsychic problems, with patients receiving DSM-III diagnoses of major depression, adjustment disorder, and conditions not attributable to a mental disorder. Treatment outcome was evaluated on the basis of proband self-report in addition to therapist and researcher assessments using a variety of measures.

The research team examined four groups of predictive variables: content and process of intake sessions; mental health; extra-therapeutic conditions; and level of distress. Several intake session factors predicted treatment success, including affect, psychological-mindedness, motivation, response to interventions, and, to a lesser degree, focality. The most significant predictor was affect, indicating the essential nature of the TLP client's ability to engage rapidly in an intense emotional experience. High level of distress demonstrated a significant positive correlation with treatment success, whereas mental health factors and extra-therapeutic conditions were not significantly related to treatment outcome. It is important to note that the intake session factors were evaluated by the clinician, while the level of distress was based on proband self-report. These results bolster the impression that it is important to utilize a variety of selection and assessment measures both in research and clinical practice.

Overall, the small base of time-limited psychotherapy outcome literature is characterized by a lack of controlled studies based upon diversified and balanced outcome measures. Koss and Butcher (1986: 656) recommended that outcome studies 'employ more diverse measures of outcome (i.e., standardized interview procedures, target symptoms ratings, clinical observer ratings of improvement, evaluations of social functioning, objective tests, etc.) and untreated control groups for comparison.'

The Jerusalem Time-Limited Psychotherapy Project (JTLPP)

In response to the paucity of diverse and well-controlled outcome studies, our research team conducted a controlled comparison (Shefler et al. 1995). Our experimental group received time-limited dynamic psychotherapy immediately after intake. Concordant with the length of therapy in the experimental group, the members of the control group were asked to wait three months before undergoing TLP. Both groups were followed up at six and twelve months after therapy termination. Three hypotheses were formulated:

1   In the experimental group, recipients of TLP were expected to demonstrate significantly greater improvement on outcome measures as compared with the waiting-list control group. We anticipated that the control group patients would show no improvement and perhaps even deteriorate during the three-month waiting period.
2   After TLP, the control patients were expected to show a degree of improvement comparable to the experimental group.
3   Results were expected to remain stable in both groups throughout the six- and twelve-month follow-up intervals.

The study was conducted at the Herzog Ezrat-Nashim Community Mental Health Center in Jerusalem. The center services the North Jerusalem catchment region (about 150,000 citizens), delivering a wide range of outpatient psychiatric and psychological services to clients of various socioeconomic levels and cultural backgrounds.

Approximately fifteen new referrals per week are invited to a screening interview, conducted by the mental health worker on duty. The initial half-hour screening session is utilized primarily to pinpoint the factors contributing to the client's distress. The staff member uses the information gathered in the screening interview to make initial treatment decisions regarding the need for hospitalization, medication, further assessment, or referral to another treatment facility. Cases that require further assessment, such as candidates for TLP or any other form of psychotherapy, are presented at the weekly staff meeting for a more thorough discussion of the optimal treatment. See Shefler and Greenberg (1991) for a detailed outline of the Center's procedures.

Patients

Thirty-three participants were selected from the walk-in service of the Center's adult outpatient clinic over the course of two years and three months. The patients were selected in two phases. First, the walk-in screening procedure was used to exclude candidates who seemed absolutely unsuitable for TLP after the application of Mann's predefined exclusion criteria (i.e., schizophrenia in any of its subtypes, bipolar affective disorders, schizoid characteristics, obsessive characteristics with major and almost exclusive defenses of isolation and intellectualization, borderline conditions, and psychosomatic disorders). Of 404 screened patients, forty-five (11 per cent) seemed suitable for TLP at the screening phase. In our community mental health center, about 15 per cent of the referrals are suitable for psychodynamic psychotherapy. This somewhat low percentage is explained by the higher percentages of patients with psychoses and many severe social and personality disorders in the Center's catchment area.

The forty-five suitable candidates were then referred for further evaluation and assessment administered by TLP team members. Finally, the team carefully evaluated the patients' capacity to delay therapy for three months. Patients who were found unsuitable for therapy within the research design were referred for other forms of treatment in the clinic. Of the forty-five patients who underwent the evaluation process, thirty-three were selected to take part in the research. Eight patients preferred a referral to private practice, and four patients in crisis condition were unable to take part in the randomization procedure. The thirty-three selected patients were divided randomly into the experimental group (n = 16) and the control group (n = 17).[1]

Therapists

The patients were also randomly assigned to available therapists. Nine therapists took part in the study: six senior clinical

---

1 One control group proband dropped out of the study after the waiting period. Upon arrival to the first treatment session, he notified the therapist that he would be out of the country for several weeks. Although both the therapist and the client agreed that it was preferable to begin treatment upon his return, the client never returned for treatment. Thus, the control group was composed of seventeen patients for intergroup comparisons and only sixteen patients for the intragroup comparisons.

psychologists, two psychiatric social workers, and one senior psychiatrist. The therapists participating in the study were all successful graduates of previous TLP courses conducted by experienced TLP supervisors (Gaby Shefler and Haim Dasberg – both of whom were trained in TLP by James Mann). The courses consisted of twelve weekly meetings (similar to TLP itself), emphasizing the parallel process that occurs in the supervision of psychotherapy. Therapist resistance is a critical factor in the treatment process. As described by Witztum and Dasberg (1986), the training courses dealt thoroughly with the manifestations of resistance in the supervision process. The structure and didactic principles of the courses are detailed in Winokur and Dasberg (1983) and Dasberg and Winokur (1984, 1989).

The minimum requirement for participation in the TLP courses was two years of supervised experience in long-term psychotherapy. From the ten to twelve participants in each course, two to four were chosen to continue their training. After a period of individual supervision, the trainees were invited to join the permanent team of TLP therapists. The TLP team met regularly for group supervision of TLP cases, theoretical and clinical discussions, and updates on recent literature published in the field. Consequently, all the therapists underwent thorough and uniform training in TLP and had at least two supervised TLPs before joining the study. Furthermore, each therapist received individual supervision for the first four therapy sessions conducted as part of the study and participated in a weekly supervision group throughout the study.

Evaluators

The pre- and post-therapy assessment procedures were conducted by evaluators other than the actual therapists. These evaluators were also TLP-trained therapists, with special training in the use of the measuring instruments and procedures. The training included discussion of anticipated problems in the administration of the measures as well as the differential responses of clients in various situations. The training process was designed to ensure uniform administration of the measuring instruments. Additionally, tape-recorded assessment interviews were used in exercises designed to sharpen the evaluators' ability to recognize and improve upon their work with stumbling blocks within the interviews. Finally, each evaluator was supplied with very specific directions to follow throughout the assessment process.

Judges

Ten therapists, experienced in both long-term psychotherapy and TLP, were trained in the administration of two specific measurement scales, the Goal Attainment Scale and the Health–Sickness Rating Scale (see measures below). Each judge attended three full-day 'hands-on' workshops to attain proficiency in administration of the instruments. The workshops began with group evaluations of previously transcribed clinical material, and moved on to work in pairs. Each pair of judges evaluated a minimum of five cases, followed by discussions on the strategies utilized in the judgment process. The trainers emphasized the consistent use of uniform operational terms to create a shared language among the judges. By the end of the three workshops, the judges demonstrated high levels of reliability in the administration of both instruments.

Supervisors

Three senior therapists with at least five years experience in brief psychotherapy, training and experience in Mann's TLP, in addition to formal clinical supervisory experience, served as supervisors for this study.

The team

The same ten therapists served as therapists, evaluators, and judges. Over the course of the study, each proband had contact with four members of the research team: the evaluator, the therapist, and two judges. Ideally, the judges would not have been members of the research team. However, the financial and technical constraints necessitated the selection of judges from the research team. Nonetheless, the thorough training and ongoing supervision of both the specific therapy method under investigation (TLP) and the administration of measurements enabled us to meet one of the chief criteria for reliable and standardized outcome studies of brief therapy methods, as discussed by Crits-Christoph (1992).

Instruments and measures

The battery of assessment scales was based on both nomothetic and individualized idiographic principles, thus achieving some balance between patients' self-reports and the independent observers' judgments of outcome. The following measures were used:

General Information Questionnaire

This is a standard sociodemographic questionnaire that elicits the family, social, demographic, occupational, and economic status of the patient.

Selection Intake Questionnaire (SIQ)

The evaluator completed this fifty-seven-item questionnaire at the conclusion of the assessment process. The following variables were rated on a scale of 1–5: the relationship with the evaluator, relationships with others, relationships with parents, affect, psychological-mindedness, motivation for therapy, responses to evaluator interventions, focus, social support network, and presumed suitability for TLP. Hovne (1984b) found that certain items were effective predictors of TLP outcomes.

Diagnostic and Statistical Manual of Mental Disorders (3rd edn; DSM-III)

All patients were diagnosed on the five axes of the DSM-III (American Psychiatric Association 1987) for descriptive purposes. Because the research was conducted during the late 1980s and early 1990s, diagnoses were made according to DSM-III-R, which are identical to the relevant DSM-IV (American Psychiatric Association 1994) diagnoses, with one exception of the lack of quantitative definition of the severity rating scale on Axis IV. The DSM-IV was modified to include only the short descriptions of social stressors, rather than the ranking system used in the DSM-III-R. Therefore, for any practical reason, the DSM-IV can be used to describe the diagnostic profile of the research sample. The diagnostic procedure took place after the pre-therapy assessment. All cases were presented by the evaluator to a trained psychiatrist, who made the diagnoses.

Target Complaints Scale (TCS)

This individualized scale (Battle et al. 1966) requires the client to specify three main complaints in ranked severity and to rate the severity of each. Mintz and Kiesler (1981) reported a test-retest reliability of .68 for this scale. A low score indicates adequate functioning on this scale.

Sentence Completion Test (SCT)

This scale, developed by Shanan (1967), is a semi-projective universal test that evaluates the quality of active coping by the client. The instrument is composed of forty uncompleted sentence stems that the client is asked to complete. It has been validated for Israeli populations. The inter-rater reliability of this instrument is .88, $p < .01$, and the test-retest reliability is .60, $p < .05$ (Hess 1976; Shanan 1967, 1973). A higher score indicates better functioning on this scale. The test was scored by an independent (masked) judge with special training in this test. In addition to the results of the full scale, the SCT's Category 4, which relates to self-esteem, held particular bearing for Mann's TLP, because changes in feeling toward the self are among the major declared objectives of this therapy.

Brief Symptom Inventory (BSI-53, Derogatis and Melisaratos 1983)

This brief revision of Derogatis, Lipman, and Covi's complex Symptom Check List (SCL-90, 1973) is a universal scale that measures psychiatric symptoms on five levels and across ten categories. It has been translated into Hebrew and validated in various studies conducted in several centers in Israel (Baider et al. 1984; Canetti et al. 1994; Roskin and Dasberg 1983). Of the various indices that were computed from this scale, we chose to use the General Severity Index (GSI), transformed into t scores, which reflects the severity of the client's general symptom level. Derogatis and Spencer (1982) reported a test-retest reliability of .90 for this index. A lower score indicates better functioning on this scale.

Health—Sickness Rating Scale (HSRS)

The HSRS (Luborsky 1975; Luborsky and Bachrach 1974) is constructed of sixty-five clinical descriptions based on seven dimensions. The dimensions include the need for protection and support, severity of symptoms, subjective level of suffering, influence on the surroundings, ability to use capacities, quality of interpersonal relationships, and the breadth and depth of a client's interests. For each proband, we selected randomly from a pool of eleven clinicians, two independent, experienced, and trained judges who were absolutely uninformed as to whether the proband belonged to the treatment or to the waiting group. These judges evaluated the seven dimensions of the HSRS, choosing a clinical profile that is most similar to the proband's condition and clinical description based on the full transcripts of the proband's evaluation sessions.

This evaluation procedure was repeated at each stage of the study (during intake, after TLP, and at the follow-ups), and the mean score of the two raters was used for the data analyses. A higher score on this scale indicates better functioning. Because several pairs of clinicians evaluated small sub-samples of patients, we computed the Pearson correlation coefficient for each pair at each stage and estimated the reliability between raters by the average correlation across pairs of raters. These means ranged from .57 (during intake) to .82 (after TLP). The average correlation across all evaluation periods was .72; this corresponds to a reliability of .84 for the average of the two raters, which was the actual measure used in the study (after applying the Spearman-Brown formula on the between-raters correlation). A test-retest reliability of .77 was reported for this scale (Luborsky 1962).

Goal Attainment Scale

This scale (Kiresuk 1973; Kiresuk and Sherman 1968) is a highly individualized measure that uses an external method of evaluating patients' conditions and the degree of success or failure in achieving individually predefined goals in therapy. On the basis of the transcripts of the pre-therapy assessment sessions, masked judges were asked to create a set of five scales relating to (a) symptoms, (b) self-esteem, (c) relationships with the same sex, (d) relationships with the opposite sex, and (e) other areas of social functioning for each proband. If the judge felt there was a need to create an additional scale for a specific proband, he or she was encouraged to do so.

After formulating the scales, the judges rated the patient's status on the basis of the pre-therapy transcripts. In the post-therapy and follow-up procedures, each judge received a set of his or her own scales and, on the basis of the post-therapy or follow-up transcripts, re-rated the patient's status on the same scales. Scores on these idiographic scales were quantified using Kiresuk and Sherman's (1968) procedures. The means of the two judges' scores were calculated using the Kiresuk-Sherman formula. A higher score indicates better functioning on this scale. Reliability between judges was estimated using the same procedure described for the HSRS. The average correlation at the different measurement periods ranged between .41 (at six months follow-up) and .63 (after TLP). The average correlation across periods was .56, which corresponds to a reliability of .72 for the average of the two raters. Mintz and Kiesler (1981) reported test-retest reliabilities of .70, .77, and .87 for this scale in three studies. A recent study in our center (Shefler et al. in press) evaluated the reliability and validity of GAS in assessing outcome in TLP. Mean interrater reliability of scores between pairs of judges was $r = .88$. Convergent validity of the GAS was confirmed by moderate to high correlations with the Health–Sickness Rating Scale ($r = .70$, $p < .0001$), the Target Complaint Scale ($r = .50$, $p < .01$), and the Brief Symptom Inventory ($r = .38$, $p < .05$).

Procedure

The procedure is outlined schematically in Figure 11.1.

Subsequent to the initial screening process described above, candidates for the study were referred to the research center for further assessment. The candidates were selected according to the following criteria:

Positive indicators for TLP   High motivation, psychological awareness, formation of a relationship with the interviewer, affective expression during the interview, ability to pinpoint the presenting complaints.

Counterindicators for TLP   Severe depression, strong suicidal tendencies, psychotic episode/s, excessive and chronic preoccupation with phobias or obsessions, addictive tendencies, tendencies toward acting out, borderline or narcissistic personality disorders, heavy reliance on primitive defenses such as massive denial or splitting. According to a previously fixed

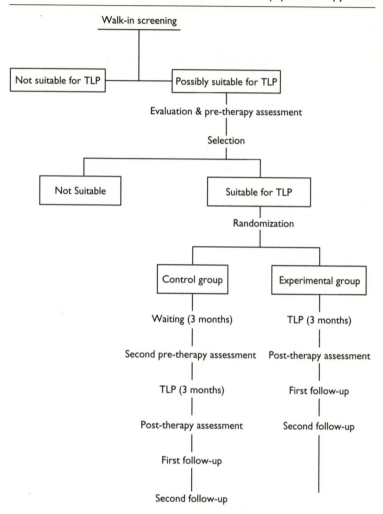

Figure 11.1   A schematic flow chart of the research procedure

schedule, each candidate was randomly assigned to an evaluator. The assessment process consisted of two fifty-minute semi-structured intake interviews that were tape recorded and transcribed. The sessions were conducted according to the formula suggested by Mann (1973) and by Mann and Goldman (1982). At the end of the first session, the candidate completed the three self-assessment scales: BSI-53, SCT, and TCS.

After the second session, the evaluator completed the SIQ and assigned a DSM-III diagnosis with the aid of a psychiatrist. The clinical material was discussed by a clinical selection committee of at least three TLP therapists, and the candidate's suitability for TLP was evaluated. Selection criteria (Mann 1973; Mann and Goldman 1982) were based on the evaluated impact of the candidate's life history (e.g. losses, harsh changes, early deprivations, etc.), the type of psychopathology, levels of ego functioning, the quality of past and current relationships established by the candidate, the ability to relate to the evaluator, the ability to present problems in a circumscribed manner, the capacity for affective expression, the candidate's responses to the evaluator's interventions (e.g. link interpretations, confrontations, empathic statements, etc.), psychological-mindedness, and motivation for therapy.

Blind protocols of the transcribed intake material were assigned randomly to two judges, each of whom administered the GAS and HSRS scales based on the clinical material.

The final selection of patients was made and the patients were assigned to either the control group or the experimental group based on a lottery procedure. The experimental patients were assigned to therapists previously selected by random assignment. The control patients were notified by telephone of their acceptance for therapy beginning in three months. The controls were assured that in three months, they would be invited to an additional session with the evaluator and assigned a therapist.

The experimental patients began TLP with a pre-therapy session, in which the therapist gathered details missing from the intake sessions and formed a rudimentary therapeutic alliance with the proband. The therapist presented the central issue and formed a therapeutic contract with the proband, consisting of twelve fifty-minute sessions and a prearranged termination date.

Throughout each therapy, the therapists received both individual and weekly group supervisions. Due to the extensive framework of training and supervision, a high level of treatment uniformity was preserved throughout the study. At the conclusion of each session, the therapist wrote a summary of the session in a standardized format.

Throughout the waiting period, none of the control patients were contacted by the Center nor did any of them contact the Center to request immediate or earlier treatment.

In the termination sessions, the therapists notified the experimental patients that they would be invited to a post-therapy session with the evaluator approximately ten days later. In the evaluation sessions, the patients completed the same self-report scales they had completed during the pre-therapy assessment procedure (BSI-53, SCT, TCS). Then they were interviewed to establish their current mental condition, as well as feelings and attitudes toward themselves. The evaluation sessions were recorded and transcribed.

At this time, the control patients were invited for a second pre-therapy assessment. They underwent the assessment procedure described earlier for the second time and then were informed of who their therapist would be, as well as the time and place of their first therapy session.

The controls then received the same TLP treatment as the experimental patients according to the format described in stages six through eight, including the post-treatment assessment phase.

Each pair of judges received unscored copies of both judges' original GAS assessments for each proband as well as a transcript of the post-therapy evaluation session. Each judge was required to assess the patient's post-therapy condition on the scales created by both judges in the pair and to assign an HSRS level. Any indications of group assignment were removed from the transcripts.

Six- and twelve-month follow-up assessments were conducted for all patients in the same format as the post-therapy assessment used at stage eight. Subsequent to each follow-up assessment, the judges repeated the procedure described in stage nine. All follow-up sessions were tape recorded and transcribed.

Results

Sociodemographic characteristics

The nine male and twenty-four female patients ranged in age from 23 to 42. Sixteen of the patients were married and seventeen were single. All patients were relatively well educated (mean years of education = 14.6) and most occupied white-collar positions. Twenty-five of the patients were Israeli-born, four were from Eastern Europe, one from Western Europe, two from North America, one from South America, and one from South Africa. No

Table 11.1 Summary of background variables in the sample: control group vs. experimental group

	Experimental group (N = 16)	Control group (N = 17)	Total (N = 33)
Gender			
Male	4	5	9
Female	12	12	24
Age			
Range	23–39	23–42	23–42
Mean	31	31	31
Mode	28	29	29
Country of origin			
Israel	12	13	25
Eastern Europe	3	1	4
Western Europe	1	–	1
North America	–	1	1
South America	–	1	1
South Africa	–	1	1
Marital status			
Married	8	8	16
Single	8	9	17
Education			
High school	6	4	10
Professional	2	4	6
Academic	8	9	17
Occupation			
White collar	12	12	24
Academic	3	3	6
Unemployed	1	2	3

significant differences were found between the experimental and control groups on the various sociodemographic variables (see Table 11.1).

Diagnoses

On Axis I of the DSM-III and DSM-IV, nine patients received no diagnosis, seven had anxiety disorders, six had depressive disorders, ten had adjustment disorders, and one had a life-phase problem. On Axis II, twenty-eight patients had no diagnosis, but a wide range of personality traits was found. Most of the patients had no physical diagnosis, and most of them had low to moderate

Table 11.2   Summary of DSM-III (and DSM-IV) diagnoses for the
control and experimental groups

	Total (N = 33)	Experimental group (N = 16)	Control group (N = 17)
Axis I Primary diagnosis			
No diagnosis	9	4	5
Anxiety disorder	7	2	5
Depression	6	2	4
Adjustment disorder	10	7	3
Phase-of-life problems	1	1	–
Axis II Personality disorder			
No diagnosis	28	15	13
Avoidant	1	–	1
Obsessive-compulsive	1	–	1
Narcissistic	1	–	1
Not otherwise specified (NOS)	2	1	1
Personality features			
Dependent	15	9	6
Avoidant	5	3	2
Passive	2	1	1
Obsessive-compulsive	6	3	3
Histrionic	4	3	1
Passive-aggressive	5	3	2
Narcissistic	3	2	1
Axis III Physical disorders and conditions	6	2	4
Axis IV Psychosocial stressors			
1-none	–	–	–
2-mild	14	10	4
3-moderate	16	6	10
4-severe	2	–	2
5-extreme	1	–	1
Axis V Global assessment of functioning (GAF)			
Current	50–80	50–73	53–80
Highest past year	53–85	50–85	53–80

psychosocial stressors. There were no differences in diagnoses
between the experimental and the control groups (see Table 11.2).

To ensure the equivalence of the experimental and the control
patients, we examined the differences between these two groups
on all of the pre-therapy assessment measures using *t* tests for

independent samples. No significant differences between the two groups were obtained on any of the outcome measures, and therefore it can be assumed that the groups are equivalent.

The mean and standard deviation of each measure was computed across patients within each group (experimental and control) for each stage (four stages for the experimental group and five for the control group). These data are displayed in Tables 11.3 and 11.4 for the experimental and control groups, respectively. In addition, Figure 11.2 displays the means of each group on each measure as a function of the experimental stages.

Outcome at therapy termination

The research hypotheses were examined using several multivariate analyses of variance (MANOVA) procedures. First, the impact of the TLP on the experimental patients was assessed by comparing the means of all the outcome measures after treatment with the means of these measures before introduction of TLP. The overall F test for the before-and-after TLP comparison was statistically significant, $F(8,8) = 11.47$. An improvement was indicated in all eight outcome measures displayed in Table 11.3, and a Bonferroni procedure revealed that in three of them (the first two target complaints and the goal attainment scale) the improvement was statistically significant. A similar analysis was conducted for the control patients, this time comparing the eight outcome measures before and after the waiting period. As expected, these differences were not statistically significant, $F(8,8) = 1.57$. Moreover, none of the individual measures revealed a significant change by the Bonferroni test, and only in three of the eight measures were the observed differences in the direction of improvement. A second analysis conducted with the control patients revealed a relatively large and significant improvement after these patients were exposed to TLP (see Table 11.4). The overall difference before and after TLP was statistically significant, $F(8,8) = 14.18$, and a significant improvement was found for each of the eight measures when the Bonferroni procedure was applied to the individual measures.

Second, the differences between the experimental group and the control group on the outcome measures after three months (after termination of TLP for the experimental patients and at the end of the waiting period for the controls) were examined. We compared these differences using a MANOVA that was performed on the gain

Table 11.3 Group means and standard deviations of outcome measures for experimental group

Scale	Before TLP (n = 16)	After TLP (n = 16)	First follow-up (n = 16)	Second follow-up (n = 15)
Target Complaints Scale				
First complaint	10.68 (1.70)	8.25 (3.21)	6.81 (2.68)	6.13 (2.53)
Second complaint	9.06 (2.97)	6.37 (3.16)	6.12 (3.77)	5.80 (3.85)
Third complaint	7.87 (3.00)	6.12 (3.13)	5.87 (3.22)	6.93 (3.43)
Sentence Completion Test				
Full scale	13.68 (4.20)	15.25 (4.56)	16.37 (4.53)	18.13 (4.77)
Category 4	3.81 (1.42)	4.50 (1.96)	5.18 (1.60)	6.13 (1.88)
Brief Symptom Inventory				
General severity index	67.56 (8.27)	64.31 (10.33)	63.18 (12.42)	61.00 (13.77)
Health–Sickness Rating Scale	67.12 (7.19)	72.40 (5.57)	73.43 (5.90)	76.13 (7.90)
Goal Attainment Scale	65.95 (1.92)	47.61 (4.90)	50.26 (4.51)	50.80 (6.03)

scores computed for the eight measures. For each measure, a gain score was defined by computing the difference ('after TLP' minus 'before TLP' for the experimental group, and 'after waiting' minus 'before waiting' for the control group), taking into account the desired direction of change (i.e., a positive gain score always indicated an improvement). This analysis revealed that the differences were statistically significant, as reflected by the overall F test, $F(8,23) = 9.18$. The differences were in the expected direction for all outcome measures, and four of them were statistically significant by the Bonferroni procedure (the goal attainment scale, the first two target complaints, and the health–sickness rating scale).

To estimate the effect size for each measure, we computed the difference between the average gain score observed in the experimental patients ('after TLP' minus 'before TLP') and the average difference score ('after waiting' minus 'before waiting') observed in the control patients divided by the common standard deviation. A global estimate for the strength of effect was derived by averaging these ratios across measures. The outcome of this computation was an average effect strength of .986.

Clinical significance of treatment outcomes

Jacobson and Truax (1991) suggested several methods for estimating the clinical significance of the changes obtained as a result of psychotherapy. Two of these methods were applied for the outcome measures used in this study:

a A criterion for a reliable change index (RC) was defined for each of seven outcome measures on the basis of the estimated standard error of the difference score (between the post-treatment and the pre-treatment values). The test-retest reliabilities reported in the literature and the sample standard deviations were used for computing these standard errors. The percentage of patients, from both the control and experimental groups, whose difference scores exceeded the RC criterion was computed for each outcome measure. These values are displayed in Table 11.5.

b A criterion for clinically significant improvement was defined for four of the outcome measures as the midpoint between the distributions of functional and dysfunctional individuals. In computing these midpoints, we adopted the procedure

Table 11.4 Group means and standard deviations of outcome measures for control group

Scale	Before wait (n = 16)	After wait (n = 16)	After TLP (n = 16)	First follow-up (n = 15)	Second follow-up (n = 14)
Target Complaints Scale					
First complaint	9.93 (1.68)	10.12 (1.99)	5.70 (2.67)	5.80 (3.25)	6.13 (2.53)
Second complaint	10.18 (2.56)	10.37 (1.70)	6.06 (3.21)	5.86 (3.21)	5.80 (3.85)
Third complaint	8.50 (2.53)	9.12 (2.57)	5.93 (2.97)	6.07 (3.65)	6.93 (3.43)
Sentence Completion Test					
Full scale	12.37 (2.30)	12.87 (4.08)	18.25 (4.28)	17.87 (4.38)	18.13 (4.77)
Category 4	2.87 (1.62)	3.18 (1.47)	5.68 (2.05)	6.06 (1.87)	6.13 (1.88)
Brief Symptom Inventory					
General severity index	71.25 (6.85)	72.31 (6.84)	62.81 (7.63)	65.20 (9.84)	61.00 (13.77)
Health–Sickness Rating Scale	66.65 (5.80)	65.18 (5.48)	74.12 (7.20)	72.20 (10.66)	76.13 (7.70)
Goal Attainment Scale	35.22 (1.12)	35.65 (2.43)	50.75 (6.14)	50.49 (6.27)	50.80 (6.03)

Table 11.5 Percentages of reliable improvement and clinically significant improvement of the whole sample

Scale	Percentage of reliable improvement	Percentage of clinically significant improvement
Target Complaints Scale		
First complaint	78	–
Second complaint	68	–
Third complaint	45	–
Sentence Completion Test		
Full scale	47	47
Category 4	–	63
Brief Symptom Inventory		
General Severity Index	75	28
Health–Sickness Rating Scale	72	78
Goal Attainment Scale	97	–

Note
Empty cells indicate that data for functional patients are unavailable for these measures.

suggested by Jacobson and Truax (1991). The means and standard deviations for the dysfunctional distributions were extracted from the pooled data of the control and experimental groups taken just before the administration of TLP, and the values for the functional distributions were taken from the literature (Derogatis and Spencer 1982, for the BSI; Hess 1976, for the two SCT measures; and Luborsky, personal communication 1994, for the HSRS). This criterion was applied only for the four measures mentioned earlier, because no information about functional individuals is available for the other measures, which are idiographic in their nature and are specifically designed for dysfunctional individuals. The percentage of patients, from both groups, whose difference scores exceeded this criterion was computed for the four outcome measures, and are displayed in Table 11.5.

Stability of changes after TLP

To test whether the improvement observed in both groups after TLP is stable, we conducted two additional MANOVAs. The outcome measures after six- and twelve-month follow-ups were compared with the same outcome measures taken immediately after TLP. These analyses were conducted for the entire group of patients (the experimental and control groups combined). After six months, five measures showed a small improvement, whereas in three measures a small decline was observed. The overall F test revealed that the changes were not statistically significant, $F(8,23) = 1.16$. After twelve months, seven of the eight measures changed in a direction of improvement, but again the overall F test was not significant, $F(8,21) = 1.54$.[2]

An examination of a therapist's effect

Finally, we examined the possibility of a therapist's effect by comparing the gains obtained on the outcome measures after treatment among the different therapists. This was done by a MANOVA performed on the gain scores ('after TLP' minus 'before TLP') computed for each measure taking the desired direction of change into account. For this analysis, the two groups were combined, but one proband had to be omitted from the analysis because he was treated by a single therapist (leaving thirty-one patients). Eight therapists were included in this analysis, and each treated between two to six patients. Using the Pillais statistic, we obtained no significant difference between the mean gain scores of the therapists, $F(64, 184) = 0.95$.

Discussion

Background variables

The socioeconomic similarity between the experimental and control groups confirms successful randomization in the study. Therefore, we can discuss the demographic makeup of the entire sample, rather than examining each group separately (Brockman et al. 1987; Piper et al. 1984; Sloane et al. 1975, 1976). The ratio of women (72 per cent) to men (28 per cent) in our sample was similar to or slightly higher than previous studies (Alexander and Eagles 1989; Piper et al. 1984; Hoglend 1988; Sloane et al. 1975), indicating that a

---

2 One patient was unavailable for evaluation at the six-month follow-up period, and an additional two patients were unavailable after one year.

higher proportion of women seek long-term and brief psychotherapies. This finding contrasts the relatively even proportions of men and women who seek treatment in psychiatric clinics.

Although the relatively young age of our sample (23 to 42 years old) is consistent with the ages reported in other outcome studies (Sloane et al. 1975, 1976; Bernard et al. 1980; Piper et al. 1984; Buckley et al. 1984; Alexander and Eagles 1989), it is younger than the average age of clients treated in community mental health centers. Similar to other psychotherapeutic research, our sample was composed solely of the stratum of clients most suitable for psychotherapy, a stratum that generally tends to be younger than other clinical populations (Alexander and Eagles 1989).

There was an equal distribution of married and single patients in our sample, although the sample contained fewer divorced patients than previous studies (Alexander and Eagles 1989; Piper et al. 1984). A greater proportion of our sample had received higher education (51 per cent) than some samples reported in the literature (Sloane et al. 1975, 1976; Piper et al. 1984; Brockman et al. 1987); however the overall educational level of our sample was lower than those in three studies conducted at university mental health centers whose samples had unusually high educational levels (Muench 1965; Keilson et al. 1979; Bernard et al. 1980). The distribution of patients into white-collar (72 per cent) and academic (18 per cent) professions underscored the absence of blue-collar workers in our sample. Finally, only 10 per cent of our sample were unemployed.

The profile of our patients as young, highly educated, white-collar professionals is typical of clients who are suitable for any kind of dynamic psychotherapy. The acronym YAVIS summarizes the profile of these clients: Young, Attractive, Verbal, Intelligent, Student.

Diagnostic variables

In contrast to the relatively equal demographic distribution, there were slight diagnostic differences between the experimental and control groups in our study. The primary Axis I diagnoses in the experimental group were anxiety disorders and depression, whereas the control group was characterized by adjustment disorders. Nonetheless, both groups contained a relatively high percentage (27 per cent) of patients who did not receive any Axis I diagnosis. These results support previous findings (Alexander and Eagles 1989) suggesting that the majority of clients suitable for any type of dynamic psychotherapy suffer from neurotic disturbances rather than severe psychiatric disorders.

MacKenzie (1988) asserts that a DSM-III Axis I diagnosis should serve solely as a counter-indicator for brief dynamic therapy. Our results clarify this point in terms of Axis II diagnoses. Clients who reveal severe personality disorders are not suitable for TLP (Mann 1973; Mann and Goldman 1982) and were eliminated during the initial selection process. Consequently, 84 per cent of our sample did not receive an Axis II diagnosis. Instead, our sample was characterized by a wide range of neurotic and idiosyncratic personality trends, typical of clients treated by dynamic psychotherapy. Although the variance in personality trends within this client population makes it difficult to identify universal inclusion criteria for outcome studies, the diagnostic nature of our sample is similar to other samples reported in the outcome literature (Frank 1959; Sloane et al. 1975, 1976; Piper et al. 1984).

In our study, only six patients (four controls and two experimental patients) received Axis III diagnoses such as hair loss, hearing loss, enlargement of the heart's chambers, lower back pain, a peptic ulcer, a dislocated hip and eczema. Notwithstanding the lack of a significant correlation between the Axis III diagnoses and the outcome results, these somatic difficulties undoubtedly influenced the individual therapeutic processes (for example, the case of the woman who suffered from a hearing loss).

In terms of Axis IV psychosocial stressors, the severity was diagnosed as moderate for 90 per cent of the patients who were evenly distributed between the experimental and control groups. In both groups, the levels of global functioning assessed on Axis V tended toward the moderate range (GAF = 50–85).

Beyond its utility as an outcome measure, the Target Complaints Scale can function as a subjective description of client distress, broadening our understanding of the sample profile from the perspective of the patients themselves. The abundance of complaints regarding self-image (28 per cent), affective state (24 per cent), and interpersonal relationships (19 per cent) was striking, and consistent across both groups. The reported complaints closely resemble the TLP client populations described by Mann (1973) and Mann and Goldman (1982), in both theoretical writings and case studies.

Overall the patients were not psychiatrically ill but showed a variety of depressive and anxious reactions, including a wide range of personality trends. From a socioeconomic and diagnostic perspective, the experimental and control groups were remarkably similar both to each other and to samples found in the previous dynamic psychotherapy outcome studies cited above. Likewise, the population under study typified the clients who are positively indicated for TLP as well as long-term dynamic psychotherapies.

Our results demonstrate the efficacy of TLP in treating clients with profiles of this type. The specificity of the sample raises the question of the degree of generalizability of our results. Several researchers (Frank et al. 1959; Shlien et al. 1962; Sloane et al. 1975, 1976; Piper et al. 1984) contended that the effectiveness of brief psychotherapy is comparable to the effectiveness of long-term psychotherapy for suitable clients. The stringent selection of clients who were positively indicated for Mann's TLP created a sample that is also representative of clients suitable for long-term therapy. Consequently, the results can be generalized to the overall population of clients suited to Mann's TLP which is also the same population of individuals suited to long-term therapy. Future studies should employ less rigid inclusion criteria in order to ascertain the effectiveness of TLP in treating clients who suffer from more severe psychopathology, based on the models of Malan (1963), Lazarus (1982), Sjodin (1983), Svedlund (1983), Krupnick and Horowitz (1985) and Hoglend (1988), who demonstrated reasonable success with 'difficult' clients. Hobbs (1989) proposed a broadening of the scope of TLP outcome studies to include specific groups such as older adults, trauma victims, personality disorders and individuals under stress.

The focus of this particular study, however, was to investigate the effectiveness and stability of TLP. The strict inclusion criteria helped minimize the risk of selecting inappropriate patients who would create false negative results. Thus, the avoidance of false negative results took priority over broadening the population under study.

Treatment outcome

The report of pre-treatment levels on the outcome measures distinguishes this study from its predecessors. The initial lack of significant differences between the experimental and control groups on the eight outcome measures strengthens the impression of inter-group uniformity created by the sociodemographic and diagnostic variables. The experimental group, however, showed a slight, though statistically insignificant, advantage over the controls.

Both groups started at the same point in terms of sociodemographic, diagnostic, and outcome measure factors. After three months of either TLP or waiting, however, the experimental group demonstrated a distinct advantage over the controls on all outcome measures. The control patients showed no improvement, and their situation seemed to worsen, although the deterioration was merely a trend that did not attain statistical significance. With the exception of the full-scale SCT, the differences between the experimental and control groups were significant, demonstrating the positive outcome of Mann's TLP as compared to receiving no treatment. Similar results have been found in previous comparisons of an experimental treatment group versus a non-treatment or waiting-list control group (Frank et al. 1959; Shlein 1962; Sloane et al. 1975, 1976; Keilson et al. 1979).

The experimental group showed post-therapy improvement on all of the outcome measures, attaining significant improvement on four of the measures. In stark contrast to the lack of improvement after the waiting period, the controls demonstrated significant post-therapy improvements on all measures. The improvement in the control group reinforces the acceptance of the first and second hypotheses.

These findings are similar to those obtained by researchers who studied other forms of brief dynamic psychotherapy (Frank et al. 1959; Sloane et al. 1975, 1976; Piper et al. 1984). Following Smith, Glass, and Miller (1980) we calculated the effect size of the therapeutic change. The average effect size computed across outcome measures was 0.986 SD. This considerable effect size clearly demonstrates the effectiveness of TLP, especially in comparison to previously reported effects (the average effect size reported by Smith et al. (1980) for long-term dynamic psychotherapy was 0.69 SD, and the effect sizes reported by Crits-Christoph (1992) range between 0.81 to 1.1 SD for different measures).

The results of this study clearly support the second hypothesis that the application of TLP would yield improvements in the control group similar to the improvements made by the experimental group. The controls showed improvements on all eight outcome measures. On three of the measures (SCT full scale, SCT

category 4, and BSI-53) the controls' improvements were significantly higher than the improvements in the experimental group.
These results differ from a previous controlled comparison in
which Gottschalk, Fox, and Bates (1973) reported a similar
improvement pattern both in their treatment group who received
six weeks of crisis intervention treatment and in the waiting list
controls. There have been no controlled comparisons in the literature demonstrating an experimental group advantage over the
control group after the control group had received the same
treatment.

Among the sociodemographic variables, only marital status
demonstrated a significant correlation with treatment outcome.
Previous findings (Frank et al. 1959; Sloane et al. 1975, 1976; Piper
et al. 1984) indicate that married clients tend to have a better
prognosis than unmarried clients. Because the ability to form an
interpersonal relationship is crucial to the success of brief psychotherapy, it follows that marital status is a relevant variable.

The more drastic improvements in the control group might seem
to indicate an advantage to waiting three months rather than
providing immediate treatment. Thus, it is important to examine
alternate explanations for the dramatic results found in the control
group. One possibility is that during the three-month waiting
period, the development of higher expectations engendered higher
motivation. Consequently, the control patients may have worked
harder in therapy. Frank's (1959) and Wilkins's (1973) contention
that the client's expectations influence the outcome of therapy has
been supported empirically by McKitrick and Gelso (1978).

In the current study, the assessment experience in addition to
the assurance from the evaluators that they would be treated in
another three months may have influenced the controls. It is
important to emphasize that at the initial assessment point neither
the clients nor the evaluators knew the patient's future group
assignment, yet there was no difference between groups on the
assessment measures. Therefore, the waiting period somehow
altered the degree of post-treatment improvement as compared to
the patients who received immediate treatment. The remarkably
low dropout rate from the control group bolsters the impression of
an expectancy effect among the control patients.

A complementary explanation construes the waiting period as a
period of deprivation that instilled a 'hunger' for therapy in the
control patients. When therapy was finally supplied, the satiation

of that hunger elicited powerful results. This hunger effect can be considered an intensification of the waiting period expectation effect.

A third explanation for the control results is linked to control difficulties in clinical research. It is reasonable to contend that the experimental group received three months of treatment, whereas the control group actually received six months of treatment. The six months included assessment, waiting, and eventual intervention. Perhaps the increased length of overall treatment engendered more impressive results. This explanation rests on the assumption that the assessment and selection processes are actually intervention processes (Davanloo 1972, 1978; Sifneos 1972, 1979) and is supported by the lack of control dropouts during the waiting period. It is feasible that the intensive assessment procedure and the expectation of change positively influenced the treatment outcome in the control group. This explanation is weakened, however, by the lack of change on outcome measures in the control group subsequent to the waiting period.

The final explanation relates to the composition differences between the experimental and control groups. The controls tended to suffer from adjustment disorders and clients of that type generally respond more strongly to therapeutic intervention than depressive or anxious clients.

Analysis of the entire sample as a single group demonstrated the clear positive effect of TLP on all eight outcome measures. Applying two of the methods recommended by Jacobson and Truax (1991), the results suggest that across measures and methods for significant improvement, the rate of overall reliable improvement is about two-thirds (the median percentage across the eleven entries of Table 11.5 is 68 per cent).

Moreover, the significant improvements yielded by TLP remained stable in both groups. Our follow-up results showed trends toward continued improvement and consistent declines in the experimental and control groups respectively, though neither of the trends attained statistical significance. These trends, however, narrowed the gap between the two groups indicating nearly equal levels of achievement by the twelve-month follow-up (a form of regression toward the mean). Both groups maintained significant levels of post-therapy improvement as compared to pre-therapy starting points on all outcome measures. Thus, the third hypothesis was confirmed.

Similarly, Witztum, Dasberg and Shefler (1989) reported stable positive treatment outcomes over the course of two years. Frank (1959), Shlein et al. (1962), Heiberg (1978), Sloane et al. (1975), and Piper et al. (1984) reported similar results at follow-ups ranging from six months to two years post-therapy. Although these researchers found some long-term changes in therapeutic achievements, the significant changes that transpired between pre- and post-therapy measurements were preserved.

There may not be a clear-cut resolution of the outcome differences between the experimental and control groups. Nonetheless, the results touch upon the ethical issue involved in the use of a control group. Not only did the controls not suffer from the three-month delay in treatment, they appeared to benefit from it. Therefore, the results can allay ethical concerns regarding the random assignment of research controls. The follow-up results confirm the lack of harmful consequence in random group assignment; ultimately, both groups showed equivalent positive outcomes. The fact that none of the patients returned for further treatment within the one-year follow-up period strengthens the impression of outcome stability (although returning to therapy does not necessarily indicate treatment failure).

The primary goal of the study: to demonstrate the effectiveness and stability of Mann's time-limited dynamic psychotherapy, was achieved. In addition, the outcomes are consistent with the rationale behind Mann's technique, because the changes occur in self-esteem, social functioning, and target complaints.

Methodological difficulties

Several strategies were employed to maintain control over both the independent and potentially confounding variables, such as stringent adherence to a reasonably standardized therapy format, separation of the therapy process from the assessment and follow-up processes, uniform training of the research team members, and accurate time interval measurements. These same strategies contained several problematic elements:

a   The randomization of group assignment necessitated an exclusion criterion that may have sacrificed the generalizability of the results to a certain extent. Clinically, an acute state of crisis does not counterindicate brief psychotherapy. Nonetheless, we tried to minimize the possible deleterious effects of waiting three months for treatment by excluding candidates who presented with an acute crisis situation.

b Adopting the suggestions of Wascow and Parloff (1975) and Mintz and Kiesler (1981), we selected a balanced battery of universal and individual outcome measures based on the judgments of the patients, evaluators, and independent judges. Toward the goal of reducing assessment bias, none of the measures included therapist assessments. Consequently, we were unable to examine the extent to which therapists are reliable evaluators of therapy outcome. The addition of measures based upon therapist assessment would have contributed to the database, however the additional information was superfluous in terms of our central research questions.

c Although the judges were independent, they were colleagues at the same mental health center as the therapists and evaluators. Notwithstanding the efforts to maintain separation between the judges and other team members in discussions of the patients they were judging, it is reasonable to assume a bias among the judges. The judges may have tended (consciously and unconsciously) toward judging what they construed as desirable outcome results for the sake of loyalty to the research team and to the center. It is also possible that information was passed on within the research team, despite the efforts to avoid occurrences of this sort. The judgment bias derived from these factors may have contributed to the extremely high levels of significance attained on changes measured by the GAS and HSRS. Nonetheless, the combination of corroborative results from additional objective measures and high interjudge correlations render the judges' assessments acceptable.

d The prerequisite of clinical expertise among the judges precluded the creation of a truly double-blind situation. Despite the deletion of identifying details, group assignment, and timing indications (e.g. whether they were six- or twelve-month follow-ups), the judges could easily detect if a protocol was from a pre-therapy, post-therapy, or post-waiting period evaluation. This difficulty was most significant in the evaluation of the three-month protocols (post-therapy for the experimental group and post-waiting period for the controls), when it was virtually impossible to conceal group membership.

e   The inclusion of an alternative treatment group for comparison with another method of short-term dynamic psychotherapy would have improved the research design. We limited the design to one treatment and a waiting period control for two reasons: (1) we were unaware of an alternative short-term therapy model that was as sharply defined as Mann's TLP. Because time was one of the controlled variables, a comparison with a twelve-week excerpt from a long-term treatment would have weakened the research design; (2) the research team did not possess a level of expertise in another type of treatment (e.g. group or behavioral therapy) that would enable the development of a comparable twelve-week treatment program. Co-operation with another treatment facility with complementary resources was a potential, although less viable, solution, due to the technical and administrative problems involved (e.g. research team training and population problems). The use of a placebo group is not only complicated technically; it is absurd in the realm of psychotherapy (Parloff 1986).

f   The absence of a standardized treatment protocol may be construed as problematic. Our therapy method, however, adhered to Mann's clear-cut guidelines for selection criteria, formulation of the central theme, and demarcation of the three stages of therapy, which can be considered a reasonably standardized treatment formula. Proband selection was based on the SIQ, which provides a selection protocol of sorts.

Its limitations notwithstanding, this study makes several valuable contributions to the field of psychotherapy research. Solid empirical support for the effectiveness and stability of James Mann's time-limited dynamic psychotherapy derived from a controlled outcome study does not exist elsewhere in the literature. In the absence of abundant controlled outcome studies of other methods of brief psychotherapy, these findings can be considered applicable to other forms of short-term psychotherapy. Furthermore, the practical and successful methodology provides a paradigm that can be replicated in future studies of alternative brief psychotherapies, as well as long-term psychotherapies, in public health centers. Finally, the controlled nature of the research design presents a solid foundation for the next step: empirical investigation of the curative processes involved in time-limited psychotherapy.

Meta-analysis of outcome studies on brief therapy

In addition to the findings of the aforementioned studies, three meta-analytical studies were conducted on the outcomes of brief dynamic therapy. Svartberg and Stiles (1991) found brief dynamic therapies demonstrated poorer outcome than extensive dynamic therapies. Crits-Cristoph (1992), however, showed that the results of brief dynamic therapies do not fall short of the outcomes of other dynamic therapies. Barber and Ellman (1996) explain the contradictory findings of the two meta-analyses as due to the fact that the latter analysis was based upon studies which met clear and rigid research criteria and employed detailed, manualized therapy protocols, as required for therapy and research of this type (Barber 1994). Andersen and Lambert (1995) conducted a meta-analysis of twenty-six studies that examined the efficacy of brief dynamic therapy (not just TLP). They found the brief dynamic therapies were significantly more effective. Like the previous study, stronger effects were found in studies based on the work of experienced therapists using treatment manuals. Reviewing the results of these three meta-analyses, there were appreciable improvements in the research designs and in the adoption of therapy manuals, which considerably improve the outcomes of the brief therapies, as well as the meta-analytical findings. To date, no comparison studies have been conducted between TLP and extensive dynamic therapies.

II PROCESS STUDIES

Empirical investigation of the effectiveness of any particular form of therapy inevitably leads the researcher to ponder the fundamental question of *how* treatment success is achieved. What are the therapeutic processes that effect change in the client's overt symptomatology and underlying dynamic structures? Empirical studies of the curative processes involved in TLP are natural outgrowths of outcome research.

In one of the earliest empirical investigations of TLP, Bernard et al. (1980) examined the relationship between patients' in-process feelings about their treatment and treatment outcome. The twenty-eight university students who participated in the study presented

with difficulties typical of a student population and were diagnosed as suffering mostly from adjustment reactions and neurotic
disturbances. The therapists were trained in psychodynamic
therapy, however they did not receive formal training in Mann's
TLP nor were most of the therapists supervised on a regular basis.

A seven-item feedback questionnaire, designed to assess the
patients' feelings toward each session, was administered at the
conclusion of each session beginning from the second session. The
outcome measures focused on patient and therapist evaluations
of treatment outcome, the degree of self-actualization achieved,
changes in state and trait anxiety, life satisfaction, and goal
achievement. A combination of self-report questionnaires and
semi-structured interviews (audiotaped and assessed by independent raters) were utilized to gather the outcome data. The therapists did not adhere strictly to the twelve-session format, therefore
the treatment phases were determined by dividing the total
number of sessions into thirds.

The results revealed significant positive correlations between the
patients' in-process therapy evaluations and two outcome
measures (raters' judgments of goal achievement and patients'
evaluation of treatment outcome) in the initial and termination
phases of treatment. These findings suggested that patients tend to
be goal-oriented in the initial treatment phase, whereas in the
middle phase patients shift their focus to the 'session-to-session
vicissitudes' of the treatment, experiencing therapy as a primary
experience rather than as a means to an end. In the termination
phase, the patients returned their focus to issues of goal achievement, linking their in-process feelings to their overall goals.

Based on the premise of divergence in client and therapist
perceptions of the treatment process, the same patients and
methodology were used by Schwartz and Bernard (1981) to
compare client and therapist evaluations of therapy as well as the
consistency of their respective evaluations in each treatment phase.
The patients tended to evaluate their therapy experience more
positively than the therapists at all phases of treatment, however
the overall mean only approached, but did not attain significance.
Clients and therapists significantly differed in their evaluations of
the therapy as positive only at the post-treatment follow-up.

The clients' and therapists' session-by-session evaluations
appeared to be the most congruent in the initial and post-treatment
phases of treatment, whereas in the middle and termination phases,

their evaluations tended to be more discrepant. The authors attributed this discrepancy to differences in prior therapy experience and variant images of the treatment process. The therapists' familiarity with the full course of therapy stabilized their session evaluations at each phase of treatment. In contrast, the clients, less familiar with therapy, based their evaluations on each session separately rather than in the context of the overall therapeutic process. Furthermore, the therapists' evaluations were modestly consistent across all three phases of treatment, while the clients' evaluations grew increasingly inconsistent in the progressive treatment phases.

Joyce and Piper (1990) conducted 'a stronger and more comprehensive test of the validity of Mann's model of TLP.' They critiqued Schwartz and Bernard's (1981) methodology on four counts: (a) the lack of monitoring therapists' adherence to Mann's TLP model; (b) the unknown psychometric properties of the rating scales used; (c) the lack of outcome measures; and (d) weaknesses in the correlational analyses. In their study of fourteen patients, Joyce and Piper improved upon Schwartz and Bernard's research design by incorporating weekly TLP supervision for the participating therapists in addition to independent raters of therapist behaviour. They also used two self-report rating scales to measure client and therapist session evaluations. Three self-report outcome measures were used to assess symptomatology, social functioning, and overall treatment evaluation. Finally, 'mixed' analyses of variance were performed on the data.

The overall sample demonstrated significant improvement on nearly all of the outcome measures and both patients and therapists evaluated the therapy experience as highly positive, providing further evidence of TLP treatment success. However, neither analyses of client and therapist consistency nor analyses of client and therapist congruence yielded significant results. Thus, the TLP model was not supported. Overall evaluation ratings indicated that clients and therapists generally evaluate therapy in increasingly positive terms as treatment progresses. Furthermore, good outcome appeared to correlate with a well-managed and satisfying termination phase. Analyses of therapist practice revealed a significantly better outcome in cases built on thorough therapist assessment of the focal problem in the initial phase of treatment. Therapist phase effects suggested that the treatments adhered to the TLP format.

Joyce and Piper summarized their study as an attempt at 'more careful and systematic assessment of the propositions regarding the dynamic sequence [that] did not provide confirmation of this aspect of Mann's model.' I suggest an alternative outlook to the clinically erroneous line of thinking proposed by Joyce and Piper and their predecessors: research based upon an improved methodology cannot substitute for basic clinical understanding.

The three studies cited above typify the earliest paradigm used in the field of process research. This paradigm rests heavily on the assumption of a uniform distribution of events throughout the course of therapy and relies upon the correlation between positive or negative outcome and the counting of in-process phenomena.

Sledge, Moras, Hartley, and Levine (1990) chose to investigate the impact of the time-limitation factor in TLP on the staying power of the patient in therapy. They examined two brief therapy methods: TLP and a second brief therapy without a specific delimitation of sessions. The variable they examined was the attrition rate. They found an attrition rate of 32 per cent in TLP, roughly half the attrition rate of the non-time-limited brief therapy. Because attrition represents, at a minimum, an inability to maintain the therapy over time, it appears the time-limitation factor enabled patients to remain in therapy, presumably transforming them into more effective treatments for the patients.

Although the following process studies were not conducted on TLP, I find them very relevant to TLP. These investigations and studies consist of attempts to designate transference as a primary curative factor in brief therapy. The study conducted by Hoglend and Piper (1995) demonstrated a substantial relationship between the degree to which the therapist adhered to transference interpretations and positive outcome upon termination of the therapy, which remained stable both six months and four years subsequent to therapy termination. Hoglend and Heyerdahl (1994) showed that clear and focused formulation of a conflict or of a central issue in therapy was a good predictor of successful therapy outcome. Even though these studies did not investigate TLP directly, they are extremely relevant to TLP theory and technique, as stated above. In this context, it is worthwhile remembering that during the first stages of his work on TLP, Mann (1973) dealt with the question of patient suitability to TLP. One of the criteria he proposed was the extent to which it was difficult or easy to identify and formulate a central issue. Though the study conducted by Hoglend and

Heyerdahl dealt with Malan's approach to brief and circumscribed therapy rather than TLP, their findings provide empirical support for Mann's early clinical observations.

The central issue as a process variable

To date, three process studies have emerged from the data gathered in the Jerusalem Time-Limited Psychotherapy Project, all focused on various aspects of the central issue as a process variable. The following section describes two of the studies in detail and briefly summarizes the third.

One innovative research method developed for the study of therapeutic process assumes that significant events in therapy, 'change events,' are distributed unevenly throughout the course of therapy. Therefore, these events cannot be investigated based on segments of a particular therapy, as they are dispersed throughout the therapy.

In the first study (Wiseman et al. 1993), we used the 'events paradigm' (Rice and Greenberg 1984) to compare two patients treated by the same therapist (see Strupp 1980a–d) drawn from the JTLPP. Based on their outcome batteries, one patient was defined as a treatment 'success' and the other was labeled as a treatment 'failure.' The purpose of the study was twofold: (1) to demonstrate that a change event in Mann's TLP, the central issue (CI) event, can be identified, and to carry out the initial steps of event analysis; and (2) to compare TLP success and failure in relation to in-therapy event processes across the three phases of treatment (initial, middle, and termination).

The first step in the events-based methodology involves the selection of a 'marker' that will signify the beginning of the change event (Greenberg 1986). The CI events were selected as the class of significant events for intensive scrutiny of the change process due to the highly charged affective state created by the CI's focus on the client's 'present and chronically enduring pain.'

The process analyses of success and failure in Strupp's case studies were based on the Vanderbilt Psychotherapy Process Scale (VPPS). Studies on the predictive validity of the VPPS differentiate between three dimensions of process: (1) exploratory processes; (2) patient involvement; and (3) therapist-offered relationship (Suh et al. 1986). In our study, VPPS rating of the central issue events served two separate functions. First, VPPS ratings of the central issue events served as indicators of productive in-session process. Events that rated high on patient participation and exploration, as well as on therapist exploration, were considered successful events, worthy of in-depth description of client performances and therapist operations (i.e., task analysis, see Rice and Saperia 1984). Second, using the CI event as the unit of analysis, the VPPS rating of in-therapy processes during these events were used to compare the two cases across the three phases of TLP.

It was expected that there would be a differential pattern of client and therapist in-therapy event behaviors across the three phases for the two cases. Specifically, in the successful case we anticipated a rise in positive patient processes (i.e., involvement and exploration) and a decline in negative process (i.e., hostility) from the ambivalence phase to the termination phase. In the unsuccessful case the opposite pattern was expected, that is, a decline in positive patient processes and a rise in negative processes from the ambivalence phase to the termination phase. With respect to therapist differential behavior, it was expected that in the successful case therapist exploration would be highest in the ambivalence phase and therapist-offered relationship would be highest at the termination phase, whereas in the unsuccessful case exploration and therapist-offered relationship would be lowest at the ambivalence phase.

Method

Two single, 30-year-old female patients were selected from the larger pool of JTLPP patients. Both women had completed courses of higher education, held white-collar positions, and received similar DSM-III-R diagnoses.

The female therapist was a clinical psychologist with twelve years of experience in dynamic psychotherapy. She underwent the therapist training described in the JTLPP section above. Two graduate students in clinical psychology served as VPPS raters, and identified and demarcated the CIs. They had at least one year of supervised experience in dynamically-oriented psychotherapy, and a theoretical background in TLP. The third judge, who identified and demarcated the CIs, was a clinical psychologist (five years post-Ph.D.) with training in TLP.

Measures

The battery of outcome measures is detailed above in the outcome study (see p. 221).

In-session process was rated on the Vanderbilt Psychotherapy Process Scale, developed for assessing significant aspects of two-person interactions in counseling or psychotherapy (Strupp et al. 1974; Suh et al. 1986). Raters read transcripts and/or listen to audio or visual recordings of a whole therapy session, or segment of a session, and rate the items on a five-point scale, ranging from 'not at all' (1) to 'a great deal' (5). We used the revised form of the scale consisting of sixty-four items, which make up eight subscales. Of the eight subscales, five pertain to the patient's behavior and demeanor (participation, exploration, psychic distress, hostility, and dependency), and three pertain to the therapist's behavior and demeanor (exploration, warmth and friendliness, and negative attitude).

Procedure

The twelve therapy hours of each case were fully transcribed. The rating procedure had two steps. The first step involved the identification and demarcation of the central issue events. The two raters read the transcripts of the twelve therapy sessions to identify the CIs, first independently, and then to discuss disagreements. The third rater served as a final, independent judge, ensuring that all events were identified and demarcated. Following this process, the CI events were copied verbatim on separate cards.

The second step involved ratings on the VPPS, using the event as the unit of analysis. Interjudge reliabilities of the VPPS subscales were calculated, resulting in Pearson correlation coefficients between the independent ratings of the two raters. The raters encountered difficulty in reaching acceptable interjudge agreement on the hostility and dependency subscales, therefore the results on these subscales should be considered as only suggestive. After the raters completed their independent VPPS rating of the data, they discussed disagreements until a consensus was reached (Suh et al. 1986). The final agreed-upon VPPS ratings were the ones used for the study. It is important to note that at the time of rating the events on the VPPS, the two raters were blind to the final treatment outcome of the two cases, as well as to the hypotheses of the study. The qualitative events analysis, which was undertaken after completing the VPPS ratings, was carried out by the three judges (who at this point were not blind to outcome). The head of therapist training for the outcome study provided informant validity for the qualitative analysis of the CIs.

Results

Treatment outcome for the two cases

Case A was drawn from the outcome study experimental group; case B participated in the control group. Overall, case B showed greater improvement than case A after therapy and follow-up, as assessed by the Target Complaints Scale, the Brief Symptom Inventory, and the Goal Attainment Scale. Rating of psychopathology on the HSRS and the client's responses on the Sentence Completion Test, presented a somewhat less clear-cut picture of differential treatment outcome. However, considering the overall picture of outcome scores at termination and follow-up in the two cases, we defined the treatment of case B, which ended with the client's improvement, as a 'success,' and the treatment of case A, which ended with no improvements, as an 'unsuccessful' case.

Identification and preliminary discussion of the CI event

Initially, the central issue event was defined in a broad manner:

> The event begins when the patient, or therapist, mentions the central issue that was presented at the beginning of therapy (as formulated originally, or some variation of it), and it ends when the patient or therapist changes to another topic of discourse and the focus on the central issue or its derivatives phases out.

When the CI event began with a therapist intervention referring to the CI, the subsequent client response was considered as the 'patient marker' for the event. The issue of defining the marker in this way will be discussed later.

In order to identify the CI marker, the raters must have knowledge of the exact wording of the central issue that was presented in the particular case under consideration. In case A, the central issue was formulated around the conflict of adequate self-esteem versus diminished self-esteem, and in case B, around the conflict of independence versus dependence.

A combined total of twenty-three CI events were identified for the two cases. Careful scrutiny of the ten events (taken from both cases) that rated highest on the VPPS subscales of patient participation, patient exploration, and therapist exploration, enabled us to explicate the patient and therapist processes involved in this kind of event. This resulted in an initial description of the four components of an event – marker, therapist operations, patient performances, and event outcome (Greenberg 1986) – for the CI event identified in the study. The following example of a CI event highlights the four components:

Marker

The CI marker consists of the patient bringing up the CI conflict in a given context. The client's statement of the conflict may be explicit, using wording similar to the original formulation of the CI, or it may appear as an implicit allusion to the CI.

In case B, the CI was presented to the client as follows:

> You have tried very hard to build an independent life for yourself and you have succeeded, yet all along you have longed for support and respect from others.

The following marker appeared in the fifth session:

> P: This week may be because of the crisis that I went through when *I moved out to live on my own*. A girlfriend of mine came over and asked if it didn't bother me to live alone, and I said no, it doesn't bother me . . . but that night I went out to a show and when I came back, *I felt extremely lonely, alone!* It really bothered me. Usually I can manage. It also *frightened me going into my house*; it was quite dark. On the last step I always run and enter quickly, as fast as I can. I was also with two girlfriends, they are also single. They came to the show, and after the show I left without saying goodbye. At home I thought that I should have said goodbye, because they could

have given me a lift home. *But I didn't want them to take me home. I wanted to be alone. I wanted to feel sorry for myself.*

This example illustrates the three elements of a CI marker: (1) an allusion to the CI conflict that was presented as the focus of the twelve-session therapy; (2) a given context for the playing out of the conflict; and (3) an indication of feeling.

Therapist operations

The therapist responds to the CI marker with an intervention aimed at focusing the client on the CI. Thus, the therapist restates the CI within the specific context indicated by the client in the marker:

> T: To feel sorry for yourself or to be independent, not to be dependent on them . . .

Bringing up the client's central conflict of 'independence versus dependence' instills meaning into the behavior and/or feelings reported in the marker. After identifying the above marker (the 'when' of the event), the therapist attempts to raise the client's awareness of various aspects of the conflict using a variety of dynamic techniques. In the events that we analyzed, four types of therapist interventions (the 'then' of the event) were identified at the central issue marker: (a) refocusing on the central issue; (b) exploration of the specific aspects of the central issue in the given context; (c) uncovering additional aspects of the conflict (broadening out); and (d) connecting the current expression of the conflict to its psychogenetic sources.

Generally, the therapeutic work during the events consisted of explorations of the particular situation that raised the conflict (reported at the marker), and explorations of the thoughts, feelings, and images that accompanied it. The process of deepening the client's feelings and thoughts surrounding the conflict is facilitated by therapist interventions aimed at broadening out to take in additional aspects of the conflict and linking the current context to sources in the client's history.

In the example, the client connected the attempt to show her girlfriends that she doesn't need a lift to her fear of becoming too dependent on them. The therapist then responded by pointing out the patient's pain:

T   The part that really hurts is that now you are left all alone.
P   Very much so! I feel like I don't want anybody to come to my
    house, to see that I am alone.

Subsequently, the client and therapist engaged in a collaborative
exploration of the client's conflictual feelings about her recent
move to living on her own.

Patient performances

In examining patient performances during the events, two major
levels of performances were identified: (1) a willingness to explore,
and deal with, the feelings raised by the conflict and (2) an
increased awareness of other aspects of the conflict and broadening
out. In the current example, the client explored her feelings about
being single and not having a partner.

Event outcome

The successful completion of the central issue event appears to be
characterized by the client's expressed acceptance of new aspects
of the conflict which rose to awareness during the event. This new
self-understanding is coupled with some indication that the patient
has emerged from this intensive exploration with a more mature
ability to form a relationship with 'a man that I will love and that
will love me.' Most of the events analyzed did not reach this final
step. Nonetheless, there was evidence of partial acceptance of
various aspects of the conflict that both patients became aware of
during the CI events.

Evaluation of event-processes in the two cases

With regard to the number of events identified for each case, there
were more events in the successful case as compared to the
unsuccessful case: thirteen and ten, respectively. In examining the
events of each case, we found that the two patients differed
markedly in their performances. Although case A (the unsuccessful
case) was able to explore the feelings raised by the conflict, the
nature of her conflict required tremendous energy just to deal with
the difficult feelings. Hence, she was unable to progress and see
other aspects of the conflict. In contrast, case B (the successful

case) was able to stay with the difficult feelings and look at the various sides of the conflict leading to the exploration of alternatives and solutions to the problems. This difference also led to a difference in the event outcomes of each case. In case A, there were events that ended with some indication of partial acceptance, but there was no indication of a more mature coping ability. In case B, the two most successful events ended with the patient expressing acceptance of the various sides of the conflict, and there was a clear indication of newly acquired coping abilities.

Examining the occurrence of the events in relation to Mann's three phases of therapy showed an interesting difference in the distribution of the events in the two cases. In the successful case, the central issue marker appeared consistently across the three treatment phases (initial-5, middle-4, and termination-4). In contrast, most of the events took place in the initial phase of treatment in the unsuccessful case (initial-7, middle-2, and termination-1), and there were only three events from the fifth to the last session. Once the 'ambivalence' phase began, work on the CI decreased dramatically. The different pattern of development over the three phases of treatment is further evidenced by the VPPS ratings of in-therapy event processes in each case.

In order to describe the development of the events over the course of the twelve treatment sessions, we calculated the means of the VPPS scales for the three phases of treatment. The nonparametric Wilcoxon test was applied to compare the VPPS scores of the two cases. Because case A had only one event in the termination phase, the middle and termination phases were combined. The Wilcoxon tests showed that in the initial phase of treatment the two cases did not differ on both client and therapist subscales. In the middle and termination phases combined, case B's participation was significantly higher than that of case A ($z = -1.65$, $p < .10$), while case A's scores on hostility ($z = 1.82$, $p < .10$) and psychic distress ($z = 2.38$, $p < .02$) were significantly higher than those of B. With respect to the therapist, her warmth toward case B was significantly higher than that toward case A in these phases ($z = -1.86$, $p < .10$).

The combination of the middle and termination phases limited the above tests, thus, Multiple Regression Analysis (MRA) was used to examine the prediction of client and therapist processes by time. MRA was applied to each case separately, testing the extent to which time predicted the VPPS event scores, with the three phases of treatment serving as the time variable (t1, t2, t3). Two MRA models were tested: the first treating the scores as a straight line (intercept + time), wherein a significantly positive beta weight indicates a rise of the line with time and a significantly negative beta weight indicates a decline of the line with time; and the second treating the scores as a parabolic (intercept + time + time squared) (Reiser and Barkan, personal communication, March 1992). In all analyses, due to the small sample and exploratory nature of the study, the significance level was set at $p < .10$.

The VPPS subscale scores of the events were treated as the observations for each case according to their occurrence in the three phases (for case A there were 7 scores at t1, 2 at t2, and 1 at t3; for case B there were 5 scores at t1, 4 at t2, and 4 at t3). Testing the prediction of the VPPS ratings that pertain to the client showed that time was a significant predictor of case B's participation (beta = 1.888; $p < .02$), but not of case A's participation. As expected, case B's participation increased with time, whereas case A's participation tended to decline across time, though not significantly different than a straight line. Case B's exploration remained steady with time, while case A's exploration showed a significant decline with time (beta = -1.954; $p < .05$). With respect to negative processes, time was not a significant predictor of hostility for both patients. The psychological distress, however, of case B showed a significant decline with time, (beta = -1.664; $p < .05$), consistent with her positive final outcome, while case A's distress remained the same throughout. In contrast, case A's dependency increased with time (beta = 1.273; $p < .02$), while case B's dependency remained steady.

The MRAs of the VPPS ratings pertaining to the therapist showed that the therapist's exploration in case B followed a parabolic function, with time (beta = 18.25; $p < .05$) and time-squared (beta = -4.75; $p < .05$) as the predictors. That is, in her treatment of case B the therapist's exploration peaked at the middle phase, whereas in her treatment of case A, the therapist's exploration was lowest in the middle phase (only a trend). The therapist's warmth and friendliness increased significantly with time toward case B (beta = 2.155; $p < .05$), but remained steady toward case A. Similar to therapist exploration, the negative attitude of the therapist in case B followed a parabolic function, reaching a peak at the middle phase, with time (beta = 6.125; $p < .10$), and time squared (beta = -1.375; $p < .10$) as the predictors. In case A, time was not a significant predictor.

Discussion

This preliminary examination of the central issue event is the first attempt to identify an event in Mann's time-limited psychotherapy. Further work is need to develop this model. Although the therapist's close adherence to the techniques prescribed by Mann and the clients' homogeneity (both met pre-determined selection criteria) imply a certain degree of generalizability to other cases, the model was still constructed on the basis of the in-session behaviors of only two patients and one therapist. Therefore, it is reasonable to assume that certain aspects of the event, such as those pertaining to therapist operations and client performances, would have to be revised to include the behaviors of other therapists and clients who might engage in other event-specific processes.

Furthermore, in terms of the validity of the model, the researchers were not blind to the outcome of the two cases while developing the CI model. This may have influenced their description of the components of the model. In the future, verification studies of the CI model should first show that independently rated successful CI events indeed contain the components predicted by the model, and then show that these components are predictive of treatment outcomes (Greenberg 1984).

The central issue event that was identified and described appears to be a significant event in Mann's TLP worthy of further study. Although the identification of the marker requires knowledge of the central issue that was defined by the therapist at the beginning of treatment, further analysis of the CI markers revealed that the patient's readiness for a therapist intervention aimed at the central issue is crucial for the productive process. This point has important clinical implications for the practice and training of TLP therapists. The analysis of the events showed that when the therapist uses the central issue in a flexible manner, guided by the client's readiness, this facilitates a collaborative, focused exploration that opens up avenues for deeper, more meaningful work on the central issue. In contrast, when the therapist's timing of a central issue intervention is misguided (without a true sign of readiness on the part of the patient), this interferes with the patient's productive process. Moreover, the consequent lack of agreement on goals and tasks seems to disrupt the working alliance (Bordin 1979).

The differential pattern of occurrence of the CI markers in relation to the phases of therapy that was observed for the two cases speaks to the effectiveness of using the central issue as a pivot for the therapeutic work in the twelve-session therapy. It appears that in the unsuccessful case, once ambivalence set in, the central issue lost its potency as a focus, requiring the therapeutic work to continue without a crucial ingredient of short-term therapy (Malan 1976a).

The pattern of VPPS ratings of patient behavior found for the successful case in this study appears consistent with an earlier finding that 'good' outcome cases showed a trend toward more positive evaluations as therapy progressed (Joyce and Piper 1990). Our analysis by time suggests that awareness of Mann's phases is particularly important for the therapist who must work harder during the ambivalence phase, whereas for the client the successful pattern is of increased participation and steady exploration. Moreover, ratings of productive client and therapist behavior toward the end of therapy (e.g. high therapist warmth and friendliness; low client hostility) could be viewed as sub-outcome measures, reflecting the therapist's and client's satisfaction with treatment and a sense of accomplishment.

Joyce and Piper (1990) suggest that observing the emotional stance of the participants as they actually engage in interaction could provide a more adequate assessment of the phenomenology of TLP. It appears that the VPPS ratings of patient and therapist behaviors, as they engage in CI events, at least partially served this function, resulting in clinically meaningful findings. This fits the notion that studying in-therapy client and therapist behaviors in the context of a particular change event provides the researcher-clinician with theoretically and clinically relevant findings (Wiseman and Rice 1989).

Further research can be pursued in two directions. The first direction is further development of the components of the CI event, using moment-to-moment process measures, such as the Experiencing Scale (Klein et al. 1986) and post-session measurement of event suboutcome (e.g. Greenberg et al. 1991). The second direction is to further test Mann's model of the three sequential phases of TLP by applying the context-specific approach taken in this two-proband study to a group design. Finally, we would like to advocate this kind of events approach to the analysis of single cases. Focusing the comparison between success and failure on theory-based events seems to provide a useful blend of a theory-based approach and an exploratory approach to change process research.

Therapeutic alliance, the central issue, and change

In a second study (Tishby, Shefler and Sargel-Zvieli in press) the same two patients were examined in terms of the relationship between the therapeutic alliance, the therapist's adherence to the central issue, and the process of change. The strength of the therapeutic alliance was evaluated with the Penn Helping Alliance Scale. A scale developed for the study was used to assess the degree of therapist's adherence to the central issue and the process measures were based upon the VPPS. There were no differences between the two therapies on any of the variables when the entire therapies were evaluated, however analyses of treatment phase revealed differences between the successful and unsuccessful therapies. The successful therapy developed in accordance with Mann's theoretical formulations, showing a gradual process unfolding around the central issue. In contrast, the unsuccessful therapy demonstrated three major differences: (1) the therapeutic alliance did not develop rapidly in the initial stage of treatment; (2) the therapeutic process was 'arrested' and even deteriorated during the middle phase of treatment; and (3) a 'recovery' occurred during the third stage, unlike the consolidation and separation work that appeared in the successful therapy.

The researchers attempted to explain the differences in the two therapies in terms of the central issue. One possibility was a shift of the central issue at the end of the initial phase of the unsuccessful therapy that may have enabled the proband to deny the crucial time-limitation factor. Another suggestion was that the client of the unsuccessful therapy could not cope with the boundaries imposed by the central issue nor with the time limitation. The final alternative centered on the conjecture that the client was not a suitable candidate for TLP in the first place.

Patient progress in TLP as measured by the RPPS

Assa (1999) conducted an additional comparative investigation of the progress of TLP patients. This study examined the same patients whose therapies were studied by Wiseman et al. (1993) and Tishby et al. (in press). Assa utilized the Rutgers Psychotherapy Process Scale (RPPS), developed by Spillman (1991) at Rutgers

University. This scale focuses on the appraisal of progress and therapeutic change as they become manifest over the course of each therapy session. Unlike other measurements (for instance, the Experience Scale or the VPPS, which only measure general emotion or engagement), this scale relates to specific variables drawn from psychodynamic conceptual systems.

The scale is composed of eight different dimensions, derived from an analysis of the clinical-psychodynamic literature. The dimensions include: expression of significant material, development of insight, focus on emotion, collaboration, clarity and vividness, focus on the self, new behavior in session, and direct references to therapist and/or therapy. Holland, Roberts, and Messer (1998) conducted thorough reliability and validity research for each of the eight dimensions. As a result of their findings, the last two dimensions were dropped from the scale, i.e. new behavior in session and direct reference to therapist and/or therapy. Thus, only six dimensions remained in the scale.

The scale is used to analyze verbatim therapy hours. The Rutgers research group selected coding units of five minute blocks of time. Consequently, each therapy hour was divided into ten blocks of time, of which the researchers coded every other block. Due to technical considerations related to the nature of the therapy hour transcripts and the fact that not all therapy hours were fully recorded, Assa delineated each quarter of a session as a coding unit, whereupon each session contained four fully scored blocks. The RPPS requires prior experience in psychodynamic therapy in order to score it reliably. Two independent judges performed the scoring in this study after practicing first on other TLP texts. Inter-rater reliability for scoring ranged from 0.85–0.90.

Like previous studies based upon the paradigm of comparison between a successful and an unsuccessful therapy, the independent variable in this study was therapy outcome, according to the outcome measurements utilized by Shefler et al. (1995). Because the study was a first-time study using the Hebrew language version of the scale as well as using the scale outside of the original research group that developed it, tests of the scale's reliability are very important. The reliability of the scale was examined by means of interclass correlation coefficients. The average correlations between judges across the six dimensions of the scale was $R = 0.8566$ for the successful therapy, and $R = 0.8232$ for the unsuccessful therapy.

For the remaining data analyses, Assa utilized scores consisting of the averages of the judges' scores on each variable, for each block. Consistent with other studies conducted by our research group (Tishby et al. in press; Wiseman et al. 1993), we treated each therapy as a three-phase treatment, according to Mann's original delineation.

In a comparison of the two therapies across the three phases of TLP according to Mann and across the six RPPS dimensions, multiple regression analysis revealed significant differences between the stages, the progress achieved on the dimensions, and the interactions. These findings indicate the presence of significant effects, which differentiate between the two therapies. Although no differences were found between the two therapies on the overall RPPS score, statistically significant differences were found on three dimensions: expression of significant material, collaboration, and clarity and vividness.

The most important finding in this study was the differentiation between the two therapies in terms of the manner in which the patients entered into therapy and into the therapy process. The treatment of the patient whose therapy was defined as successful revealed significant differences between the first and second phases of therapy across all six dimensions, and, therefore, on the overall score as well. During the second stage, all of her scores were very high. In other words, this patient progressed steadily from one phase to the next. In the treatment defined as unsuccessful, no such differences were found, and there was even a certain decline, though not significant, during the second phase of therapy.

Another meaningful finding in this study was the change in the dynamic profile of the two patients in terms of the dimensions. The patient in the successful therapy exhibited a marked linear development as she progressed from the first phase through the last phase. The more significant difference was found between the first and second phases, whereas between the second and third phases there was lesser, albeit significant, progress in terms of effect size.

The patient in the therapy defined as unsuccessful exhibited regression in her dynamic work during the second phase in comparison to the first phase, and a significant slowing down of progress in the transition from the second to the third stage, which marks the final phase of therapy. Thus, in effect, she did not successfully work through the separation phase of therapy, as reflected in the outcome.

The RPPS examines the degree of dynamic depth in therapy, enabling the tracking of development and regression throughout the two therapies, within the context of the patients' personalities and their respective levels of awareness at the beginning of therapy. For example, the patient who began therapy with a lower level of insight was rated according to the progress achieved in relation to her starting point. The distinctions between the various dimensions of the scale enabled observation of the differential course of development across the scores for each of the six dimensions, for each of the patients. This distinction also enabled observation of the relationships between various dimensions and the success of the therapy. The dimensions of collaboration, expression of significant material, and clarity and vividness were highest in the therapy defined as successful.

Based on this study, we essentially learned that rapid entrance into therapy (which, on a practical level, implies rapid development of a working alliance and initial capabilities of the patient) supports better therapy outcome.

A trend found throughout the several process studies underscores the critical nature of the second phase of therapy. Wiseman et al. (1993) discovered a proliferation of positive change events at the second stage of therapy. Tishby et al. (in press) pointed to development and progression in the therapeutic alliance during the second phase of the successful therapy, and Assa (1999) demonstrated an increase on measures of the quality of the dynamic work during the second phase of the successful therapy.

It appears the next stage in TLP process studies should focus on therapy content, including the search for relationships between interpretations and outcome, central issue contents and outcome, and the development of affective depth between therapist and patient and outcome.

Interjudge reliability and agreement about the patient's central issue and TLP outcome

The data gathered in the JTLPP was utilized recently in a process-related investigation of the relationship between the central issue and treatment outcome (Shefler and Tishby 1998). Our exploratory study focused on two questions, based upon the two indirect approaches to evaluating the accuracy of clinicians' formulations suggested by Persons (1991) in his proposal of the Case Formulation Approach.

The first question focused on interjudge reliability and agreement about the patient's CI in TLP. We were interested in finding out whether different clinicians who read the same clinical material, and followed Mann's instructions closely, would agree on the CI that was 'most accurate' for a particular patient, or whether they would differ in their choices. Strong agreement would support the notion that there is one CI issue that is the 'most accurate' for a patient and that most TLP-trained clinicians would arrive at that 'accurate' formulation. Low agreement would suggest that there are several plausible formulations, reflecting differences in understanding and organization of clinical material. Thus, even within Mann's structured model, there may be room for variability and flexibility.

The second question pertains to a possible relationship between consensus and outcome. We wondered whether the cases on which judges agreed were also the cases that had a better outcome, based on the rationale that more readily agreed upon cases lend themselves more easily to creating a dynamic focus. In those instances, the presentation and organization of the clinical material may make it easier for judges to discriminate 'accurate' from 'inaccurate' CIs. Mann and Goldman (1982) argue that cases which are easier to focus also have a better chance of positive outcome. Several studies have supported this notion (e.g. Crits-Christoph et al. 1988). The 'focality' of the clinical material is considered predictive of successful therapy, and as such, is one of the selection criteria used in TLP.

Patients

Fifteen cases, ten females and five males, were randomly selected from the patients treated in the JTLPP. All patients were diagnosed according to the DSM-III-R: five patients had no Axis I diagnosis, three showed anxiety disorders, two presented depressive disorders, and five had adjustment disorders; fourteen patients had no Axis II diagnosis, and one had an avoidant personality. The researchers were 'blind' to the patients' outcomes.

Therapists and judges

Nine senior therapists in the Herzog Ezrat-Nashim Community Mental Health Center conducted the TLPs that were used in this study (see JTLPP section above for description of training). The judges, fifteen experienced clinicians, were *not* affiliated with the Jerusalem Community Mental Health Center, nor were they familiar with the case material. They participated in a four-year seminar on TLP in which they received substantial training on formulating the patient's CI. Additional training, provided especially for this project, included lectures on the conceptual and technical components of the CI, the principles of constructing the CI, and exercises in formulating the CI.

Measures

The Accuracy Rating Scale A rating scale, which assesses the suitability of the CI for a given case, was constructed for this study. The scale consists of two parts: in the first part judges are asked to rate accuracy of the CI to the specific patient, based on a reading of the initial evaluation. The ratings range from 1 (highly inaccurate) to 5 (highly accurate). The second part of the scale is used to rate discrete components of the central issue. In this part, the CI is broken down into its four components: (1) support and acknowledgment of strengths, (2) sense of time, (3) the affective mode, and (4) the relation to one's self. Judges are asked to rate *each component separately* for accuracy, on a scale from 1 to 5. Whereas in the first part they have to decide whether or not the entire CI is accurate, in the second part they may rate some components as accurate and others as less accurate.

Outcome measures

Outcome scores were obtained on six measures: the Brief Symptom Inventory (Derogatis and Spencer 1982), The Health–Sickness Rating Scale (Luborsky 1975), the Target Complaints Scale (Battle et al. 1966), Goal Attainment Scale (Kiresuk and Sherman 1968), Sentence Completion Test (Shanan 1967), and the Rosenberg Self-Esteem Scale (Rosenberg 1979).

Procedure

Each of the fifteen transcribed intakes was distributed to three different judges, who worked independently on the two tasks in the procedure:

1 Formulating the CI

The judges were asked to read the two initial intake sessions of each case, and formulate a CI that fitted the clinical material. They were instructed to include Mann's four CI components in their formulations. They were then asked to write down an alternative CI that seemed plausible for the case but of lesser relevance than their initial formulation, for use in step two. Once this task was completed, all formulations were reviewed by one of the researchers, who checked their adherence to Mann's model.

2 Rating the accuracy of the CI

In the second step of this study judges rated the CIs on their goodness-of-fit to the case material. Transcripts of the intakes were redistributed to the same group of judges, but in a different order, so they did not rate the same cases for which they had formulated CIs in step one. Again, each judge received three cases. The judges evaluated three CIs per case: the original CI used by the therapist in the JTLPP and two additional formulations created in step one of this study. The set of alternative CIs formulated by the step one judges were used instead of completely irrelevant 'dummy' formulations. The judges worked independently, assigning each of these CIs a global accuracy score, and four component scores. They were not aware that one of the CIs they were rating was the actual one used in therapy.

Results

Inter-rater reliability

In this study we were interested not only in reliability of ratings, but also in the judges' agreement in terms of the actual values assigned to the CIs and their components. Prior to calculating agreement, interjudge reliabilities for each case (fifteen items) were computed, using the interclass correlation coefficient (Rosenthal 1987), for two or three judges. Reliabilities were low for three of the cases ($R < .40$), and moderate to good for the remaining twelve, ranging from $R = .46$ to $R = .85$. The mean interclass correlation for the fifteen cases was $R = .54$.

The Lawlis and Lu (1972) chi-square test was calculated to determine whether agreement between raters for each case was greater than could be expected by chance. We were interested in detecting *similar* clinical perceptions of the cases, not necessarily an exact match. Therefore, agreement was defined as a discrepancy of no more than one point between judges. In ten out of fifteen cases, inter-rater agreement was greater than would be expected by chance. The strength of agreement was calculated using the T index, recommended by Tinsley and Weiss (1975). T values range from moderate ($T = .30$) to good ($T = .74$).

Agreement on the central issue as a whole

We were interested in looking at agreement on the CI as a whole, separate from the component ratings. Therefore we looked at the number of CIs the judges agreed upon in each case. The trend seems similar, with agreement for roughly two-thirds of the CIs. In five cases, judges agreed on all three CIs, in eight cases, judges agreed in their ratings on two out of three CIs, in one case, judges agreed only on one out of three, and in one case judges did not agree on any of the three CIs.

The original CIs, formulated in the JTLPP, did not receive consistent ratings. In only four out of fifteen cases did judges agree on a high accuracy rating of the original CI. In the remaining cases, judges either disagreed on the accuracy rating of the original CI, or agreed on a low rating. Thus, the original CI was not 'identified' by the judges in this study as the most suitable for the patients.

Agreement about the components

The Lawlis and Lu chi-square test was applied to the component ratings (affect, self, support, and time) in each case. The results were the same as those achieved in the agreement test which combined the CI ratings and the component ratings. That is, judges agreed on component ratings in ten out of fifteen cases.

Relationship between accuracy of CI and final therapy outcome

The availability of outcome data made it possible to check whether the cases on which judges agreed were also cases with better outcome, compared to cases on which judges did not agree. The cases were divided into two groups: the ten cases on which the judges agreed formed the agreement group, while the five cases on which the judges did not agree formed the disagreement group. T-tests were computed between mean outcome scores of the two groups, on each of the six outcome scores available. Outcome scores were calculated as the difference between pre-therapy and post-therapy scores on each measure. Significant differences were found for three out of six outcome measures: the Brief Symptom Inventory, $(t(13) = 2.251, p < .05)$, the Rosenberg Self-Esteem Scale $(t(13) = 2.282, p < .05)$, and the first complaint on the Target Complaints Scale $(t(13) = 2.457, p < .05)$. That is, the cases in which judges agreed about the CI, were also cases with better outcome scores on the above three measures.

Discussion

This study was designed to test whether (a) different therapists would construct similar central issues for the given clients, and (b) whether they would agree on the 'most accurate' central issue for these clients.

The CIs constructed in the first part of the study differed both in their wording and in their dynamic content. Some possible explanations of these findings may lie in the differences between clinical reality and the experimental situation. First, because judges had to formulate the CIs on the basis of transcripts, they did not have access to the subtle non-verbal communications pertinent to the dynamic understanding of the client. The absence of such data may have increased individual differences between judges in their interpretation of the clinical material.

Another difference between the experimental situation and clinical reality concerns the procedure for constructing CIs. In the clinical setting created for the TLP project, the CI was created in a group process, whereby clinicians discussed several possible CIs, shaping each other's thinking until they reached a consensus.

The experimental situation in this CI study represents only the preliminary step in which the individual therapist attempts to formulate a CI before the group discussion. Thus, as long as therapists work in isolation, agreement is more difficult to achieve. Still, in private practice and in many instances where group discussion is not possible, the actual situation of the therapist is similar to the one in this study. It is important to find out the degree of reliability that can be achieved under these circumstances, and not just in instances where work is conducted in teams (Barber and Crits-Christoph 1993).

Finally, in clinical practice, work on the CI combines two different functions: the psychodynamic-intellectual activity that leads to the initial formulation of the CI and the therapist's anticipation of the client's possible emotional reactions to different aspects of the CI. The combination of these two functions determines the final choice of the CI and the particular way of presenting it to the patient. Our study involved only the first function, which is rather technical and lacks the interpersonal component essential in any psychodynamic treatment. The importance of these two functions is highlighted in the following examples, formulated in the experimental and clinical setting, respectively:

> In terms of achievements in your work and family life, you have been successful. However, when it comes to interpersonal warmth and closeness, you feel that something is missing. Whenever there is an opportunity for closeness, you burst out with emotion and drive away the other person. This arouses a great deal of sadness in you.

> You are a woman with strengths and talents, and you have succeeded in many areas in your life. However, you also experience intense emotions which you believe must be kept under control, and when you lose that control you feel like a failure.

The first CI contains several 'dynamic observations' strung together to reflect a theoretical analysis of the patient's issues, whereas the second CI reflects a similar dynamic understanding but is formulated in a more personal and direct way. The second CI focuses on the patient's self-experience in contrast to the first CI's description of an interpersonal pattern viewed by an outsider.

With the initial CIs seeming quite different from each other, we proceeded to the second task of this study in which the judges rated the accuracy of the CI. We were interested in finding out whether choosing rather than formulating would lead to greater similarity. Our small-sized sample showed moderate levels of reliability for almost all cases, and moderate-to-good values of agreement in ten out of fifteen cases. Thus, in two-thirds of the cases, clinicians were able to agree on the accuracy of the CIs presented to them. A closer inspection of these results showed that even in two cases where agreement was not achieved, the reliability was quite high. In these cases, although judges did not agree on the absolute degree of accuracy, they did assign ratings in a similar rank order.

The similarities in judgment can be attributed to standard training and a common background as psychodynamic therapists. Disagreements, on the other hand, seem to reflect the judges' personal reactions to the clinical material, so that different central issues became salient for different clinicians. A second reading of the central issues formulated for each case supported this interpretation by showing that the CIs seemed to tap into similar dynamics but the different emphases and wording lowered agreement among the judges. For example, the following three formulations were constructed for the same case:

> On the surface your life has been quiet and calm. Although there have been many changes, you have tried to please everyone, while ignoring your own deep needs. Now that you can no longer contain all that is bursting forth from within you, you find it hard to recognize yourself, and you feel guilty about it.

> All your life you have always had to be a strong and supportive person. However, this has left you isolated and distressed, feeling that you never had anyone to lean upon, or to count on.

> You have always given of yourself to others, but inside, you have always felt, and still feel, that you are undeserving and unsupported.

All three formulations address the patient's giving to others at the expense of fulfilling her own needs. The variations relate to the pain the patient felt in these situations: the first CI emphasizes her **guilt, and difficulty acknowledging her own needs**, the second CI focuses on her **isolation and distress**, and the third CI stresses the feeling that she is **undeserving**. In this example, all three judges rated the first CI as the most accurate of the three CIs, however, they did not agree that this was the *best* CI for the patient. Two judges rated it as highly accurate whereas the third judge rated it as only moderately accurate.

Although our results show some uniformity in the general psychodynamic understanding of a given case, the variability in the emphases chosen by different clinicians reflects somewhat different reactions to the clinical material. Differences and disagreements may also reflect on the nature of the cases, and the extent to which they lend themselves easily to a therapeutic focus. Perhaps inter-judge agreement was achieved in those cases that were easier to focus, where one CI clearly predominated. Alternatively, cases where agreement was not achieved, may have been those that could not be easily focused. Further research utilizing a larger caseload is necessary, in order to delineate the pattern of similarities and differences.

When the central issues were broken down into their components, there was greater agreement among the judges. Thus, it appeared easier to rate the components as individually accurate or inaccurate than to rate the accuracy of the central issue as a whole. It is possible that it was difficult to assign accuracy ratings in instances where judges agreed with some part of a formulation and not with other parts. These results further support the notion of a general similarity between judges in their psychodynamic understanding of the cases.

The low level of agreement on the component of time, a universal issue, was surprising. Re-examination of the central issues showed that each CI contained an allusion to time, although often it was vague (for example, 'all your life . . .', 'you have always . . .') and devoid of personal meaning. It is possible that clinicians found it easier to recognize other distinguishing features of patients, whereas time was more difficult to grasp and, therefore, stated mechanically. The vagueness of the time phrases may have presented a rating problem for the judges, who could not distinguish 'suitable' time phrases from 'unsuitable ones.'

An interesting finding was that the original CIs formulated by a group of clinicians in the Jerusalem TLP project, were not often rated as highly accurate by judges in this study. Although these CIs were derived by means of group consensus, they did not stand out as the 'most accurate' CIs in this study. This finding raises the question of whether there is one CI which is the 'most accurate', or whether there could be several plausible CIs for a given patient. According to Persons (1991), the accurate formulation is the one which will ultimately lead to better outcome, compared with other formulations. Garfield (1990), on the other hand, doubts that there is a 'correct' formulation, arguing that a formulation which is accepted by the patient will be therapeutically effective. Several possibilities exist for such a formulation, depending on the patient-therapist dyad. To further explore this question we are currently conducting another study, in which two CIs are compared in terms of their effects on in-session patient progress in TLP.

Regarding the question of relationship between agreement and outcome, our hypothesis was that cases on which it would be easier to agree, would also be the cases with better outcome. Our results, based on a small sample, lend modest support to this hypothesis: for three out of six outcome measures, a positive relationship was found between agreement and outcome. It is possible that cases on which judges could agree were those in which the clinical material lent itself more easily to a clear therapeutic focus. The ability to focus might be related to the presence of themes that are more familiar and salient to therapists conducting psychodynamic therapy, and also to the level of organization with which patients present themselves. According to the basic theoretical assumptions of TLP, patients whose presenting problems can be easily focused, have a better chance of gaining from this type of therapy (and thus achieve a better outcome). In addition, several studies have shown that therapists' adherence to the therapeutic focus throughout treatment, increases the likelihood of a positive outcome (Crits-Christoph et al. 1988; Norville et al. 1996). Thus, cases which were easier to focus, may have also been the ones where therapists found it easier to maintain the CI throughout treatment, thereby contributing to a better outcome. This line of reasoning is supported by the results of the first process study described above in which there was an increase in the number of 'CI events' in the successful case as compared to the unsuccessful case. In a similar study, currently in progress, we are comparing the relationship between therapist's adherence to the CI throughout treatment and patient progress.

Our findings are somewhat disappointing from the point of view of statistical reliability. However, they are valuable in terms of disproving a common criticism: that CIs are technically formulated as a set of clichés (Witztum and Dasberg, 1986). This study demonstrates that creativity and individual variance remain at the heart of psychodynamic treatment, even when it is short-term. The moderate relationship found between CI accuracy and outcome in TLP indicates that even though the CI is a main process variable in TLP, it is nevertheless only *one of several* process variables contributing to positive change in TLP, which need to be further investigated.

Conclusion

This chapter provides a thorough and focused review of the current body of empirical research on TLP. In addition, the suitability of TLP to empirical investigation was established.

The uncontrolled outcome studies demonstrated positive posttherapy results for TLP and durability of the results for time periods of six months to two years. This does not imply that the positive results do not endure for longer than two years, rather that time periods beyond two years have not yet been measured empirically. Notwithstanding the lack of extensive longitudinal empirical studies, evidence of long-standing positive results has been gathered from both clinical observations and the non-systematic contact maintained between therapists and clients. The controlled outcome study, described in great detail, indicates both the striking advantage of TLP over non-treatment and the longevity of the results. In the comparative studies, TLP yielded the second most effective results in contrast to both group and individual long-term dynamic therapies, and demonstrated a similar positive outcome when compared to cognitive-analytical therapy.

Additionally, the process studies reviewed in this chapter provided the opportunity to empirically trace curative factors in TLP, indicating that various processes are involved in the generation of change. The clear demarcation and passage from one stage of therapy to the next correlated positively with successful treatment outcome. Another group of studies focused on the central issue: its structure, the frequency with which it was used, its strength as a focal point, and the degree of interjudge agreement on its accuracy. Each aspect of the central issue was correlated with positive treatment outcome.

In terms of future TLP research directions, the range of therapeutic processes under investigation should be broadened. This includes processes unique to TLP, such as the influence of the time restraints and separation processes in the treatment, as well as further investigation of other dynamic curative factors. Among these factors are the therapeutic alliance, transference and counter-transference relationships, and the way that particular types of clients interact with the fundamental characteristics of TLP.

Chapter 12

Teaching, learning, and training in time-limited psychotherapy

During the four decades since the establishment of brief approaches to dynamic therapy and their appearance as eccentric psychotherapeutic approaches, the study and teaching of TLP has undergone many vicissitudes. It has today reached the point where these methods have become a common, essentially inseparable, component among the repertoire of professional tools utilized by many therapists (Messer, in press). I believe the essence of the change lies in the attitudes of therapists experienced in extended therapy. The essence of this change is the transition from a position of fear, suspicion, and resistance toward an innovation perceived as threatening to a realistic and practical stance which views these therapies as an existent and widespread clinical fact. A second change relates to who employs brief therapy methods. In the past, TLP was always studied by therapists already experienced in the techniques of extensive dynamic psychotherapy, whereas in the current reality, more and more novice therapists, without experience in extended long-term therapy, are involved in learning and acquiring TLP and other dynamic therapy methods. This change leads to the fact that advancement in the instruction and supervision of TLP today no longer concerns the processing of resistance to TLP, but focuses instead upon ways of coping with the lack of clinical experience among beginning therapists.

Despite these vicissitudes, the teaching and learning of time-limited dynamic psychotherapy (TLP) still entails many of the same difficulties and dilemmas that typify the training processes of extended dynamic psychotherapies. Among the issues that arise are the shaping of individual therapeutic style, striking a balance between therapeutic supervision and directed teaching, the nature of the supervisory relationship and its influence on the supervisor-therapist dialogue, maintaining the appropriate degree of supervisor responsibility for the therapist's clinical performance, and providing a suitable amount of support in supervision. Each of these difficulties is an integral component of the process of professional development regardless of the particular therapeutic approach or techniques used.

In a survey conducted by Davidovitz and Levenson (1995), approximately 4,000 American therapists were questioned about the frequency with which they practice brief therapy, their training in the field, and their degree of satisfaction with this training. The results of the survey were surprising: only 25 per cent of the respondents defined themselves as psychodynamically oriented psychotherapists in their approach. Among those (i.e., out of a sample of roughly 1,000 respondents), 82 per cent reported conducting any type of brief therapy as part of their practice. They reported that roughly 30 per cent of their work time in private practice and 50 per cent in public practice was dedicated to brief therapy. The researchers asked the survey participants to what extent they were satisfied with their work, and only 7 per cent of therapists practicing brief therapy reported satisfaction with practicing this type of therapy. When asked about their training in brief therapy, the responses were astonishing. Of those who responded positively to the question whether they practiced brief therapy, 82 per cent reported acquiring their knowledge of brief therapy through reading books and articles in the field. In other words, 20 per cent had done no reading about brief therapy. Approximately 40 per cent had not participated in any seminars or academic courses on brief therapy. For most therapists, the most effective means for learning brief therapy was through supervision and ongoing consultation. Academic courses were found only slightly helpful, and, likewise, participation in workshops, study days, and professional conferences. In their evaluations of themselves as therapists or on the quality of their brief therapies, most therapists described a state of mediocrity.

Evans and Levenson (1997) examined instructional and training techniques in brief therapy methods at the internship and residency sites of APA accredited therapy institutions in the United States. They found that 60 per cent of graduate institutions, and 81 per cent of residency institutions, defining themselves as psychodynamically oriented, provided some type of training or supervision in brief dynamic therapy methods. The overall portrait described by

Levenson and Strupp (1999) portrays the widespread practice of brief therapy despite insufficient training, if any, among therapists who do not even affiliate themselves with the practice of this type of treatment. Apparently, therapists practice brief therapy due to a lack of choice, under pressure from their employers or their clientele. Some therapists do not admit to practicing brief therapy, even though they dedicate significant blocks of time to these therapies.

The question that ought to be asked is not whether or not therapists practice brief therapy, but rather which therapists do not yet practice brief therapy. In regard to this question, I often think of the issue of practicing TLP with children. The prevailing attitude is that TLP is not an approach geared toward children. Nevertheless, there have been attempts here and there to write about brief therapy with children, though no books or comprehensive articles on the topic of TLP with children have as yet been published. On the other hand, a sizable proportion of therapies conducted with children are time-limited psychotherapies. Therapies last for the duration of the school year, until summer vacation, and, in many cases, the number of therapy sessions is delimited in advance in order to overcome the child's fear of becoming attached to therapy. These limitations take place without necessarily viewing the therapy as brief. With that, I would like to claim that while the previous state of affairs required justification of brief therapy and its practice, alongside coping with resistance and deep-seated change processes, the current situation differs. Today, we must cope with a reality in which the practice of brief therapy has become a fact on the ground.

Similar to the treatment process itself, the teaching and training processes of time-limited psychotherapy differ from those of extensive psychotherapy in the centrality of the time element. The stringently defined time restraints significantly impact upon the development of the therapist-supervisor relationship, typically generating the feeling that there is not enough time to learn and accomplish all that is desired. Although this feeling can appear throughout longer therapies and in their supervision, the parallel process experienced in TLP supervision serves as a medium for deeper understanding of the client's therapeutic experience.

What sort of therapist is suitable for TLP?

The answer to this question considers the dimensions of both professional skills and personality. Often, there was a tendency to view brief therapies as most suitable for inexperienced clinicians or clinicians with minimal experience. The logic behind this trend was based upon the schematic nature of brief therapy models, the well-defined supervisory frameworks, and the abundance of new clinical and theoretical literature in the field. Additionally, the beginning clinician's enthusiasm, an essential component of any brief therapy, creates the impression of suitability to this type of therapy. Unfortunately, that enthusiasm is often a by-product of the mistaken belief that brief therapies shorten the lengthy process of therapist training.

Previously, we remarked that many therapists practice TLP and other brief therapy methods without undergoing training or supervision. Some of these are indubitably therapists experienced in therapy in general, and in extended therapy in particular. This experience has advantages for the TLP therapist in anything related to the ability to implement rapid clinical assessment, identify dynamic processes, distinguish between primary and secondary material, and link various states and processes. Nevertheless, none of these guarantee that the therapist with experience in the observation and diagnosis of the aforementioned phenomena will put these observations into practice or process the material while directly facing the patient. In the literature (Dasberg and Winokur 1984; Winokur and Dasberg 1983) concerning the treatment of resistance to TLP among seasoned therapists, we found that many experienced therapists avoided acting in accordance with the treatment guidelines. I believe a balance has been created in the field of TLP teaching and supervision today between the necessity, which has decreased but still exists, for dealing with the habits and resistance to change among seasoned therapists on the one hand, and the inexperience of novice therapists on the other. Teaching and supervision systems must cope separately with each of these two generalities.

In addition to prior experience, the therapist's personality plays an important role. Therapists with separation difficulties or therapists with passive or dependent tendencies are less suitable for TLP. From a theoretical perspective, the therapist must be active and directive in therapy. It seems reasonable to assume that therapists with active, or even domineering, personality features will be drawn naturally to TLP more than other therapists. Undoubtedly, the therapeutic process will bring out the problematic elements integral to active and directive personalities. Those elements should be considered when planning the supervisory process.

An additional problem should be added, which is the role of personal therapy in the professional development of the therapist. A therapist's personal therapy, which is a formal demand of training programs in some fields and standard practice in others, is conventionally considered to impact heavily upon the therapy approach studied and adopted by the novice therapist (Botermans 1996; Norcross et al. 1988; Strupp et al. 1988).

Despite the advantages of brief therapies and their efficacy in a wide variety of circumstances, they are not the therapies of choice for deepening the therapist's knowledge of his or her self, personality, and problems. Usually, therapists seeking therapy for professional reasons would not request brief dynamic therapy, just as they would not request cognitive or behavioral therapy. A therapist would seek out those types of therapy if he or she were struggling with a problem that required a very focused solution. In order to increase self-awareness, the therapist-in-training typically turns to psychoanalysis or psychodynamic therapy. Identification with the therapist exerts strong effects upon the novice therapist, and, to a large extent, dictates his or her choices. It seems a large number of therapists identify themselves as dynamic therapists due to their identification with their own therapists, and consequently are unable to view themselves as brief therapy therapists.

As we see later in the chapter, the solution to these problems lies, in my opinion and in the opinions of others, neither in debate nor in a struggle regarding the superiority and efficacy of any particular therapy methods. Furthermore, these debates do not determine which therapy methods survive and which become extinct. If therapists and their supervisors were trained to recognize that expanding the reservoir of divergent therapy methods, varying in theoretical outlook, time duration, and the processes involved in their acquisition, then this recognition would enable them more easily to acquire new, effective approaches, such as TLP and others.

The final point relates to the therapist's motives in choosing to practice TLP. A therapist whose choice is a response to disappointment, failure, or impatience in regards to long-term therapy will be equally, if not more, disappointed by TLP. The choice should be based on an understanding of the significance of both focusing and separating processes in therapy. Thus, the initial stages of supervision must include clarification of what led the therapist to choose the TLP method.

Old habits die hard: altering previous therapeutic style and practice

The primary challenge to the TLP therapist is the responsibility of remaining consistent in the role of staunch guardian of the central issue. Experienced clinicians are well-practiced in attending to every thread of detail and connecting those many details to one broader fabric of understanding. In contrast, TLP requires the therapist to maintain a singular focus on details related to the central issue while ignoring any other issues that arise. Along those lines, the supervisor, the therapist, and the client each sort through and select particular focal issues throughout long-term therapy. In the supervision of TLP, the supervisor must channel the therapist's previously acquired skills toward continual emphasis of two fundamental therapeutic principles: focality and separation.

The elimination of previous long-term therapy practices primarily involves practices grounded in the illusion that there is unlimited time to understand fully the client's entire emotional world. A typical refrain heard in long-term psychotherapy supervision is 'it will come up again' in regard to undetected or neglected elements from the previous session. However, the luxury of having 'another time' is generally not part of the TLP experience, nor does it usually arise in supervision. Moreover, the centrality of the focal issue elevates the importance of directly and consistently relating to any material connected to the selected issue, be it from an experiential angle or a technical angle. The constant focus on development of the central issue may apply pressure to therapists experienced in long-term therapy, as they are likely to perceive the stringent focus as a limitation of, or deficiency in, the therapeutic framework. At this stage, the supervisor must enable the therapist to encounter the theoretical and clinical importance of the focal issue and the time constraints in a way that is experientially and conceptually intertwined. In this manner, the supervisor can bring the therapist to view the strict focus and time constraints as a therapeutic impetus rather than as a limitation.

Another problem that arises is the therapist's tendency to compare the different atmospheres of long-term and time-limited psychotherapies. Whereas long-term therapy engenders a more relaxed atmosphere, the TLP atmosphere may feel too intensely goal-directed. In this regard, the supervisor must facilitate an understanding of the distinction between the consistent maintenance of a specific focus and the presentation of an overly directive demeanor. Sometimes, the therapist's excessive activity or directive demeanor serve as resistance tactics. (See Witztum and Dasberg 1986, for a detailed discussion of therapist resistance.)

Individual vs. group supervision

Dasberg and Winokur (1984, 1989) and Winokur and Dasberg (1983) described a group training model based upon an integration of theoretical knowledge and clinical implementation of the theoretical principles. In the proposed group model, the supervisor facilitates both intellectual and experiential coping with the issues that arise in TLP training. Although I firmly support the centrality of the group learning experience as part of the training for any form of therapy, the beginning therapist must be provided with a more intimate supervisory setting as well. Individual supervision is crucial for the therapist grappling with the paramount questions likely to arise, whether the issues concern personal conflicts or struggles with the therapeutic work itself. Therefore, group supervision should only supplement, but not replace, individual supervision, particularly in the initial training stages.

Group supervision does, however, provide a valuable forum for dealing with technical matters. The group process tends to increase creativity and accuracy in the formulation of the central issue. In addition, the group setting proves useful in focusing the therapist and helping to maintain focus on the central issue throughout treatment. There is no substitute for group support when therapists struggle with feelings of isolation or separation difficulties. In my experience, group supervision is highly effective whether the group members are therapists experienced in TLP or beginning TLP therapists.

Levenson and Strupp (1999) claim, justifiably, that the situation today has changed in terms of practical and future outlooks. They claim clinical training should not be continued with the attitude of business as usual, and therapists must equip themselves for the new reality that has formed in the market of psychotherapy methods. They propose a few key suggestions: idealistic and perfectionist goals should be abandoned, shifting the focus toward realistic goals. The demands of the treatment-seeking community cannot be ignored, and people are voting with their feet for brief and circumscribed therapy methods. It is preferable to conduct intentional training of these methods than to continue denying the reality depicted in the survey taken by Davidovitz and Levenson (1997). Specialized clinical abilities should be developed for the new methods, such as reflection in action, a concept considered by Strupp and Binder (1984) to be a basic requirement of the ability for meta-communication. It would be ideal for more experienced therapists to learn brief therapy techniques, but because that is not the reality, emphasis should be placed upon training the available therapists, even if they lack experience in extended therapy methods. Even with all of their limitations, I believe it is preferable to train inexperienced therapists than not to train them or to 'turn them' into brief therapists without training, supervision, or affiliation with this therapy approach. As demonstrated by Davidovitz and Levenson, that is precisely the way in which some therapists who feel reluctant, unenthusiastic, and uninspired become brief therapists. Finally, Levenson and Strupp claim brief therapy methods and training for their practice should be viewed as an ongoing task and not as it was initially acceptable to assume, a brief process (Dasberg and Winokur 1984; Winokur and Dasberg 1983).

Levenson and Strupp (1999) found that therapists changed their minds and altered their positions toward brief therapy through participation in extensive workshops on the approach. They found it relevant and effective for treating therapist resistance to brief therapy and, therefore, proposed workshops of this nature as part of the therapist-training program for brief dynamic therapy.

The supervisor – missionary of therapeutic innovation

Despite considerable resistance from many therapists, there is a growing trend among public institutions toward encouraging the practice of brief psychotherapy, which is due to more than merely the low cost of these therapies. In these cases, TLP may be forced upon therapists to a certain extent. Consequently, the therapists may express their resistance by doubting the therapy's effectiveness. The therapist may place the supervisor in the position of 'cheerleader' who vigorously attempts to spark the therapist's faith in the utility of TLP. As a result, the supervisor can be cast in the role of the 'heretic' who, from a therapist's point-of-view, betrays the principles of long-term therapy.

In this situation, the supervisor might mistakenly resort to convincing and explaining tactics. Instead, the supervisor should aim to listen actively and draw attention to the parallels between the client's experience in therapy and the therapist's experience in supervision, particularly in terms of expectations and feelings of disappointment. The supervisor's awareness should be based on the understanding that long-term and time-limited dynamic psychotherapy fundamentally run parallel to, rather than oppose, each other. Furthermore, the supervisor should bear in mind that these two treatment modes represent only a fragment of the range of possibilities available to clients.

Additionally, the supervisor is often looked upon as a source of 'just another opinion,' particularly in the supervision of experienced therapists. Particularly in light of the limited time and the 'fatefulness' of therapeutic interventions, the supervisor must maintain a balance between providing the therapist with another ear or opinion and offering his or her TLP expertise.

It is also important to remember that some of the therapist's resistances will be expressed nonverbally, through acting out. For example, the therapist may insist that none of the patients are suitable for TLP, disrupt the fluidity of the treatment process by taking excessive breaks, or cancel therapy or supervision sessions. The various forms of resistance apply pressure to the supervisor, whether the source of the pressure be individual therapists, the group, or the system within which the supervisor works. It is especially important to identify these resistances and to process them within the training and supervision process.

Binder (1999) writes that notwithstanding the importance of supervision in any therapy, we ought to change the supervision strategy for brief therapy methods. He believes the model adopted from the psychoanalytic approach, in which experiential learning occurs through the accompanying supervision, is inappropriate for brief therapies. Binder is not convinced that modification of these outlooks indeed influences the acquisition of the abilities for brief therapy and, therefore, suggests the adoption of approaches taken from the cognitive sciences and the development of psychotherapy training through the use of computerized multimedia tools.

He focuses on two main modes. The first is the ability to improvise within the framework of the definitive parameters of the therapy model. He also suggests focusing upon taped therapy hours, defining clear tasks for supervision, and focusing upon specific skills for the therapist and clearly defined interactions between therapist and patient. It is important for feedback to center upon positive actions taken by the supervised therapist more than giving general praise.

Vakoch and Strupp (2000) discuss the advantages of training and supervision for manual-based therapy methods. They cite the advantages of using a manual for therapy (consistency, clear formulation of principles, researchability, overcoming severe problems) and the limitations of a manual (does not include the entire human spectrum of interpersonal states). Despite the far-reaching advantages of advanced and future-oriented methods in psychotherapy instruction, they underscore the fact that in both the immediate and the more distant future, psychotherapy and the change it engenders will always be the fruit of a human encounter between the personality of the patient, prevented from growing and flourishing, and the personal skills and dedication of the therapist.

Flexibility of the treatment format

Innovators of new therapeutic techniques and approaches often perceive their approaches as needing more solid footing than already well-established approaches. This perception may function as a defense against those who employ other approaches or it may be an expression of genuine internal doubt regarding the treatment's effectiveness and the durability of treatment outcome. One means of substantiating a new therapeutic approach is the creation of a very clear-cut treatment manual. To date, no TLP treatment manual exists that is as precise as the format for, say, the cognitive treatment of depression (Beck et al. 1978; Klerman et al. 1979). Nonetheless, Mann's (1973) extremely lucid directions dictate the treatment style and interventions used in TLP.

Perhaps the best example of this is the specification of the central issue components and the precise outline for formulation of the central issue. In fact, the limited degree of flexibility and personal touch allowed in the formulation of the central issue may even lead the therapist to view the TLP process as rigid and dogmatic. When this occurs, the feeling of rigidity may be carried over into the supervision process as well. Because the practice of any dynamic psychotherapy is quite broadly based on the emotional experiences of the therapist, the supervisor should guide the therapist-in-training toward finding the nuances of individuality and creativity in the practice of TLP. Otherwise, the supervision process will likely be reduced to merely a lifeless handing out of technical advice.

Therapists' struggles with separation and termination

Therapists are, first and foremost, human beings comprised of complex emotional structures. For therapists and clients alike, many of the complexities of human emotion are intimately linked to processes of separation. Thus, it is not surprising that problems surface among therapists suffering from separation and detachment difficulties when they embark on a therapeutic process based upon imminent separation. Dealing with this issue in supervision is likely to bring certain people to the mature realization that their ability to conduct TLP is limited or that perhaps a reasonable degree of treatment success is not really feasible for them. Alternatively, genuine coping with these questions in supervision can encourage the therapist to seek personal therapy for separation difficulties.

The supervisor plays a central role in the termination phase, possibly the most difficult and critical stage of TLP. The supervisor functions as the therapist's compass, and sometimes his or her own compass, navigating the therapist toward termination of the treatment despite the separation difficulties. In addition, the supervisor and therapist might have to contend with the client's attempts to sabotage the termination.

At this critical juncture, the parallel processes of supervision and therapy are emphasized. Must the supervisor delve into the therapist's own experience of termination and separation from the supervisory relationship while simultaneously guiding the therapist through the TLP termination process? In reality, it is not always possible and this schema cannot always be fully realized. Furthermore, the supervisor need not manipulate an intensification of the parallel process nor must he or she scrutinize the fine details of the process. Instead, the metaphoric and symbolic understanding of the process developed by the therapist and supervisor is sufficient.

Coping with follow-up evaluations

Unlike long-term dynamic psychotherapies, the TLP 'treatment package' almost always includes some form of post-termination follow-up, considered fundamental to the therapy. The demand for follow-up evaluations can pose a significant threat to the therapist practiced in long-term therapy. The idea of placing a value on treatment results or the suggestion that those results are measurable presents an ideological problem for some therapists. As a supervisor, I drew immense support from the fact that I had undergone a significant transformation in my perception of post-treatment follow-up as a TLP trainee. Coming from an extensive long-term psychotherapy background, I encountered serious difficulty when I was first required to conduct follow-up evaluations. Although I initially struggled with the formidable task of facing the results of my work, the combination of supportive supervision and personal processing of my inner conflict dissipated the emotional threat and eventually transformed the follow-up evaluations into satisfying and rewarding experiences.

Supervision of outcome research

Due to its brevity, TLP appears more readily given to systematic scientific observation (Shefler 1989, 1990, 1991, 1993, 1994) than most long-term psychotherapies. Some community mental health centers have engaged in empirical follow-up of their treatments (Witztum et al. 1989; Shefler et al. 1995), thus enabling researchers to observe the transformations that participating therapists undergo as they learn to view the research as educational rather than threatening and invasive. The once-threatening precept that 'we will conduct a systematically controlled investigation of the results of your work' can be altered when the therapist discovers the supportive and satisfying aspects of working as part of a research team. Similar to the other phases of therapy, the supervisor attempts to cultivate a broad understanding of the necessity for research and follow-up evaluation and to enable the therapist to come to terms with the exposure of his or her treatment results to systematic investigation.

Conclusion

TLP is unique not only in its function as a specialized therapy method, but it also stands out in the learning and supervision processes connected to it. A prevalent issue among short-term therapy methods, TLP included, concerns the demands and challenges that confront experienced and beginning therapists alike. The pressure upon inexperienced therapists who attempt short-term therapy early in their training will not contribute to, and may even harm, the consolidation of therapeutic proficiency on a higher professional level.

It was emphasized that TLP is intended for therapists well versed in the fundamentals of psychoanalytic theory, as well as the long-term therapy approaches that stem from it. Familiarity with psychoanalytic theory combined with a solid base of clinical experience will bring the TLP therapist to an understanding of the basic principles of all psychodynamic psychotherapies: transference, countertransference, resistance, and the basic intervention strategies of interpretation, confrontation, and clarification. Likewise, and perhaps more so than in long-term therapies, rapid and accurate diagnostic abilities are essential. Upon this foundation of experience and sharpened clinical skills, and with the help of a clearly directed and well-focused supervision, the interested therapist's talents and abilities can be channeled into the practice of TLP. Of course, this rests upon the condition that the therapist's motives are appropriate and his or her personality is able to withstand the tremendous emotional load accompanying this form of therapy.

References

Alexander, D. A. and Eagles, J. M. (1989) 'Which neurotic patients are treated with psychotherapy?' *The International Journal of Social Psychiatry*, 35: 173–80.

Alexander, F. (1951) 'Principles and techniques of briefer psychotherapeutic procedures.' *Research Publication of the Association of Nervous and Mental Disease*, 31: 16–20.

American Psychiatric Association (1987) *Diagnostic and statistical manual of mental disorders* (third edn rev.) (DSM-III-R). Washington DC: American Psychiatric Association.

American Psychiatric Association (1994) *Diagnostic and statistical manual of mental disorders* (fourth edn) (DSM-IV). Washington DC: American Psychiatric Association.

Anderson, E. M. and Lambert, M. J. (1995) 'Short-term dynamically oriented psychotherapy: a review and meta-analysis.' *Clinical Psychology Review*, 15: 503–14.

Anderson, E. M. and Lambert, M. J. (in press) 'A survival analysis of clinically significant change in outpatient psychotherapy.' *Professional Psychology: Research and practice*.

Arieti, S. and Bemporad J. (1978) *Severe and mild depression. The psychotherapeutic approach*. New York: Basic Books.

Arlow, J. A. (1984) 'Disturbances of the sense of time with special reference to the experience of timelessness.' *Psychoanalytic Quarterly*, 53: 33–7.

Arlow, J. A. (1986) 'Psychoanalysis and time.' *Journal of the American Psychoanalytic Association*, 34: 507–28.

Assa, T. (1999) *Patient progress during two short-term psychodynamic treatments as measured by the RPPS*. Unpublished masters thesis, The Hebrew University, Jerusalem.

Baider, L., Amikam, J. C. and Kaplan De-Nour, A. (1984) 'Time-limited thematic group with post-mastectomy patients.' *Journal of Psychosomatic Research*, 28: 323–30.

Baker, H. S. and Baker, M. N. (1987) 'Kohut's self psychology: an overview.' *The American Journal of Psychiatry*, 144: 1–9.

Balint, M., Ornstein, P. P. and Balint, E. (1972) *Focal Psychotherapy*. London: Tavistock.

Barber, J. P. (1994) 'Efficacy of short-term dynamic psychotherapy: past, present, future.' *Journal of Psychotherapy Practice and Research*, 3: 108–21.

Barber, J. P. and Crits-Christoph, P. (1993) 'Advances in measures of psychodynamic formulations.' *Journal of Consulting and Clinical Psychology*, 61: 574–85.

Barber, J. P., Crits-Christoph, P. and Luborsky, L. (1996) 'Effects of therapist adherence and competence on patient outcome in brief dynamic therapy.' *Journal of Consulting and Clinical Psychology*, 64: 619–22.

Barber, J. P. and Ellman J. (1996) 'Advances in short-term dynamic psychotherapy.' *Current Opinion in Psychiatry*, 9: 188–92.

Battle, C. C., Imber, S. D., Hoehn-Saric, R., Nash, E. R. and Frank, J. D. (1966) 'Target complaints as criteria of improvement.' *American Journal of Psychiatry*, 20: 184–92.

Beck, A. J., Rush, A. J., Shaw, B. F. and Emery, G. (1978) *Cognitive Theory of Depression. A Treatment Manual*. New York: Guilford Press.

Bennett, M. J. (1984) 'Brief psychotherapy and adult development.' *Psychotherapy*, 21: 171–77.

Bergman, Z. and Witztum, E. (1987) 'Using letters in psychotherapy.' *Sichot, the Israel Journal of Psychotherapy*, 1: 116–22.

Bernard, H. S., Schwartz, A. J., Oclatis, K. A. and Stiner, A. (1980) 'Relationship between patients' in-process evaluations of therapy and psychotherapy outcome.' *Journal of Clinical Psychology*, 36: 259–64.

Binder, J. L. (1999) 'Issues in teaching and learning Time-Limited psychodynamic psychotherapy.' *Clinical Psychology Review*, 19: 705–19.

Binswanger, L. (1912) 'Analyse einer hysterichen Phobie.Jb.' *Psychoanalyse Psycholpathologie Forsch.*, 3: 228–39.

Bordin, E. S. (1979) 'The generalizability of the psychoanalytic concept of the working alliance.' *Psychotherapy: Theory, Research and Practice*, 16: 252–60.

Botermans, J. F. (1996) 'The training of psychotherapists: impact on confidence and mastery, self efficacy and emotional reactivity.' Unpublished doctoral dissertation, Catholic University of Louvain, Belgium.

Brockman, B., Poynton, A., Ryle, A. and Watson, J. P. (1987) 'Effectiveness of time-limited therapy carried out by trainees.' *British Journal of Psychiatry*, 511: 602–10.

Buckley, P., Conte, H. R., Plutchik, R., Wild, K. V. and Karasu, T. B. (1984)

'Psychodynamic variables as predictors of psychotherapy outcome.' *American Journal of Psychiatry*, 141: 742–48.

Canetti, L., Shalev, A. Y. and Kaplan De-Nour, A. (1994) 'Israeli adolescents' norms of the Brief Symptom Inventory (BSI).' *Israel Journal of Psychiatry*, 31: 13–18.

Chambless, W. D. and Task Force (1998) 'Update on empirically validated therapies, II.' *The Clinical Psychologist*, 51: 3–16.

Colarusso, A. C. and Namiroff, R. A. (1979) 'Some observations and hypotheses about psychoanalytic theory of adult development.' *International Journal of Psychoanalysis*, 60: 59–71.

Colarusso, A. C. and Namiroff, R. A. (1987) 'Clinical implications of adult developmental theory.' *American Journal of Psychiatry*, 144: 1263–70.

Crits-Christoph, P. (1992) 'The efficacy of brief dynamic psychotherapy: a meta-analysis.' *American Journal of Psychiatry*, 149: 151–58.

Crits-Christoph, P., Cooper, A. and Luborsky, L. (1988) 'The accuracy of therapists' interpretations and the outcome of dynamic psychotherapy.' *Journal of Consulting and Clinical Psychology*, 56: 490–95.

Crits-Christoph, P. and Barber, J. P. (1991) (eds) *Handbook of Short-Term Dynamic Psychotherapy*. New York: Basic Books.

Dasberg, H. and Winokur, M. (1984) 'Teaching and learning short-term dynamic psychotherapy: parallel processes.' *Psychotherapy*, 21: 184–88.

Dasberg, H. and Winokur, M. (1989) 'An exercise in reliability of short-term dynamic psychotherapy.' In H. Dasberg, Y. Isaacson and G. Shefler (eds), *Short-term psychotherapy – background, technique, and application*. Jerusalem: Magnes Press. (In Hebrew.)

Davanloo, H. (1972) 'Techniques of short-term psychotherapy.' *Psychiatric Clinics of North America*, 2: 11–12.

Davanloo, H. (1978) 'Evaluation and criteria of selection of patients for short-term dynamic psychotherapy.' *Psychotherapy and Psychosomatics*, 29: 307–8.

Davidovitz, D. and Levenson, H. (August 1995) 'A national survey on practice and training in brief psychotherapy: comparison of psychologists, psychiatrists and social workers.' Paper presented at the annual meeting of the American Psychological Association, New York.

Derogatis, L. R., Lipman, R. S. and Covi, L. S. (1973) 'SCL-90: an outpatient psychiatric rating scale (preliminary report).' *Psychopharmacology Bulletin*, 9: 13–27.

Derogatis, L. R. and Melisaratos, N. (1983) 'The brief symptom inventory: an introductory report.' *Psychological Medicine*, 13: 595–605.

Derogatis, L. R. and Spencer, P. M. (1982) *The brief symptom inventory (BSI-53): administration, scoring and procedures manual – I.* Baltimore: Johns Hopkins University Press.

Deutsch, F. (1949) *Applied psychoanalysis: selected lectures on psychotherapy*. New York: Grune and Straton.

Deutsch, F. and Murphy, W. (1955) *Clinical interview: Associative explora-tion*. New York: International University Press.

Erikson, E. H. (1968) *Identity: Youth and Crisis*. New York: W. W. Norton.

Evans S. and Levenson, H. (August, 1997) 'Brief therapy training in APA approved graduate programs and internships.' Paper presented at the annual meeting of the American Psychological Association, Chicago.

Ferenczi, S. and Rank, O. (1925/1986) *The Development of Psychoanalysis*. Madison CT: International Universities Press.

Frank, J. D. (1959) 'The dynamics of psychotherapeutic relationships.' *Psychiatry*, 33: 17–39.

Frank, J. D., Gleidman, L. H., Imber, S. D., Stone, A. R. and Nash, E. H. (1959) 'Patients' expectancies and relearning as factors determining improvement in psychotherapy.' *The American Journal of Psychiatry*, 115: 961–68.

Freud, S. (1895) 'Katharina, studies on hysteria.' In: J. Strachey (ed.) (1968) *Standard Edition of the Complete Psychological Works of Sigmund Freud*, ed. James Strachey, 24 volumes. London: Hogarth Press, 1953–73, vol. 2.

—— (1913) 'On beginning the treatment (Further recommendations on the technique of psychoanalysis.' *Standard Edition*, 12.

—— (1914) 'On narcissism.' *Standard Edition*, 14.

—— (1923) 'The ego and the id.' *Standard Edition*, 19.

Garfield, S. L. (1990) 'Issues and method in psychotherapy process research.' *Journal of Consulting and Clinical Psychology*, 57: 273–80.

Goldberg, A. (1973) 'Psychotherapy of narcissistic injuries.' *Archives of General Psychiatry*, 28: 722–26.

Gorkin, M. (1986) 'Countertransference in cross cultural psychotherapy. The example of Jewish therapist and Arab patient.' *Psychiatry*, 49: 69–79.

Gottschalk, L. A., Fox, R. A. and Bates, D. E. (1973) 'A study of prediction and outcome in a mental health crisis clinic.' *American Journal of Psychiatry*, 130: 1107–111.

Greenberg, L. S. (1984) 'A task analysis of interpersonal conflict resolution.' In: L. Rice and L. Greenberg (eds), *Patterns of change*. New York: Guilford.

Greenberg, L. S. (1986) 'Change process research.' *Journal of Consulting and Clinical Psychology*, 54: 4–9.

Greenberg, L. S., Rice, L. N. and Elliot, R. (1991) 'Approaches to analysing session change.' Panel session presented at the 22nd Annual Meeting of the Society for Psychotherapy Research, Lyon, France.

Grinker, R. R. and Spiegel J. P. (1944) 'Brief psychotherapy in war neuroses.' *Psychosomatic Medicine*, 6: 123–313.

Hartocollis, P. (1975) 'Time and affect in psychotherapy.' *Journal of the American Association of Psychoanalysis*, 23: 383–95.

Heiberg, A. (1978) 'The main lines of the short-term psychotherapy.' *Psychotherapy and Psychosomatics*, 29: 309–11.

Hess, N. (1976) 'Coping styles and defensive styles as components in mental health and sickness.' Unpublished masters thesis. The Hebrew University, Jerusalem.

Hobbs, M. (1989) 'Short-term dynamic psychotherapy.' *Current Opinion in Psychiatry*, 2: 389–92.

Hoglend, P. (1988) 'Brief dynamic psychotherapy for less well-adjusted patients.' *Psychotherapy and Psychosomatics*, 49: 197–204.

Hoglend, P. (1993a) 'Suitability for brief dynamic psychotherapy: psychodynamic variables as predictors of outcome.' *Acta Psychiatrica Scandinavica*, 88: 104–10.

Hoglend, P. (1993b) 'Personality disorders and long-term outcome after brief dynamic psychotherapy.' *Journal of Personality Disorders*, 7: 168–81.

Hoglend, P. (1996) 'Motivation for brief dynamic psychotherapy.' *Psychotherapy and Psychosomatics*, 65: 209–15.

Hoglend, P. and Heyerdahl, O. (1994) 'The circumscribed focus in intensive brief dynamic psychotherapy.' *Psychotherapy and Psychosomatics*, 61: 163–70.

Hoglend, P. and Piper, W. E. (1995) 'Focal adherence in brief dynamic psychotherapy: a comparison of findings from two independent studies.' *Psychotherapy*, 32: 618–28.

Holland, S. J., Roberts, N. E. and Messer, S. B. (1998) 'Reliability and validity of the Rutgers Psychotherapy Progress Scale.' *Psychotherapy Research*, 8: 428–81.

Hovne, R. (1984) 'Assessment and outcome in short-term dynamic psychotherapy.' Unpublished doctoral dissertation, State University of New Jersey.

Howard, K. I., Kopta, S. M., Krause, M. S. and Orlinsky, D. E. (1986). 'The dose-effect relationship in psychotherapy.' *American Psychologist*, 41: 159–64.

Jacobson, N. S. and Truax, P. (1991) 'Clinical significance: statistical approach to meaningful change in psychotherapy research.' *Journal of Consulting and Clinical Psychology*, 59: 12–19.

Joyce, A. S. and Piper, W. E. (1990) 'An examination of Mann's model of time-limited individual psychotherapy.' *Canadian Journal of Psychiatry*, 35: 41–9.

Keilson, M. V., Dworkin, F. H. and Gelso, C. J. (1979) 'The effectiveness of time-limited psychotherapy in a university counseling center.' *Journal of Clinical Psychology*, 35: 631–36.

Kernberg, O. F. (1975) *Borderline Conditions and Pathological Narcissism*. Northville: Jaxo Inc.

Kiresuk, T. J. (1973) 'Goal attainment scaling at a county mental health service.' *Monograph Evaluation*, 1: 12–18.

Kiresuk, T. J. and Sherman, R. E. (1968) 'Goal attainment scaling: a general method for evaluating comprehensive community mental health programs.' *Community Mental Health Journal*, 4: 443–53.

Klein, M. H., Mathieu-Coughlan, P. L. and Kiesler, D. J. (1986) 'The experiencing scales.' In L. S. Greenberg and W. M. Pinsof (eds), *The psychotherapeutic process: a research handbook*. New York: Guilford Press, pp. 21–71.

Klerman G. L., Wissman M. M., Rounsaville B. J. and Chevreon E. S. (1984) *Interpersonal Psychotherapy of Depression*. New York: Basic Books.

Kohut, H. (1968) 'The psychoanalytic treatment of narcissistic personality disorders.' *The Psychoanalytic Study of the Child*, 23: 86–113.

—— (1971) *The Analysis of the Self*. New York: International Universities Press.

—— (1977) *The Restoration of the Self*. New York: International Universities Press.

—— (1978) 'The disorders of the self and their treatment: An outline.' *International Journal of Psychoanalysis*, 59: 413–25.

Koss, M. P. and Butcher, J. N. (1986) 'Research on brief psychotherapy.' In S. L. Garfield and A. E. Bergin (eds), *Handbook of Psychotherapy and Behavior Change*. New York: John Wiley & Sons.

Krupnick, J. L. and Horowitz, M. J. (1985) 'Brief psychotherapy with vulnerable patients: an outcome assessment.' *Psychiatry*, 48: 223–33.

Lambert, M. J., Hansen, N. B. and Finch, A. E. (in press) 'Patient-focused research: using patient outcome data to enhance treatment effects.' *Journal of Consulting and Clinical Psychology*.

Lawlis, G. F. and Lu, E. (1972) 'Judgment of counseling process: reliability, agreement, and error.' *Psychological Bulletin*, 78: 17–20.

Lazarus, L. W. (1982) 'Brief psychotherapy of narcissistic disturbances.' *Psychotherapy: Theory, Research and Practice*, 19: 228–36.

Levenson, H. and Strupp, H. H. (1999) 'Recommendations for the future of training in brief dynamic psychotherapy.' *Journal of Clinical Psychology*, 55: 385–91.

Luborsky, L. (1962) 'Clinicians' judgments of mental health.' *Archives of General Psychiatry*, 7: 407–17.

Luborsky, L. (1975) 'Clinicians' judgments of mental health: specimen case descriptions and forms for the Health–Sickness Rating Scale.' *Bulletin of the Menninger Clinic*, 39: 448–80.

Luborsky, L. and Bachrach, H. (1974) 'Factors influencing clinicians' judgments of mental health.' *Archives of General Psychiatry*, 31: 292–99.

MacKenzie, K.R. (1988) 'Recent developments in brief psychotherapy.' *Hospital and Community Psychiatry*, 39: 742–52.

McKitrick, D. S. and Gelso C. J. (1978) 'Initial client expectancies in time-limited counseling.' *Journal of Counseling Psychology*, 24: 246–49.

Mahler, M. (1972) 'On the first three sub-phases of the separation-individuation process.' *International Journal of Psycho-Analysis*, 53: 333–38.

Malan, D. H. (1963) *A study of brief psychotherapy*. London: Tavistock.

Malan, D. H. (1976a) *The frontier of brief psychotherapy*. New York: Plenum.

Malan, D. H. (1976b) *Towards the validation of dynamic psychotherapy: a replication*. New York: Plenum.

Mann, J. (1973) *Time-limited psychotherapy*. Cambridge, MA: Harvard University Press.

Mann, J. (1991) 'Time limited psychotherapy.' In: P. Crits-Christoph and J. P. Barber (eds), *Handbook of Short-term Dynamic Psychotherapy*. New York: Basic Books.

Mann J. (1981) 'The core of time-limited psychotherapy: time and the central issue. In: S. H. Budman (ed.), *Forms of Brief Psychotherapy*. New York: Guilford Press.

Mann, J. and Goldman, R. (1982) *A casebook in time-limited psychotherapy*. New York: McGraw-Hill.

Meeks, J. E. (1971) *The Fragile Alliance*. Baltimore: Williams and Wilkins.

Messer, S. B. (2001a) 'What makes brief psychodynamic therapy time efficient.' *Clinical Psychology: Science and Practice*, 8: 1–4.

Messer, S. B. (2001b) 'What allows therapy to be brief: introduction to the series on brief therapy.' *Clinical Psychology: Science and Practice*.

Messer, S. B. and Warren C. S. (1995) *Models of Brief Psychodynamic Therapy: A Comparative Approach*. New York: Guilford Press.

Messer, S. B. and Warren, C. S. (2001) 'Brief psychodynamic therapy.' In: R. J. Corsini (ed.), *Handbook of Innovative Psychotherapies*. New York: John Wiley & Sons.

Mintz, J. and Kiesler, D. J. (1981) 'Individualized measures of psycho-therapy outcome.' In P. Kendall and J. Outcher (eds), *Handbook of research methods in clinical psychology*. New York: John Wiley & Sons.

Muench, G. A. (1965) 'An investigation of the efficacy of time-limited psychotherapy.' *Journal of Counseling Psychology*, 12: 294–98.

Norcross, J. C., Strausser-Kirtland D. and Missar, C. D. (1988) 'The process and outcomes of psychotherapists' personal treatment experiences.' *Psychotherapy*, 25: 36–43.

Norville, R., Sampson, H. and Weiss, J. (1996) 'Accurate interpretations and brief psychotherapy outcome.' *Psychotherapy Research*, 6: 16–29.

Oberndorf, C. P. (1947) 'Constant elements in psychotherapy.' *Yearbook of Psychoanalysis*, 3: 175–97.

Offer D. (1987) 'In defense of adolescents.' *Journal of American Medical Association*, 257: 3407–08.

Parloff, M. B. (1986) 'Placebo controls in psychotherapy research: a sine qua non or a placebo for research problems?' *Journal of Consulting and Clinical Psychology*, 54: 79–87.

Persons, J. B. (1991) 'Psychotherapy outcome studies do not accurately represent current models of psychotherapy.' *American Psychologist*, 46: 99–106.

Phillips, E. L. (1985) *Psychotherapy revised: new frontiers in research and practice*. Hillsdale, NJ: Erlbaum.

Pine, F. (1989) 'Motivation, personality organization and the four psychologies of psychoanalysis.' *Journal of the American Psychoanalytic Association*, 37: 31–64.

Piper, W. E., Debbane, E. G., Bienvenu, J. P. and Garant, J. (1984) 'A comparative study of four forms of psychotherapy.' *Journal of Consulting and Clinical Psychology*, 52: 268–79.

Piper, W. E., Azim, H. F. A., Joyce, A. S. and McCallum, M. (1991a) 'Transference interpretations, therapeutic alliance and outcome in short-term individual psychotherapy.' *Archives of General Psychiatry*, 48: 946–53.

Piper W. E., Azim, H. F. A., Joyce, A. S., McCallum, M., Nixon, G. W. H. and Segal P. S. (1991b) 'Quality of object relations versus interpersonal functioning as predictors of therapeutic alliance and psychotherapy outcome.' *The Journal of Nervous and Mental Disease*, 197: 432–39.

Piper, W. A., Boroto, D. R., Joyce, A. S., McCallum, M. and Azim, H. F. A. (1995) 'Patterns of alliance and outcome in short-term individual psychotherapy.' *Psychotherapy*, 32: 639–47.

Reik, T. (1960) *The Haunting Melody: Psychoanalytical Experience in Life and Music*. New York: Grove Press.

Rice, L. N. and Greenberg, L. S. (eds) (1984) *Patterns of change: intensive analysis of psychotherapy process*. New York: Guilford Press.

Rice, L. N. and Saperia, E. P. (1984) 'Task analysis and the resolution of problematic reactions.' In L. N. Rice and L. S. Greenberg (eds), *Patterns of change: intensive analysis of psychotherapy process*. New York: Guilford Press, pp. 29–66.

Rosenberg, M. (1979) *Conceiving the self*. New York: Basic Books.

Rosenthal, J. (1987). *Judgment studies: design analysis and meta-analysis*. New York: Cambridge University Press.

Roskin, M. and Dasberg, H. (1983) 'On the validity of the Symptom Check List (SCL): a comparison of diagnostic self ratings in general practice patients and normals.' (Based on the Hebrew version.) *International Journal of Social Psychiatry*, 129: 225–30.

Sargel-Zvieli, L. (1997) 'The relationship between the therapeutic alliance and the degree of therapist adherence to the central issue and change processes in time-limited dynamic psychotherapy.' Unpublished masters thesis. The Hebrew University, Jerusalem.

Schwartz, A. J. and Bernard, H. S. (1981) 'Comparison of patient and therapist evaluations of time-limited psychotherapy.' *Psychotherapy: Theory, Research and Practice*, 18: 101–8.

Shanan, J. (1967) 'The tendency for active coping, a basic element in mental health.' (In Hebrew.) *Megamot*, 15: 188–95.

Shanan, J. (1973) 'Coping behavior in assessment of complex tasks.' Proceedings of the 17th International Congress of Applied Psychology, Vol. 1.

Shapiro, D. (1965) *Neurotic Styles*. New York: Basic Books.

Sharar, D. (1995) 'Termination in short-term dynamic psychotherapy, and the therapist's personality.' *Sichot, the Israel Journal of Psychotherapy*, 10: 13–19. (In Hebrew.)

Shefler, G. (1988a) 'Application of basic psychoanalytic clinical concepts in short-term dynamic psychotherapy.' *Israel Journal of Psychiatry and Related Sciences*, 25: 203–11.

Shefler, G. (1988b) 'Short-term dynamic psychotherapies – their development and their common technical components.' *Sichot, the Israel Journal of Psychotherapy*, 2: 111–22. (In Hebrew.)

Shefler, G. (1989) 'Research in short-term dynamic psychotherapy.' In H. Dasberg, J. A. Itzigsohn and G. Shefler (eds), *Brief Psychotherapy: Background, Techniques and Application*. Jerusalem: The Magnes Press.

Shefler, G. (1990) 'Research and evaluation of short-term dynamic psychotherapy.' *Sichot, the Israel Journal of Psychotherapy*, 4: 193–97.

Shefler, G. (1991) 'Can process research teach us the essence of psychotherapy?' *Israel Journal of Psychiatry and Related Sciences*, 28, 1: 31–9. (In Hebrew.)

Shefler, G. (1993) *Time-Limited Psychotherapy*. Jerusalem: The Magnes Press.

Shefler, G. (1994) 'Research in Dynamic Psychotherapy: Realm or Dream?' *Sichot, the Israel Journal of Psychotherapy*, 2: 126–31. (In Hebrew.)

Shefler, G. (2000) 'Time-limited psychotherapy with adolescents.' *Journal of Psychotherapy Practice and Research*, 9: 88–99.

Shefler, G. and Greenberg, D. (1991) 'Clinical administration of a community mental health center. A model for improving efficacy and coping with staff burnout.' *Hospital and Community Psychiatry*, 42: 748–50.

Shefler, G., Dasberg, H. and Ben-Shakhar, G. (1995) 'A randomized controlled outcome and follow-up study of Mann's time-limited psychotherapy.' *Journal of Consulting and Clinical Psychology*, 4: 585–93.

Shefler, G. and Tishby, O. (1998) 'Interjudge reliability and agreement about the patient's central issue in time-limited psychotherapy (TLP) and its relation to TLP outcome.' *Psychotherapy Research*, 8: 426–38.

Shefler, G., Cannetti, L. and Wiseman, O. (in press) 'Psychometric properties of Goal Attainment Scaling of Mann's Time-Limited Psychotherapy.' *Journal of Clinical Psychology*, in press.

Shlien, J. M., Mosak, H. H. and Dreikurs, R. (1962) 'Effects of time limits: a comparison of two psychotherapies.' *Journal of Counseling Psychology*, 9: 31–4.

Sifneos, P. E. (1972) *Short-term psychotherapy and emotional crisis.* Cambridge, MA: Harvard University Press.

Sifneos, P. E. (1979) *Short-term dynamic psychotherapy: evaluation and technique.* New York: Plenum.

Sjodin, I. (1983) 'Psychotherapy in peptic ulcer disease.' *Acta Psychiatria Scandinavia*, 67: 39–42.

Sledge, W. H., Moras, K., Hartley, D. and Levine M. (1990) 'Effects of time-limited psychotherapy on patient dropout rates.' *American Journal of Psychiatry*, 147: 1341–47.

Sloane, R. B., Staples, F. R., Cristol, A. H., Yorkston, N. J. and Whipple, K. (1975) 'Short-term analytically oriented psychotherapy versus behavior therapy.' *American Journal of Psychiatry*, 132: 373–77.

Sloane, R. B., Staples, F. R., Cristol, A. H., Yorkston, N. J. and Whipple, K. (1976) 'Patient characteristics and outcome in psychotherapy and behavior psychotherapy.' *Journal of Consulting and Clinical Psychology*, 44: 330–39.

Smith, M. L., Glass, G. V. and Miller, T. I. (1980) *The benefit of psychotherapy.* Baltimore: Johns Hopkins University Press.

Spillman, A. (1991) 'The development of a scale measuring patient progress and patient stagnation in psychodynamic psychotherapy. Doctoral dissertation, graduate school of applied and professional psychology.' Rutgers University, New Jersey.

Sterba, R. (1951) 'A case of brief psychotherapy by Sigmund Freud.' *Psychoanalytic Review*, 38: 75–80.

Strupp, H. H. (1980a) 'Success and failure in time-limited psychotherapy. A systematic comparison of two cases: Comparison 1.' *Archives of General Psychiatry*, 37: 595–603.

Strupp, H. H. (1980b) 'Success and failure in time-limited psychotherapy. A systematic comparison of two cases: Comparison 2.' *Archives of General Psychiatry*, 37: 708–16.

Strupp, H. H. (1980c) 'Success and failure in time-limited psychotherapy, with special reference to the performance of a lay counselor.' *Archives of General Psychiatry*, 37: 831–41.

Strupp, H. H. (1980d) 'Success and failure in time-limited psychotherapy. Further evidence (Comparison 4).' *Archives of General Psychiatry*, 37: 947–54.

Strupp, H. H., Hartley, D. and Blackwood, G. L., Jr. (1974) 'Vanderbilt Psychotherapy Process Scale.' Unpublished manuscript, Vanderbilt University.

Strupp, H. H. and Binder, J. L. (1984) *Psychotherapy in a New Key: A Guide to Time-Limited Dynamic Psychotherapy.* New York: Basic Books.

Strupp, H. H., Butler, S. F. and Rosser, C. (1988) 'Training in psycho-dynamic therapy.' *Journal of Consulting and Clinical Psychology*, 56: 689–95.

Suh, C. S., Strupp, H. H. and O'Malley, S. S. (1986) 'The Vanderbilt Process Measures: The psychotherapy process scale (VPPS) and Negative Indicator Scale (VNIS).' In L. S. Greenberg and W. M. Pinsof (eds), *The psychotherapeutic process: a research handbook*. New York: Guilford Press, pp. 285–323.

Svartberg, M. and Stiles T. C. (1991) 'Comparative effects of short-term psychodynamic psychotherapy: a meta-analysis.' *Journal of Consulting and Clinical Psychology*, 59: 704–14.

Svedlund, J. (1983) 'Psychotherapy in the treatment of irritable bowel syndrome.' *Acta Psychiatria Scandinavia*, 67: 103–5.

Tannenbaum, S. A. (1913) 'Uber einen durch Psychoanalyse geheilten Fall von Dyspareunie.' *Zbl. Psychoanalyse*, 4: 373–82.

Tinsley, E. A. and Weiss, D. J. (1975) 'Inter-rater reliability and agreement of subjective judgments.' *Journal of Counseling Psychology*, 22: 358–76.

Tishby, O., Shefler, G. and Sargel Zvieli, L. (in press) 'Success and failure in time-limited psychotherapy: their relationship to therapeutic alliance and adherence to the patient's central issue.' *Psychotherapy Research*.

Vakoch, D. A. and Strupp, H. H. (2000) 'The evolution of psychotherapy training: reflection on manual-based learning and future alternatives.' *Journal of Clinical Psychology*, 56: 309–18.

Van der Hart, O. (1983) *Rituals in Psychotherapy*. New York: Irvington.

Van Der Hart, O. (1987) 'The use of farewell rituals in the treatment of mourning.' *Society and Welfare*, 7: 266–79.

Wascow, I. G. and Parloff, M. B. (eds) (1975) *Psychotherapy change measures*. (DHEW Publication No. ADM 74-120.) Rockville MD: National Institute of Mental Health.

White, H. S., Burke, J. D. and Havens, L. L. (1981) 'Choosing a method of short-time psychotherapy: a developmental approach.' In S. H. Budman (ed.), *Forms of Brief Psychotherapy*. New York: Guilford Press.

Wilkins, W. (1973) 'Expectancy of therapeutic gain: an empirical and conceptual critique.' *Journal of Consulting and Clinical Psychology*, 46: 69–79.

Winnicott, D. W. (1955) 'The depressive position in normal emotional development.' *British Journal of Medical Psychology*, 25: 89–96.

Winokur, M. and Dasberg, H. (1983) 'Teaching and learning short-term dynamic psychotherapy.' *Bulletin of the Menninger Clinic*, 47: 36–52.

Wiseman, H. and Shefler G. (1993) 'The study of the central issue as a change event in TLP: process analysis.' In G. Shefler, *Time-Limited Psychotherapy: Theory, Practice and Research*. Jerusalem: Magnes Press. (In Hebrew.)

Wiseman, H., Shefler, G., Canetti, L. and Ronen, Y. (1993) 'A systematic comparison of two cases in Mann's time-limited psychotherapy: an events approach.' *Psychotherapy Research*, 3: 227–44.

Wiseman, H. and Rice, L. N. (1989) 'Sequential analyses of therapist–client interaction during change events: a task-focused approach.' *Journal of Consulting and Clinical Psychology*, 57: 281–86.

Witztum, E. and Dasberg, H. (1986) 'Difficulties in the application of the short-term dynamic therapy method: therapist resistance.' *Sichot, the Israel Journal of Psychotherapy*, 1: 17–22. (In Hebrew.)

Witztum, E. and Chen E. (1989) 'Multi-brief psychotherapy – a case report.' *Sichot, the Israel Journal of Psychotherapy*, 3: 208–13. (In Hebrew.)

Witztum, E., Dasberg, H. and Shefler, G. (1989) 'A two-year follow-up of time-limited therapy in a community mental health center in Jerusalem.' *Israel Journal of Psychiatry and Related Sciences*, 26: 244–58.

Witztum, E. and Roman, I. (2000) 'Psychotherapeutic interventions with complicated grief: metaphor and leave-taking rituals with the bereaved.' In R. Malkinson, S. Rubin and E. Witztum (eds), *Traumatic and Non-Traumatic Loss and Bereavement. Clinical theory and Practice.* Madison, CT: Psychosocial Press, pp. 143–72.

Wolpe, J. (1958) *Psychotherapy by Reciprocal Inhibition.* Stanford, CA: Stanford University Press.

Index

abandonment: fears 133, 149, 200, 201, (*see also* separation anxiety); guilt 174, 175

Abraham (case study) 111–20; presenting complaint 112, 113; relationship patterns 112

acceptance, feelings of 151, 164, 177, 200

achievement: goal 246; as patient selection criterion 69, 70, 72–3, 191, 223; pressure 96

acknowledgment: seeking 114, 116; social 110

acting out 224

active transference 20; *see also* transference

activity/passivity conflict 44, 56, 94, 155

adjustment, disorders of 97, 216, 236, 246

adolescence 80, 92, 93; and therapy 93, 94, 109

affective: deficit 106; dimension 142; experience 7; expression, as selection criterion 69, 70, 71, 72, 97, 102, 163, 169, 216, 221, 224, 226; isolation 72; network 45–7; state 237

affects, basic 45–7, 106; fear 46, 56; gladness 46; guilt 46, 158, 271;

madness 46, 56; sadness 46, 55, 140, 141

aggression 131

Alexander, D.A. 235, 236, 237

Alexander, F. 20

alter ego needs 111, 115

'always' 7

ambivalence: to money 116, 117, 120; phase of 64–5, 115, 116, 120, 147, 172; parent/child relationship 106, 114, 115, 120, 160, 182, 198, 207, 210; to termination 175; therapist 176; to therapy 133, 148; *see also* hate-attraction dynamic

American Psychiatric Association 221

Anat (case study) 166–79; course of treatment 168–77; follow-up 177; patient therapist relationship 169, 178, 179; personal history 166–8; presenting complaint 166

anchoring 53, 65

Anderson, E.M. 19, 61, 245

anger, expressing 100–103, 115–17, 120, 129, 134; towards therapist 160, 164, 173, 201

anxiety 2, 8, 13, 56, 87, 166, 180, 206; disorders 228, 229, 236, 238; relieving 246; symptoms 13

appetite depression 144

Tinsley, E.A. 267
Tishby, O. 55, 210, 260, 262, 263
training, therapists 33, 34, 57, 219,
    275–87; and acceptance of TLP
    275, 278, 279, 282–4; alternatives
    283; in diagnosis 287; directed
    teaching 275; in directive therapy
    278, 281; evaluating 286; in focus
    on central issue 280, 281, 284; in
    follow-up 285–6; group 281–2;
    individual 281–2; lack of 276,
    277, 278; ongoing 282; in
    separation issues 280, 285;
    therapist suitability 277–9;
    therapeutic style 275, 280–81,
    284–5, 287; therapeutic
    supervision 275, 276, 282–4;
    therapy as 26, 279; in time-
    limitation 277, 280; treatment
    manuals 284
transference 163, 287; active 20;
    healing through 37;
    interpretation 147; to mother
    figure 53; negative 2, 65;
    neurosis 22; and outcomes 248;
    positive 2, 51, 64, 146, 169, 178;
    research 248, 274; self-object 67,
    78, 110, 117; and therapy length
    22
transitional: crises 74; periods 13,
    109
trauma 7; TLP for 238; see also
    stress

Truax, P. 232, 234, 241
trust 191, 195, 209

uncertainty, handling 99
understood, feeling 55, 111, 114,
    169

Vakoch, D.A. 284
validation, seeking 114, 116
Vanderbilt Psychotherapy Process
    Scale (VPPS) 249, 250, 251, 256,
    257, 259, 260
Van der Hart, O. 156

Warren, C. S. 30, 32, 66, 179
Wascow, I. G. 243
weakness 180
Weiss, D.J. 267
White, H. S. 109, 110, 119
Wilkins, W. 240
Winnicott, D. W. 40, 41
Winokur, M. 219, 278, 281, 282
Wiseman, H. 66, 210, 249, 259, 260,
    262, 263
Witztum, E. 32, 109, 156, 164, 213,
    219, 242, 273, 281, 286
Wolpe, J. 23
working alliance see patient/
    therapist relationship
worlds, moving between 187, 188,
    189, 190, 191, 192, 208, 209

Yuval (case study) 15, 16